1999

ASIAN FREEDOMS
The Idea of Freedom in East and Southeast Asia

Hegel famously held that 'the Orientals knew only that one (i.e. the ruler) is free'. Such stereotyping of Asia as uniformly despotic and enslaved was transmitted to the modern era by thinkers as diverse as Marx and Nietzsche.

Just when the new history of Asia appeared to be escaping these Orientalist stereotypes, they have been rediscovered in, of all places, Asia itself. Influential statesman and intellectuals have discerned in 'Asian values' a domain where personal freedom plays a lesser role. The universality of freedom and human rights has again come under critical attack.

Asian Freedoms uses the tools of contemporary intellectual history to challenge these trends. Inspired (and goaded) by Orlando Patterson's theory of freedom as a particularly western outgrowth of classical slavery, this book argues that authentic conceptions of freedom are found throughout the Asian region, where they have emerged in complex ways from local institutions and practices.

A prestigious group of contributors explores these adaptations and aternative genealogies of freedom from historical, religious, political and idcological perspectives. This timely book will make an important contribution to our understanding of Asian politics and culture, particularly in the light of the politically sensitive 'Asian values' debate.

David Kelly teaches in the School of Politics at the Australian Defence Force Academy, University of New South Wales. Previously he was a senior research fellow at the Contemporary China Centre, Australian National University. Anthony Reid is Professor of Southeast Asian History in the Research School of Pacific and Asian Studies, Australian National University.

CAMBRIDGE ASIA-PACIFIC STUDIES

Cambridge Asia-Pacific Studies aims to provide a focus and forum for scholarly work on the Asia-Pacific region as a whole, and its component sub-regions, namely Northeast Asia, Southeast Asia and the Pacific Islands. The series is produced in association with the Research School of Pacific and Asian Studies at the Australian National University and the Australian Institute of International Affairs.

Editor: John Ravenhill

R. Gerard Ward and Elizabeth Kingdon (eds) *Land, Custom and Practice in the South Pacific* 0 521 47289 X hardback

Stephane Lawson *Tradition Versus Democracy in the South Pacific* 0 521 49638 1 hardback

Walter Hatch and Kozo Yamamura *Asia in Japan's Embrace* 0 521 56176 0 hardback 0 521 56515 4 paperback

Alasdair Bowie and Daniel Unger *The Politics of Openness in Southeast Asia* 0 521 58343 8 hardback 0 521 58683 6 paperback

ASIAN FREEDOMS

The Idea of Freedom in East and Southeast Asia

EDITED BY

DAVID KELLY and ANTHONY REID

CAMBRIDGE
UNIVERSITY PRESS

PUBLISHED BY THE PRESS SYNDICATE OF THE UNIVERSITY OF CAMBRIDGE
The Pitt Building, Trumpington Street, Cambridge, United Kingdom

CAMBRIDGE UNIVERSITY PRESS
The Edinburgh Building, Cambridge CB2 2RU, United Kingdom
40 West 20th Street, New York, NY 10011–4211, USA
10 Stamford Road, Oakleigh, Melbourne 3166, Australia

First published 1998

Printed by SNP Offset (M) Sdn. Bhd.

Typeset in Baskerville 10/12 pt

A catalogue record for this book is available from the British Library

Library of Congress Cataloguing in Publication data

Asian freedoms: the idea of freedom in East and Southeast Asia/
edited by David Kelly and Anthony Reid.
p.   cm. (Cambridge Asia-Pacific studies)
Includes bibliographical references and index.
ISBN 0-521-62035-X (hb: alk. paper).
ISBN 0-521-63757-0 (pb: alk. paper)
1. Human rights – Asia, Southeastern. 2. Human rights – East Asia.
3. Civil rights – Asia, Southeastern. 4. Civil rights – East Asia.
5. Asia, Southeastern – Politics and government.
6. East Asia – Politics and government.
I. Kelly, David, 1948– .II. Reid, Anthony, 1939– . III. Series.
JC571.A76 1998
323.44'095–dc21   97–35128

Contents

Contributors

THANET APHORNSUVAN is an Assistant Professor of History at Thammasat University, Bangkok. His publications include *Rabob that kab amnaj kanmuang nai prawatsat sangkhom thai* [Slavery and Political Power in Thai Social History] (1990) and *Pok pluek prachathipatai nai amerika* [Peeling American Democracy] (1992).

WILLIAM J. F. JENNER is Professor of Chinese at the Australian National University. His books include *Memories of Loyang: Yang Hsüan-chih and the Lost Capital, 493–534* (1981) and *The Tyranny of History: The Roots of China's Crisis* (1992; rev. edn, 1994) and many translations from the Chinese, among them *Journey to the West*, 3 vols (1982–86 and later reprints).

DAVID KELLY teaches in the School of Politics at the Australian Defence Force Academy, University of New South Wales. Previously he was a senior research fellow at the Contemporary China Centre, Australian National University. He is co-author of *Chinese Marxism in the Post-Mao Era* (1990). His publications reflect broad interests in Chinese intellectual history, including contemporary liberal and conservative ideologies.

IAN MABBETT is Reader in History at Monash University, and a specialist in Buddhism. His publications include *A Short History of India* (1968; rev. edn, 1983) and, with David Chandler, *The Khmers* (1995).

VERA MACKIE has taught Modern Japanese History and Women's Studies for some years at the University of Melbourne. She has recently been appointed Foundation Professor of Japanese Studies at Curtin University of Technology in Western Australia. She is the author of *Creating Socialist Women in Japan: Gender, Labour and Activism, 1900–1937* (1997).

ANTHONY REID is Professor of Southeast Asian History in the Research School of Pacific and Asian Studies, Australian National University. His books include *The Indonesian National Revolution, 1945–50* (1974); *Southeast Asia in the Age of Commerce, c1450–1680*, 2 vols (1988–93); and, as editor, *Slavery, Bondage and Dependency in Southeast Asia* (1983). He was a contributor to Volume 1 of the *Cambridge History of Southeast Asia* (1992).

JAMES C. SCOTT is the Eugene Meyer Professor of Political Science and Anthropology at Yale University and Director of the Program in Agrarian Studies at Yale. His publications include *The Moral Economy of the Peasant: Subsistence and Rebellion in Southeast Asia* (1976); *Weapons of the Weak: Everyday Forms of Peasant Resistance* (1985) and *Domination and the Arts of Resistance: The Hidden Transcript of Subordinate Groups* (1990).

JOSEF SILVERSTEIN is Professor Emeritus, Department of Political Science at Rutgers University, New Jersey. His publications include *The Political Legacy of Aung San* (1972; rev. edn, 1993); *Burma: Military Rule and the Politics of Stagnation* (1977), and *Burmese Politics: The Dilemma of National Unity* (1980).

ALEXANDER WOODSIDE is Professor of History at the University of British Columbia. His publications include, as author, *Vietnam and the Chinese Model* (1971) and *Community and Revolution in Modern Vietnam* (1976), as co-author *In Search of Southeast Asia: A Modern History* (1971), and as editor *Moral Order and the Question of Change* (1983) and *Education and Society in Late Imperial China, 1600–1900* (1994).

Preface

At a time when 'Asia' is being constructed in some quarters in opposition to the 'western' preoccupation with personal freedom, we believe it is timely to examine the contexts and lineages of ideas of freedom in some parts of Eurasia outside its western peninsula. This book is the result of four years of concern with that examination.

The first step was the theme of Freedom adopted for 1994 by the Humanities Research Centre of the Australian National University. One of the three conferences on this theme was 'Ideas of Freedom in Asia', held in July 1994 and convened by the undersigned. That conference was to some extent built around an anticipated dialogue with Orlando Patterson, whose 1991 book, *Freedom in the Making of Western Culture*, had helped to galvanise our own thinking about the Asian backgrounds for ideas of freedom. Although Professor Patterson was unfortunately prevented from attending at the last moment, the occasion proved an exciting one for its many participants.

That was only the first step in many further discussions which have led to this book. Many people contributed to the discussions at the conference and our subsequent debates, without appearing as authors in the book which finally resulted. This is an opportunity to thank Dipesh Chakrabarty, Ariel Heryanto, Mark Elvin, Geremie Barme, Gu Xin, Mabel Lee, Dai Qing, Paik Nak-Chung, Marsillam Simanjuntak, Sanjay Seth, Ray Ileto and Peter Jackson, whose ideas contributed substantially to the ongoing debate.

We also wish to thank Graeme Clarke and the staff of the Humanities Research Centre for their hospitality, imagination and good humour; Linda Poskitt and Clare Guenther, successive administrators of the Economic History of Southeast Asia Project in the Research School of Pacific Studies, for assisting us in preparing the book; and Lewis Mayo and Y. S. Chan for assistance with cover illustration.

David Kelly
Anthony Reid

CHAPTER 1

Freedom – A Eurasian Mosaic

David Kelly

Freedom is not come easy
It have to fight for

T-shirt, Hong Kong, 1993
(Chocolate Creative Products, Inc.)

The Language of Freedom

In early 1995, former US Secretary of State Robert S. McNamara published a headline-making *mea culpa* regarding the US entanglement in Vietnam which included the following:

> We viewed the people and leaders of South Vietnam in terms of our own experience. We saw in them a thirst for – and a determination to fight for – freedom and democracy. We totally misjudged the political forces within the country. We underestimated the power of nationalism to motivate a people (in this case the North Vietnamese and Viet Cong) to fight and die for their beliefs and values . . .[1]

In the act of criticising himself, McNamara unwittingly recapitulates a fault which was first brought to light long ago. In a 1967 book subtitled 'Why Today's War Objectives must be Limited' General Matthew Ridgway, commander of UN forces in the Korean War, poured scorn on his sometime superior General Douglas MacArthur's professed 'knowledge of the Oriental Mind', knowledge that had in fact prompted a series of disasters not unlike what McNamara would come to regret in Vietnam. McNamara's viewpoint, at first glance stereotypically American, may embody a more widely cultivated Orientalist fallacy that we shall discuss shortly.[2] What we focus on at present is McNamara's own specific concern, namely certain non-Western understandings of freedom and democracy.

Let us approach McNamara's statement in good faith. The South Vietnamese, he implies, fought badly for 'freedom and democracy'; the North Vietnamese fought well for patriotism. An alternative reading – that the North wanted freedom from foreign (above all American) domination – seems to have eluded him. As in the case of

1

the Korean War, 'the Americans still did not see that they were, in their new postwar alliances, setting themselves up as the guardians of the status quo against the colonial peoples who were demanding freedom on their own terms'.³ Might the North Vietnamese not claim to have been fighting for 'freedom and autocracy'? This would require stretching the narrowly ideological sense of freedom subscribed to, even now, by McNamara (as well as an appropriately ironical use of 'autocracy'). But to use some terms of art, invoked more formally at a later stage of this discussion, 'organic sovereignal freedom', the power of corporate groups up to the level of the nation-state to act as they please regardless of the wishes of others, has been one of the historically dominant meanings of freedom of much of Asian and also of European history.⁴ It suffices to leave this episode with a question: if North *and* South Vietnamese died with the words *su tu do* ('freedom') on their lips – there exist certifiable accounts of such dying words – what did each mean? Were they referring to the same thing? This book attempts to shed light on such deeply fascinating and important questions.

When we say (or deny) that it's a free country, talk of free trade, freedom of speech, a free citizen, there is a hazy yet readily grasped link between the different things we are talking about. This link extends through an endless series of often highly technical, rule-defined usages in the modern world: in trade, art, culture, philosophy, religion, law and politics, just to name a few.

'Freedom' is one of the most general terms used to qualify human action. As a quality of human action, freedom is further differentiated into such abstract variants as physical and mental, positive and negative, aesthetic and ethical, before being classified as legal, political or institutional. Many a textbook goes further to root the human or existential dimension in a more ontological one. Western culture is strewn with attempts to lodge freedom within some transcendent concept such as chance, fate or determinism. More widely, the contrast of freedom (as free will) and necessity is the source of key notions of moral and legal responsibility, often seen as contemporary counterparts of classical theological conceptions of sin and guilt. So good and edifying does freedom seem to be in modern Western thought that special argument must be entered to qualify certain of its manifestations as undesirable or evil. As Chandran Kukuthas has noted, the value of freedom is so positive that political ideologies as diverse as liberalism and Marxism all vie to claim an exclusive title to its use.⁵

If we accept Orlando Patterson's controversial perspective that freedom was first a fact, then a value, all the commonplace genealogies of our taken-for-granted intellectual lexicon involve a reversal of historical fact. According to Patterson, whose work informs some of the essays in this book, freedom has been a 'widely held vision of life' only in the medieval and above all modern West.[6] For most ancient peoples, and more recent ones resistant to 'Western values', freedom, which for certain reasons entailed a loss of communal identity, was a very artificial and far from desirable state, one to be taken on most reluctantly. Only after its *reinvention* – as we shall see, a critical term of historical art – did freedom become accepted as a core value. This reinvention began with the institution of Greek slavery in ancient times. Only then could it ramify into the series of usages outlined in the preceding paragraphs.

However it emerged or is now understood, freedom is clearly an indispensable premise. Wars have been and still are fought in its name, nations unified and propelled into modernity, eras judged and regimes brought before the bar of their subjects. It would be astonishing if ideological distortions did not enter into the way such judgements are made. Nowhere is this more the case than in the nations, regions and cultural mosaics that form what for want of a better term is known as Asia. The Korean and Vietnam wars are only two – monumentally tragic – cases where ideological constructions of freedom and liberation have left a mark on world history.

Nowhere are reports about degrees of freedom – its perilous ascendancy in Taiwan or its suppression in Rangoon, its exuberance in Manila or its mediocrity in Singapore – in greater currency than in this Asian region. All the registers of freedom as an idea are of potential interest to the observer of humanity here. Nevertheless there is a key cluster which seems repeatedly to claim centre stage and to describe itself as *real* freedom. This is the cluster centring around ethics, politics and law. More esoteric uses of the idea – the freedom of creative artists, of the individual soul before God, of the existential subject and so on – are bracketed out. This may be so only temporarily, and indeed some chapters of this book demonstrate how freedom's higher metaphorical registers, its metaphysical dimensions, may reawaken with a vengeance, reconstructing the givens of cultural identity. But for much of the time, freedom really matters in social history when it figures as social practice, an idea, indeed even a 'shared vision of social life', but more specifically as the underlying source of criteria of legal, ethical, and political practices – human rights, the rule of law, civil society, democracy and so on. This begs the question whether the key meanings or language games embedded in the Western vocabulary are present in the non-European culture, albeit in a different format. Again and again in this book we find evidence that this is indeed the case.

The notion of a *rights-based morality* is one way of describing what is common to many of these practices, and has the advantage of being accepted political science jargon. However, we are aware of the danger of reductionism implicit in this formula. Non-European languages may lack unambiguous equivalents for either *freedom* or *rights*. Modern states are of course generally inclined to adopt some of the legal terms and concepts of Western law, not least commercial law, which is replete with 'rights' and 'freedoms'. Even in the case of Marxist-Leninist regimes, constitutional law generally emerges in the post-revolutionary 'inclusionist' phase,[7] though it rarely corresponds to any genuinely institutionalised norms of civil society, but rather to the personalised power politics of the élite. Nonetheless the systematically correlated concepts *freedom*, *autonomy*, *sovereignty*, *democracy*, *law* and *rights* emerge in these societies as well.[8]

Even so, despite some common patterns in the emergence of a modern language of freedom, we still have little ground for assuming that the referents – the things meant – are entirely interchangeable between languages. As virtually all the contributors show, there is an incessant struggle to extend or curtail the meanings of local, foreign and coined expressions to serve different purposes. Linguistic complexities aside, there remain, even within a single Western language like English, intrinsic difficulties of symbol and referent. 'Having a freedom' does not always mean 'having a right'. There are other images or language games encoded in 'freedom', such as the *removal of a restraint or impediment*, which are for some people (and peoples) the controlling ones. The *capacity to flee the reach of the state* is also one to which rights are irrelevant – or if relevant, ironically so, as when state-ordained 'rights' become something fearful, to be fled. Such circumstances are central to Scott's and Jenner's essays in this book.

Even after narrowing our conceptual scope to the social-practical, we nonetheless encounter a number of blunt value-judgements. 'Asia' figures in the minds of many as a kind of Antarctica of freedom, a cultural zone where social order is the controlling value and where well-adjusted members of family-centred communities reject Western political institutions as harbingers of alienation and chaos. It is consistent with (but logically independent of) certain other views: such as that 'folk' ideals of freedom exist, but are permanently disabled by other cultural factors. Such constructions are far from being merely Western mirages. Notoriously, they emanate from on high in Asia itself. In a 1993 interview Lee Kuan Yew stated:

> As an East Asian looking at America, I find attractive and unattractive features. I like, for example, the free, easy and open relations between people regardless of social status, ethnicity or religion. And the things that I have always admired about America, as against the communist system, I still do: a certain openness in argument about what is good or bad for society; the accountability of public officials; none of the secrecy and terror that's part and parcel of communist government.

But as a total system, I find parts of it totally unacceptable: guns, drugs, violent crime, vagrancy, unbecoming behaviour in public – in sum the breakdown of civil society. The expansion of the right of the individual to behave or misbehave as he pleases has come at the expense of orderly society. In the East the main object is to have a well-ordered society so that everybody can have maximum enjoyment of his freedoms. This freedom can only exist in an ordered state and not in a natural state of contention and anarchy.[9]

Lee's view, neatly rejecting 'their' ill-ordered freedom in favour of 'our' well-ordered one, is of unusual significance. It is consistent with the thinking expressed more obliquely in a document signed by ministers and representatives of Asian states at a meeting in Bangkok from 29 March to 2 April 1993. In their 'Bangkok Declaration' these leading spokespersons adopted a united stance on the impending World Conference on Human Rights to be held in Vienna in May of that year. Among the points affirmed they

8. *Recognize[d]* that while human rights are universal in nature, they must be considered in the context of a dynamic and evolving process of international normsetting, bearing in mind the significance of national and regional particularities and various historical, cultural and religious backgrounds.

10. *Reaffirm[ed]* the interdependence and indivisibility of economic, social cultural, civil and political rights and the need to give equal emphasis to all categories of human rights.[10]

Innocuous as these formulations sound, their intent seems highly questionable. Put in the simplest terms, the concession to the universality of human rights in Clause 8 can be viewed as disingenuous, since Clause 10, and an earlier affirmation of the priority of the principles of sovereignty, territorial integrity and non-interference, effectively disarm it. More generally, given the actual configuration of political powers at work in the region, the Declaration's mild terms constitute an ideological message condoning and legitimating illiberal policies. A factual account of current practices in these political systems would arguably reveal the hollowness of some of the 'categories of human rights' favoured by the Declaration.

The contributors to this book have been inspired to question the Bangkok Declaration. Senior Minister Lee and the signatories posit a simple dialectic of freedom and order: 'here' (in Asia) they cohabit, 'there' (in the West) they do not. One fundamental task of our joint project is to show that 'here' is not susceptible to such blanket generalisations. Asia is not all of a piece, even if there are sufficient family resemblances among its parts to establish a basis for comparison and nuanced generalisation. Nor are the parts understandable without a grasp of the evolving historical fields and communities within which social practices and ideas circulate. The first finding of the present work – and it is surely a major one – is that Western ideas of freedom *have* been widely accepted in Asia, but have had radically different careers depending on the local stock of concepts or practices onto which they have been grafted. When, as the Bangkok signatories advise, we bear in mind 'the significance of national and regional particularities and various historical, cultural and religious backgrounds', we may (and do) come to conclusions rather different to those of Mr Lee.

Social Constructionism and its Pitfalls

'I was', Orlando Patterson states, 'obliged by the findings of my own scholarship to inform my inquiring friends that the basic historical argument, if not the moral purpose of the Bangkok Declaration was fundamentally correct'.[11] Given what I have said above, this (admittedly qualified) support of the Bangkok Declaration raises some serious methodological issues. It is crucially important, as I have argued from the outset, that an account of uses of the language of freedom in Asia proceed on the basis of a thorough grasp of the ideological nature of this language in Asia *and* in the West. Historical sociologists like Patterson provide some useful tools for doing this. Without a sense of the ideological context of modern Asian countries, however, the relativist and 'social constructionist' tools of Patterson and other post-Orientalists are all too easily turned to the purposes of certain strains of nativistic anti-liberalism with which they have in fact little in common. As David Wright-Neville puts it,

> Cast as assaults upon lingering hegemonic European forms on behalf of their (increasingly disenfranchised but increasingly affluent) constituents, the cultural rhetoric of East Asian political conservatives is more accurately read as part of a wider effort to buttress their political authority by inventing an imagined enemy.[12]

In a different vein, Daniel A. Bell and his collaborators argue from the cultural particularity of the liberal project to the likelihood of 'illiberal democracy' in Pacific Asia. Patterson's argument that the modern form of freedom as an ideal was absent from the non-Western world is adduced in their account.[13]

We are happy to begin with a searching critique of Western freedom, breaking it into its component parts in order to see how these may have been – and are – put together differently. But the general methods of social constructionism do not fully support such views as those of Lee Kuan Yew and the Bangkok Declaration. Thus while Patterson writes of a 'stillbirth' of freedom in the non-Western world,[14] 'freedom' as he uses the term refers to an elaborately defined cultural complex rather different to the US-style libertarianism so often caricatured by Eastern ideologues.

It is not, however, possible to refute Patterson's ideas of freedom in Asia without refuting commonplaces of Western thinking on the subject as well. Such a procedure involves some troubling methodological and conceptual issues. A title such as *Asian Freedoms* is open to the objection that Asia is not a coherent geographical or cultural entity. Talking as if it were is the result of a kind of original sin called 'essentialism', which leads Western authorities to project a uniform Otherness onto the very different worlds of Turkey, India, Vietnam and so on. This can be seen as a move by the West to incorporate and dominate these other parts of the world.[15]

We have no wish to describe further the epicycles of a futile debate. Rather than Orientalism, what the contributors to this book are collectively pursuing is something one might rather call 'Eurasianism'.[16] Critics of Orientalism correctly point out that there is no underlying unity, no Asian essence, shared at a deep level by all cultures from Turkey to Japan. But to assert, as some seem to, a total absence of cross-cutting relationships is contrary to common experience. To use a no doubt overly familiar analogy, members of a family are recognisable as such because they each bear one or more, but not necessarily all, of a set of common traits. *No one trait is essential.* The societies and cultures of Asia – indeed of Eurasia – are linked by many such systems of family resemblance, some broader (like those associated with the world religions, e.g. Buddhism, Hinduism, Islam or Christianity) and some narrower, like those related to Chinese, or, where it applies, English, or Arabic, literary and intellectual culture. In many cases the relationship crosses the imaginary line between Europe and Asia. In certain respects, for example, Marxism-Leninism links China, Vietnam and North Korea culturally to Eastern Europe and the former Soviet Union more truly than to some of their neighbours.

We make no claims, in the manner of General MacArthur, to 'know the Oriental Mind'. Nor can we afford to incorporate 'Asia' as a secondary, dwarf variety of something 'we' in Western countries regard as authentic and privileged. Australia, with its history of penal servitude and the state-ordained enslavement of previously free peoples, the Aborigines and Torres Strait Islanders, is not a good place from which to assert an immaculately conceived sense of moral value, which might confer the right to judge those around us (though it has, partly in virtue of these factors, produced a robust civic culture). But there is a more crucial point, captured metaphorically in Patterson's book, where he notes that 'the revolutionary originality of jazz as a musical genre created by black Americans is in no way undercut by the evidently strong influence of Western popular and classical music on its development'.[17] There is a major procedural issue at stake here, one with both cultural and political dimensions. It is applied with striking clarity by Edward Friedman, who argues forcefully:

> Although it is in no way evil that Westerners feel pride that modern democracy originated in the Atlantic basin, Occidentalism, the glorification of a better part of Western culture as if it were the whole, obscures the actual sources of despotism and democracy. A spotlight on 'Western' culture permits chauvinists elsewhere to strut in traditional garments and stigmatize democrats as virtual foreigners.[18]

Patterson and Friedman stand on the following common ground: in culture, cross-fertilisation is all. Neither origins (African music, Asian culture) nor later influences (classical music, Western culture) are sufficient to determine outcomes (jazz, Asian freedoms). Nor are origins obliterated by such influences.

Our Eurasianism is as much opposed to Friedman's Occidentalism as it is to Orientalism.[19] In many of the case studies presented in this book, 'freedom' figures as a neologism coined in order to translate a Western term that previously had no clear local equivalent in the non-Western language. This, however, says nothing about the subsequent history of the concept, its political legitimacy or its realisation in sociopractical terms. When we go on to talk about the universality of certain interpretations of freedom, we mean in the sense that jazz, an African-American music, is both culturally specific (not the less 'black' for incorporating 'white' elements) and readily appreciated across cultural boundaries. Nothing intrinsically precludes the ideas discussed as 'Asian freedoms' from living a life of their own in the culture which we might perhaps now relabel as Eurasian. Equally, a constructionist approach – source of the concept of reinvention adverted to previously – in the humanities and social sciences provides no support for Friedman's chauvinists who 'strut in traditional garments and stigmatize democrats as virtual foreigners'.

This book supports Friedman's further point that the Asian experiences in political and intellectual development have valuable lessons to offer, particularly once the shibboleths of Orientalism and Occidentalism are discarded. In sum:

- 'Asian' peoples fully participate in global modernity and its paradoxes of increasing liberty and increasing discipline,[20] while differing from other regions of global modernity in ways that render contentious the appropriation of Western intellectual-cultural discourses.

- Servitude and oppression are resented everywhere; Asian peoples do not inhabit a separate planet. When they themselves appeal to freedom as a universal standard of political and other values, this can hardly be dismissed as a bourgeois Western, hegemonic invention.

What the contributors accept from current literature exemplified by Patterson and Friedman is a broad approach of *constructionism* – summed up in Patterson's view that 'freedom was socially constructed, not discovered – for it was an invented value'.[21] But this formulation is accepted with a grain of caution. The terms 'socially constructed' and 'invented' appear to imply a freedom of an extreme type, a licence to construct or invent without regard to conditions or limitations. This is not our interpretation. The constructionist formula does not imply that one throws a collection of facts into the air to see where they come down. Nor is it a view that this is what people do in making history.[22]

Also to be kept at a distance is what Roger Keesing identified as the 'cultural constructive paradigm', namely that 'neither biology nor the material world impinge directly on the human condition except as they are constructed and interpreted through locally cumulated, conventional – that is, cultural – symbols'.[23] As Wright-Neville warns, this paradigm supports 'a proliferation of cultural relativisms' among whose failings is the tendency to play down deviations from cultural norms, submerging them within an assumption of the state as the 'epitome of the organic unity of the nation'.[24]

Rather, we appropriate social constructionism as a rule of thumb for research into an intrinsically complex topic: it focuses attention on the ways in which culture and thought are subject to systems of power and privilege, yet open to defensive tactics on the part of the powerless. Neither biology nor the material world is ruled out of this field of vision, although it is the material world rather than biology that is more frequently brought into play. In the present era, the nation-state holds many strategic means of constructing or inventing values, but rarely is it successful in doing so with totalitarian efficiency. When political élites in Asia epitomise the political culture of their surrounding community in terms of an organic unity, constructionism as used here alerts us to the questions of legitimacy that such claims seek to pre-empt. What levels of censorship and surveillance operate in the background of these claims? We are tempted to speculate still further when emerging entrepreneurs in Singapore or Malaysia develop economic peripheries in neighbouring regions. In countries such as Cambodia and Burma, the defence of 'Asian values' may prove to serve still more instrumental – not to say material – purposes, such as excusing the latter from entrenching human rights, democracy and other tokens of freedom. The rhetoric operating here, while deserving closer attention, is not the central concern of this volume. As intellectual historians the contributors seek in the first place to make sense of the tangle of the past, to clear away the overlays of tradition and modernity and grasp the mosaic of competing values, interests and frames of reference that is revealed. Only then, it seems, may the claims and counter-claims about the standards of supposed 'Asian' or 'Western' or 'universal' values be themselves evaluated.

When applied to Asian societies, Patterson's thesis regarding slavery and its 'recombinants' (serfdom, debt-bondage and so on) as a moulding institution holds up somewhat less well than the general constructionist model in which it is posed. This is not to say that Asian institutions of slavery have not played a role. They certainly have, but not exclusively in the format that Patterson may lead one to expect, namely that of 'weak slavery' inducing 'weak freedom'. Slavery was a strongly developed state system in ancient China and Korea, yet freedom failed to gel in any modern sense. For much of the time in most instances, the slave's debt-bondage was at least in principle redeemable, making it a less permanent badge of dishonour than in 'classical' chattel slavery. Slavery's weakness in the nineteenth century is demonstrated in Thailand, China and Korea, where it rapidly shrivels away and virtually disappears in the face of concerted Western cultural impact. Capitalism seems easily to have brushed aside the resistance slavery, as debt-bondage, offered to the newly demanded mobility of labour. (Ironically, in the process it also tended to overthrow certain protections against other forms of exploitation which slavery sometimes offered.)

Christianity was very early transformed by Greek-inspired notions of freedom, and has ever since been a potent bearer of these values. 'In its Pauline form freedom in the literal sense of redemption from the spiritual slavery of sin became the central religious goal.'[25] Christianity is old in Asia, but not as old as Buddhism. Recognising the fundamental theme of liberation in Buddhism, Ian Mabbett surveys the early literature, turning up a series of concerns that hinge on the doctrine of *Dhamma/dharma*. This is significant for the chapters on Burma and Thailand in the modern era, where the Buddhist legacy has an important role in shaping contemporary political thought.

The capacity to flee the reach of the state, a question we glanced at above, is flagged as significant to two macro-regions, China and Southeast Asia. The chapters by Scott and Jenner throw revealing, if contrasting, light on the ambiguities of the state's modernising role. Scott finds 'a historical logic that connects the codified individual freedoms of liberal thought to the growth of the state'. In Pacific Asia this had more to do with the nation-building efforts of local powers than with foreign hegemony. In most of these cases slavery was of subsidiary economic importance. Even less were they systems of social discipline compatible with modern institutions; slave-owning classes are often bastions of conservative opposition to such institutions. Hence modernising states, wanting to put exploitation on a businesslike basis, had every reason to wield freedom and its cognates in order to delegitimise and eventually remove vestigial slavery. Jenner finds that the modern oppressive apparatus of the Chinese state had important imperial precursors. Ironically, this was less a matter of institutionalised slavery than of a bureaucratic encirclement, continuing into the present, of most if not all potentially civil institutions.

In Thailand, as in China, freedom as a modern social value was initially shaped by the élite's confrontation with colonialism and its peculiar criteria as to what constitutes civilisation. Yet as Thanet Aphornsuvan's chapter suggests, something very different resulted. This was due in large part to the strikingly distinct institution of slavery, which continued to be an *attractive* status for certain strata, but also to the pervasive political culture rooted in Buddhism.

Scott's state is an engine of calculative rationality. It organises and alienates the life-world of peoples who obstinately cling to the margins, the spaces that are the sole support of all they know and all they need to know of freedom. His synthesis focuses on land-use regimes like forestry, but threads these themes back to the grasping power of the primate cities. Jenner objects to none of this, but shows that the Chinese state had a similar set of governing principles, though not couched in calculative rational terms. In Scott's Southeast Asia, modernity replaces and overturns traditional forms of accommodation and is subtractive; Jenner's modernity has an additive effect on traditional forms of state power in the Chinese/neo-Confucian world.

China's attempt to follow the path of modernisation by way of constitutional, liberal institutions was a notorious failure. Yet freedom as a criterion of civilised modernity was never totally suppressed even under Maoism, and has returned as a powerful ideological undercurrent. David Kelly attempts to use the constructionist principle to locate some genuine 'origins of modern freedom' in China. No matter how inadequately framed, the appeals made by contemporary Chinese intellectuals to freedom and democracy as universals cannot be dismissed as a nihilistic derogation of 'traditional' values.

Vera Mackie investigates the links between patriarchal authority and the new language of freedom and popular rights in Meiji Japan. Japanese liberalism, crucially a rural rather than an urban force, cannot be encompassed in the idea of a confrontation, leading to

Confucian discourse retarding liberal democratic ideas. Mackie shows that much as Confucianism was constantly being reinvented and reconstituted, Confucianist language 'could be used to justify the most modern practices and institutions'.

The dilemmas of gender relations in Japan point to a fateful fault line in all the East Asian Confucianist cultures. Women like Kishida Toshiko unhesitatingly described their situation as one of enslavement. The education they received was merely decorative. The rise of a modern mobilised Japanese state required the end of this unquestioned common fate of women, but in the absence of Western-style buffers between the public and private spheres, little could be done to liberate gender difference from the realm of rigidly hierarchical relations. Debates on the nation-state as family set the scene for later developments in socialism and feminism early in the twentieth century (when Japan's intellectual influence over China, Vietnam and Korea was at its zenith). In all these countries community and freedom appear as twin ideals which defy a final reconciliation. The family remained an oppressive microcosm within a wider exploitative imperium.

Indonesia, like Korea, has inscribed freedom on the banners of successful political movements. Here, however, the outcomes have on the whole been far less salutary. Anthony Reid's study of the Indonesian idea of *merdeka* ('freedom') shows that this was not for lack of strong local traditions in which slavery, manumission and freedman status played a conspicuous role. The Malay, Javanese and Bugis legal codes allowed for the freeing of slaves; by the seventeenth century non-slave status was 'an aspect of the good life'. White Rajah Brooke's comment on the Bugis might well serve as a paradigm for Eurasianists: 'amid all of the nations of the East . . . the Bugis alone have arrived at the threshold of recognised rights.'

Despite this rich heritage, Indonesia remains a case of the 'Asian values' syndrome in which values of liberation, freedom or rights are given a communalistic twist. But few would put Indonesia in as harsh a category as Burma. Josef Silverstein weaves fascinatingly between the Buddhist traditions already adverted to and the modern liberation movements to which both the SLORC (the Burmese *junta*) and Daw Aung San Suu Kyi lay claim in their starkly differing ways.

Vietnam is an intriguing piece of the Asian mosaic, being cross-cut by Buddhist, Confucian, Western colonial and Marxist zones of influence. Alexander Woodside underscores the findings of other contributors who have identified important traditions of liberty within an admittedly despotic order. Woodside investigates early French reports of Vietnam as an 'academic democracy', partly through the writings of the eighteenth-century polymath Le Quy Don. These reveal a highly articulated sense of the moral autonomy required of a Confucian bureaucrat which provided a fragile limit on despotism.

Rousseau wrote that 'Man was born free, and everywhere he is in chains'. Hegel, in another well-known quotation, held that 'the Orientals knew only that one is free'.[26] Despite great efforts on the part of certain of its leaders, ideas of freedom, in a host of interpretations and practical applications, are very much alive and well throughout the Asian region today. Just as 'really existing freedom' in the West has had a chequered career and is recurrently subject to contention among rival claimants and representations, so too does Asia display innumerable variations on the broad theme of human liberation. The two sides of the Rousseauan coin are simply more obvious in the latter case.

Freedom has entered the modern Asian languages through a veritable bazaar of older expressions rooted in local institutions, practices and concepts. These have often been reworked to serve the new ideologies of nation-building, liberation, revolution and, latterly, development. Nonetheless, their origins in ancient institutions of hierarchy, dependency and personalistic ties often threaten the stability of such new contents as equality, autonomy and legality.

It is a Weberian theme that such forms of rationalisation accompany the rise of freedoms in the modern world. In a brilliant study, Max Weber pointed to a particularly cogent case study drawn from music. The conventions of modern Western music rest on the technique of equal temperament.[27] The plethora of naturally occurring tones was subjected to a mathematical simplification which was both liberating and constraining. The result is a wonderfully flexible convention that allows great interchangeability of musical materials. The contemporary orchestra and its repertoire are hard to conceive without it. But the artistic freedom that this opened up to composers and conductors came at a cost. The ancient tonal systems replaced by equal temperament contained many sounds which are actually more consonant and 'true' to the ear. Equal temperament is in fact off-key to ears trained in these systems. To the modern ear, it is the older musical intervals which sound off-key: a fine example of genuine relativism in culture. No traveller in the Asian region can fail to observe how local musical cultures have, for better or for worse, taken up equal temperament, fitting local materials and instruments to it. The needs of mass culture conspire with the fact that the simplified scale system soon (in a single generation, perhaps – often less) loses its 'off' quality and becomes the norm; it is the older instruments and sounds which sound off until they are brought into the new scheme of sound.

Freedom is in some ways like equal temperament. It is remarkable the extent to which freedom, however translated, however interpreted, has sooner or later become a standard with which to measure other values, both locally and in the West itself. While Western intellectuals have in recent years rebelled somewhat sheepishly against freedom and other conceptions rooted in the Enlightenment, there are many in Asia who are resolute in their defence.

In order to recognise the full gamut of expressions of freedom, it is necessary to free our thinking, as far as we can, of both Orientalism and 'Occidentalism'. To the extent that we see the whole history of freedom, we must accept that certain of its manifestations – mainly those associated with national sovereignty – are tainted but nevertheless authentic branches of the tree. Certain manifestations of sovereignal freedom in the West have been more destructive than any others known.[28] Those who confer a 'motherhood' aura of sanctity on freedom would do well to consider that it comes in a package with heightened social disciplines and controls. It may be that in the East there are freedoms which, in adapting freedom to their own patterns of discipline and control, will ultimately be seen as peculiarly constructive.

Notes

1 *In Retrospect: the Tragedy and Lessons of Vietnam* (New York: Times Books, 1995), p. 322.
2 Matthew B. Ridgway, *The Korean War* (New York: Doubleday, 1967), p. 78.
3 Edwin P. Hoyt, *The Day the Chinese Attacked* (New York: Paragon House, 1994), p. 84.
4 Orlando Patterson, *Freedom in the Making of Western Culture*, vol. 1 (New York: Basic Books, 1991). Thus Patterson's notion of freedom as a 'tripartite value' (p. 5): 'From the moment of their chordal fusion in classical Greece, a tension has always existed among sovereignal and civic freedoms. Yet . . . all three have remained a vital part of the Western consciousness.' See also note 25.
5 Chandran Kukuthas, 'Freedom', in Robert E. Goodin and Philip Pettit (eds), *A Companion To Contemporary Political Philosophy* (Oxford: Blackwell, 1993).
6 Patterson, *Freedom*. For critical views see R. W. Davis, *The Origins of Modern Freedom in the West* (Stanford: Stanford University Press, 1995); Dimitrys Kyrtatas, 'The Western Way to Freedom', *New Left Review*, 197 (Jan.–Feb. 1993), pp. 85–95.
7 Ken Jowitt, *New World Disorder: The Leninist Extinction* (Berkeley: University of California Press, 1992), pp. 88–120.
8 Rather than a *list* such as freedom, autonomy, sovereignty, democracy, law, rights, etc, we need a *matrix* (itself, of course, only a segment of the complex manifold needed to represent all the temporal and spatial variations). See table opposite.

Freedom: An Asian Lexical Matrix

English	Burmese	Thai	Indonesian	Vietnamese*	Chinese	Japanese	Korean
freedom (*independence*)	lut-lat-ye	seriphap	kemerdekaan				
freedom (*personal*)	lut-myauk-ye (*detached from affairs*)	issaraphap (*free situation*) thai (*non-slave*)	merdeka (*non-slave*) bebas (*unconstrained*)	(自由) tu do	自由 ziyou	自由 jiyū	自由 chayu
autonomy	ko-paing-oak-choke-khwint	kaan pokkhrong ton eeng	mandiri	(自主) tu tri	自主 zizhu	自主 jishu	自主 chachu
sovereignty	a-choke-achar-ahnar	ekkarat	kedaulatan (*Arabic*)	(主權) chu quyen	主權 zhuquan	主權 shuken	主權 chukwŏn
democracy	demokrasi	prachathipatai (*peopledom*)	demokrasi	(民主) dan chu	民主 minzhu	民主 minshu	民主 minchu
law	oo-padae	kotmai	hukum (*Arabic*)	(法律) phap luat	法律 fazhi	法律 hōuritsu	法律 pŏpchaek
rights	a-khwint-a-ye	sitthi	hak (*Arabic*)	(權利) quyen loi	權利 quanli	權利 kenri	權利 kwŏnryŏk

* Chinese characters are no longer used in Vietnamese, but have been included to show the historical origins of the words.

9   Lee Kuan Yew, 'Culture is Destiny', interview with Fareed Zakaria, *Foreign Affairs*, 73, 2 (March–April 1994), pp. 109–126.

10 'Bangkok Declaration of Asian States', April 1993; published in *Human Rights: The New Consensus* (London: Regency Press in association with the UN High Commissioner for Refugees, 1994), pp. 293, 295.

11 Freedom, Slavery and the Modern Construction of Rights, paper presented *in absentia* to a conference on 'Ideas of Freedom in Asia', ANU Humanities Research Centre, Canberra, July 1994.

12 David Wright-Neville, 'The Politics of Pan Asianism: Culture, Capitalism and Diplomacy in East Asia', *Pacifica Review* 7, 1 (1995), pp. 1–26; quote from p. 19.

13 Daniel Bell, David Brown, Kanishka Jayasuriya and David Martin Jones (eds), *Towards Illiberal Democracy in Pacific Asia* (New York: St Martin's Press, 1995), pp. 4–7.

14 See Ch. 1 of Patterson, *Freedom*.

15 It would be useless to attempt to disclaim the charge of essentialism, or its specific form of Orientalism. It is like a series of other original sins which are in common currency in the twentieth century. Such terms all too often spell the end of further questioning, of any interest in what *else* the target of such labelling happens to sustain. This is not to deny the intellectual contributions of many of the critics of Orientalism. For a useful overview of current debates on Orientalism, see Gyan Prakash, 'Writing Post-Orientalist Histories of the Third World', *Comparative Studies in Society and History* (1990), pp. 383–407.

16 Some readers have felt that like 'Oriental', the word 'Eurasian' has entrenched pejorative connotations. 'Words mean what I want them to mean. The question is – who is to be the master?' (Lewis Carroll). In the present case, our bearings have been taken from the title of the musical ensemble 'Eurasian Echoes', whose members are Korean and Japanese, and whose musical sources are East Asian, European, and African-American. The seamless fusion of universal and relativistic frames of reference on their eponymous CD was an inspiration – though admittedly hard to emulate in the written word.

17 Patterson, *Freedom*, p. 429.

18 'Democratization: Generalizing the East Asian Experience', in Edward Friedman (ed.), The *Politics of Democratization: Generalizing East Asian Experiences* (Boulder: Westview Press, 1994), pp. 19–57; quote from p. 42.

19 The sense in which this term is used here lies close to, but is not identical with, that of Xiaomei Chen, *Occidentalism: A Theory Of Counter-Discourse in Post-Mao China* (New York: Oxford University Press, 1994).

20 Peter Wagner, *A Sociology of Modernity: Liberty and Discipline* (London: Routledge, 1994).

21 Patterson, *Freedom*, pp. 2–3.

22 Our understanding of social constructionism has points of contact with what Stephen Welch usefully generalises as phenomenological social science: Stephen Welch, *The Concept of Political Culture* (New York: St Martin's Press, 1993). In similar vein is the work of Pierre Bourdieu. See *In Other Words: Essays Towards a Reflexive Sociology* (Cambridge: Polity Press, 1990). The social constructionism criticised by some as arguing that '*langue* or some sort of social structure fixes the ideas that are the content of individual minds' is not strictly relevant to the approach adopted here. See Mark

Bevir, 'Mind and Method in the History of Ideas', *History and Theory*, 36, 1(1997), p. 171.

23 Roger Keesing, 'Asian Cultures?', *Asian Studies Review*, 15, 2 (1991), pp. 43–9.

24 David Wright-Neville, 'The Politics of Pan-Asianism', pp. 12, 25.

25 Cf. Patterson, *Freedom*, part 4. Quote from p. 315. But see also Kyrtatas, 'The Western Way to Freedom'.

26 Jean-Jacques Rousseau, *The Social Contract* (London: Penguin, 1968), p. 49. Hegel's saying is cited below in Thanet Aphornsuvan's chapter: see his footnote 14.

27 Max Weber, *The Rational and Social Foundations of Music* (Carbondale, Il.: Southern Illinois University Press, 1958).

28 Patterson writes, 'it is one of the central arguments of this work that all three elements of freedom, derived as they are from the ancient relation of slavery, have the potential of being either refined upward into a civilized ideal or backward to the primal domination of slavery at its most elementary state: the savage right that inheres in one man's power of life and death over another' (*Freedom*, p. 365). He states elsewhere that while 'moralists or philosophers may rail with outrage at this seeming libel of the ideal we cherish . . . the bleak socio-historical truth remains that in their claim that what they felt was freedom, the Nazis had the whole long history of the Western tradition of sovereignal freedom on their side, (*Freedom*, p. 404).

CHAPTER 2

Buddhism and Freedom

Ian Mabbett

Christianity is sometimes seen as a major contributor to the traditions of freedom in Western civilisation.[1] It is then natural to ask whether, or how far, any other religion played a similar part in lands where Christianity was not present as a major cultural force.

As soon as we turn to Asia, Buddhism presents itself as a natural term of comparison. Like Christianity, it came to stand for universal values and acquired (though to a smaller extent) a missionary spirit. It offered believers the goal of salvation at the end of a spiritual quest, and rejected the particularistic values of any political system or social order. Although the Buddhist message was not at the outset concerned with social relationships, it is clear that Buddhism early acquired a strong emphasis on practical morality and that, to the extent that it gained wide following and the patronage of the great, it became involved in social organisation. But Buddhist teachings always held the potential to inspire an inner quest for salvation, rejecting in principle the legitimacy of social constraints on individual action and replacing them with the strict discipline of the monk's life outside the jurisdiction of political institutions. In these respects the claims of Buddhism to be accounted a force for the recognition of freedom as an important value in Asian countries appear *prima facie* quite strong.

Here I shall review some of the relevant basic Buddhist doctrines in order to assess how far one might argue for an elective affinity between Buddhism and the liberal ideas of personal freedom and human rights which have become basic assumptions in modern democratic societies. It would be possible to confine such a review to a survey of concepts in a particular set of canonical scriptures. This would provide a relatively sharp focus, but I believe that it would encourage confusion between abstract theory and historical reality, for Buddhism consists of far more

19

than any set of scriptures can encompass. Therefore, although attention will be directed especially to the Pali scriptures of Theravada
Buddhism as a way of identifying early doctrines, some comments
will also be made about the operation of Buddhism in practice, particularly about the institution of the monkhood as a state within a state. It is
only by looking at some of Buddhism's historical vicissitudes, however
briefly, that we can appreciate the complexity of the relationship
between Buddhism and the concept of freedom: in practice, Buddhism
contributed to freedom in some ways and limited it in others; in yet
others it belongs to a different universe of thought.

Liberation and Existential Freedom

One of the most striking features of Buddhist doctrine in historical
practice, common to countries influenced by Theravada (Sri Lanka,
Burma, Cambodia, Laos and Thailand) and Mahayana (China, Japan,
Korea and Vietnam) traditions alike, is the value it places on all life, not
just human. This value is embodied in ritualised acts of compassion
towards helpless creatures.

The bestowing of freedom upon living beings, known as *fang sheng*
('release life') was an ancient Chinese Buddhist custom. Monasteries
would often have a pond dedicated to *fang sheng*, where the pious
would place fish specially purchased from the fishmonger, and there
might be, at the rear of a monastery, stables, byres or sties for the care
of livestock donated and fed by the devout. The most popular benefi-
ciaries of this custom were those which could fend for themselves when
given their freedom – birds, reptiles and fish. In the 1920s and 1930s,
as Holmes Welch reports, there were ceremonial mass releases of birds
in homage to Kuan Yin, Buddhist bodhisattva and goddess of mercy;
in Hong Kong in 1963, as an act of piety intended to mediate the ending of a drought, there was a release of 300 sparrows along with turtles,
monkeys and barking deer; on later dates large numbers of other creatures were released, many bought from pet shops, and fishing boats
were seen avidly spreading nets in the vicinity of pious releases of fish.[2]

This idea of merit acquired by bestowing freedom upon sentient
beings is not just a peculiarity of Chinese Mahayana Buddhism. It can
be found in full vigour in traditional strongholds of Theravada
Buddhism such as Thailand or Cambodia, where birds can be bought
at markets specifically so that they can be released;[3] in Thailand
unwanted pet dogs are commonly deposited in Buddhist *wat*.[4]

In a sense, then, it is possible to find in Buddhist doctrine a practical
value placed on liberation. Of course it is quite proper to distinguish
between the rather cynical spirit in which many lay Buddhists no doubt

conduct such exercises[5] and the underlying spirit of compassion (*karuna*) which represents the real meaning of Buddhist teaching on the treatment of sentient beings. The latter has come to be very important in Buddhism, and it would be a grave mistake to overlook the importance of the principle of *avihimsa*, 'non-injury', as a principle of Buddhist life.[6]

In what sense, then, can Buddhism be described as a teaching of freedom? Let us go straight to the heart of the matter: early Buddhism was founded on the quest for enlightenment (*bodhi*), a state wherein the quester's ignorance (*avidya*[7]) would be dispelled. In the Buddhist view, the contents of the world lack any enduring substantial reality of their own. Ignorance produces false belief in the substantial independent reality of things in the world (pleasurable objects, other people, even one's own self) and consequently entails powerful attachment to them. This attachment or grasping is responsible for all forms of suffering. The self is not a substantial entity but a current made up of permanently unsatisfied cravings – unsatisfied because their objects are ephemeral, lacking essential reality. This current is perpetuated from life to life. Enlightenment, however, cuts the cycle. Ignorance is dispelled; all attachment, whether to self, other selves or things, is dissolved by this insight. Craving ceases, and there is no more rebirth. Clearly, then, Buddhism can be correctly described as a doctrine of existential freedom, for according to its teaching the goal of spiritual cultivation (*bhavana*) is release (*vimukti*) from the burden of suffering and rebirth.

How useful is this conclusion for the study of freedom in history? Writing about modern Burma, E. Sarkisyanz draws together a number of references supporting the association between Buddhist values and social or political liberty – for example, the Burmese poet Thakin Kudaw Hmain, who described political independence as 'nirvana within this world'.[8] Such cases show that Buddhists have appealed to their religious values in validation of a belief in freedom in some sense.

It is, however, necessary to acknowledge that the identification of political independence with *nirvana* – the extinction of ignorance and attachment whereby enlightenment is realised – is a piece of poetic symbolism and not at all a statement of Buddhist doctrine. It would be a mistake to interpret Buddhism as a manifesto for social action or a contribution to political theory. Early Buddhism, it must be emphasised, declares all worldly institutions, activities and concerns to be equally transient and unworthy of ultimate concern. The claims of rulers to rights over the lives of their subjects may indeed be founded on delusion, but so too are those of reformers and revolutionaries. No one social doctrine is accorded unique value, for life in society is vain and empty.

This much is theory. In historical practice, Buddhism was adapted to various social situations; its original indifference to the social bases of authority could be enlisted to support either a passive acceptance of established institutions of power or a positive rejection of them. Examples of either tendency can easily be multiplied; some will be noticed at various points below.

Choice, Karma and Hierarchy

The Buddhist concept of *karma* is rich in implications for the theoretical discussion of freedom. With it we may link the Buddhist doctrine of non-self, *anatman*, though this latter idea can be noticed only very briefly here.

Karma, literally 'action', is in its now most familiar meaning a moral law of cause and effect. Every action (*karma* in the literal sense) necessarily produces consequences for the actor: good actions produce good effects, bad ones produce bad – the consequence is totally inescapable. This doctrine has an important bearing on the question of freedom through its implications for free will.

Many scholars (notably Max Weber[9]) have been inclined to see *karma* as part and parcel of an Indian fatalism that makes human strivings hopeless and blights all rational endeavour for betterment of one's lot. Whether this in fact applies to Buddhism needs to be questioned. Buddhism is especially liable to attract this characterisation because it adds to the *karma* idea the concept of non-self, *anatman*, which denies substantial reality to the individual person and replaces it with a stream of events governed by *karma*, as described above. This stream is not an entity; it is more like a wave motion. From one life to the next there is no passage of a substantial soul but simply a transfer of a phenomenon. The seeker after salvation must lose any idea of self or of the reality of the senses through which the self apprehends the world.[10] Thus one is to see through the world, not seek to modify it by any act of will.

Some scholars have cogently refuted the deterministic interpretation – the denial of any scope for the initiation of a free act – which such a doctrine might seem to imply. It has been argued, for example, that Weber was misled in his interpretation of the *karma* doctrine as fatalism by identifying it too closely with the Hindu validation of the caste system.[11] In this system, birth, the product of past *karma*, determines an individual's position in society, and can be seen as an iron destiny that allows no scope for human endeavour. The mistake is to suppose that caste rules automatically go with *karma*. In Buddhism, they do not; Buddhism has carried the doctrine of *karma* to countries where there is nothing like the caste system, and where status may be achieved, not ascribed. In Thailand, for example, Buddhist teachings are well entrenched, but the social system does not ordain that an individual's rank is permanently fixed by birth; one's condition at birth is indeed the result of past *karma*, but may be changed in the course of a lifetime by action in the present.[12]

Gananath Obeyesekere convincingly argues against *karma* as determinism. For him, the responsibility for fate is placed by *karma* 'quite squarely on the individual himself';[13] the freedom to shape one's own destiny is not annulled by the action of past *karma*. Padmasiri de Silva similarly interprets the Buddhist teaching as implying that the individual can control the forces of past and present to influence the future.[14] He distinguishes between two models of *karma*: the 'judicial model', which emphasises the role of the *result* of an action (the according of just deserts), and the 'craftsmanship model', which emphasises the role of the *agent* of an action.[15] In the latter, individuals are able to shape their moral character by repeated acts of the same sort, for these tend to fix the character and create a predisposition to reproduce characteristic behaviour in the future. *Karma* is a form of self-expression.[16]

There are different versions of the *karma* doctrine, which have different implications for individuals' control over their destiny. If good actions produce good results, and bad actions bad results, can the result of past bad actions be neutralised by good actions performed in the present? Or is one doomed inevitably to experience the fated consequences?

On the whole (though with an important technical qualification[17]) early doctrine appears to have maintained that the results of each action are entirely inescapable. Good and bad *karma* are not pooled together; the results of each have to be experienced separately. Even an enlightened being, an *arhant*, still had to endure the results of past evil.[18] Thus in the *Majjhima Nikaya* we are told of the *arhant* Angulimala, who at the time of attaining *arhant* status still had to expiate the *karma* of multiple murders. During his alms round he was attacked and struck by a clod of earth, a stick, and some gravel. His head was streaming with blood and his bowl was smashed. This was the inescapable result of his past bad deeds, which still had to be paid for.[19]

The belief in the separate fruition of all *karma* persists in modern times. Thus in Burma there is told the story of U Khant, a villager who won 1320 *kyat* from a 50-*kyat* bet. Over-excited by his good fortune, he died the next morning. The *karma* of past good deeds determined his win; that of past bad deeds determined his death.[20]

There has been, however, a strong tendency in the course of Buddhist history for the less palatable consequences of the *karma* doctrine to be mitigated. Buddhist traditions observed in modern times characteristically show a strong preoccupation with 'merit-making', with practical actions which may maximise one's good *karma*, and a tradition has developed which treats *karma* as a pooling of good and bad actions in the past (like a bank balance, which is a pooling of past deposits and withdrawals); the results of past misdeeds can be effectively abolished by merit-making actions in the present.[21]

The bad effects of past deeds may (in the Theravada tradition, for example) be bought off by taking to the life of an ascetic in old age; or, again, the nature of one's rebirth may be substantially determined not just by past *karma* but by what is wished for at the moment of death.[22] Gananath Obeyesekere argues that *karma* was too stark a doctrine to accept unmodified, and various ways of influencing one's fate were sought in Buddhist countries to meet a psychological need. These included the practice of astrology, a remnant of an ancient cosmological system not strictly compatible with the *karma* doctrine, and the appeal to divine grace (strong even in Theravada countries).[23]

It is easy to see that the relationship of the *karma* doctrine to issues of freedom is complex. *Karma* does not in any simple sense represent a teaching either of free will or of determinism. It combines elements of both: in the strict interpretation of the doctrine the fate created by past deeds is indeed inescapable, but in the present moment there is perfect freedom to choose courses of action which will affect the future. The possibility of free choice in the present is emphasised. 'It is choice or intention that I call karma – mental work – for having chosen a man acts by body, speech and mind.'[24]

Buddhism shares a belief in *karma* with Hinduism, which is historically identified with an elaborate pattern of social organisation that in various obvious ways denies the freedom of the individual. While Hinduism lays down minute regulations governing all aspects of life,[25] Buddhism, by contrast, is often seen as favouring a more egalitarian form of society and as challenging social discrimination.

Proponents of this view are able to appeal to a variety of scriptural sources. The Pali canon knew the legend of the institution of kingship by contract between the first ruler, Maha Sammata ('the Great Chosen One'), and the population that elected him, making him king in return for a portion of the rice crop. The need to have a ruler arose only after the corruption of human nature, and the institution of private property was part of a process of decline that led to stealing, lying and the need for punishment.[26] As Spellman comments, 'This Buddhist legend is clearly a theory of social contract',[27] and it evinces the values of what Orlando Patterson calls civic freedom.

Buddhism also knew the ideal of the *cakravartin*, the 'wheel-turner' or universal emperor under whose benign dominion all beings enjoyed peace and well-being. A *cakravartin* should rule with right-eousness (*dhammena*).[28] A fable describes the future *cakravartin*, Cakkavatti-Samkha, who will renounce his throne, give away the contents of his treasury to the destitute, and become a wandering monk in the company of all his soldiers.[29] In the same spirit, a king is represented as saying to his successor, 'And whosoever in thy kingdom is poor, to him let wealth be given'.[30] The military and judicial functions of kingship, exalted in so many Hindu texts, were often regarded with disfavour by early Buddhist thinkers as the 'dismal science', for a king must in the course of his duties perform many acts that harm other beings; a Jataka story had a future Buddha reflecting: 'If I become king, I shall be born in hell . . . My father through being a king is guilty of grievous action which brings men to hell.'[31]

Such attitudes to kingship represent what has been called the 'anarchic spirit' of Buddhism, in contrast to the 'relativistic ethics' of Hinduism.[32] There is a variety of ways in which Buddhist lore has been enlisted in the service of modern socialist doctrines. In a Buddhist country such as Burma, the only terminology available to express modern political ideas belongs to Buddhist tradition. For example, the Buddhist term for flux (the constantly changing flow of impermanent entities that constitutes the world) was used for flux of matter in dialectical materialism.[33]

Though it must be severely qualified, quite a good case can be made out for the view that Buddhism, from the beginning, attacked social discrimination. Canonical teaching rejects the idea that birth matters: 'What has been designated as "name" and "family" in the world is only a term.'[34] The *Dhammapada* has various references to the brahmans, the priestly class which at the time of the Buddha had acquired pretensions to religious and social eminence, but what makes a brahman is not fine clothes and ostentatious lifestyle but faith, purity and the practice of non-injury – character, not family, is what makes a brahman.[35] Buddhism rejected distinctions based on birth: 'Not by birth does one become an outcast, not by birth does one become a Brahmana, by deeds one becomes an outcast, by deeds one becomes a Brahmana.'[36] The claims to pre-eminence of the brahmans had to be rejected to the extent that they depended on birth: 'Now seeing . . . that both bad and good qualities, blamed and praised respectively by the wise, are thus distributed among each of the four classes, the wise do not admit those claims which the brahmins put forward'.[37]

In his essay on the concept of equality in Theravada Buddhism, Padmasiri de Silva recognises in it 'the concept of human dignity and equal respect for all'; 'The Buddhist perspective on equality is basically orientated towards the human person as a free and rational moral agent.'[38]

But it would be an error to conclude from these selective quotations that Buddhism can have modern political or social ideas read into it in any simple way. De Silva's analysis is nuanced, emphasising that the Buddhism he describes is very different in its spirit from the intellectual framework in which modern doctrines of individual rights have evolved. Buddhist social ideas are rooted in assumptions about the claims of the family, respect for the old and wise, the reciprocity of human relations, and the stability of society; duties are as important as rights.

> Even the Buddhist five precepts which embody the content of some of the human rights like the right to life and property are not presented in the form of rights . . . They are presented in the form of a promise (or even duty) such that they ensure the basic conditions of harmonious social life and the development of individual character.[39]

It is in this context that we should assess the principles attributed to the Buddha's teaching on community organisation. The Buddha is represented as saying that a certain tribal community would remain strong as long as it observed the following seven conditions:

1 frequent assemblies
2 internal harmony
3 traditionalism in administration
4 respectfulness
5 not abducting women and girls
6 reverence for rites and shrines
7 supporting holy men.[40]

The first of these looks like an embryonic feature of civic freedom, but the values informing the list as a whole are those of stability and tradition, not individual liberty.

Other qualifications need to be made to the conclusion that Buddhism conveyed a teaching of civic liberties. In the first place, it is important to remember that at the time when the Buddhist teaching took shape, the Indian caste system, with all its proliferation of local communities and rules, did not yet exist. Buddhist criticisms of ascribed status were directed not against the caste system as it is known today but primarily against the claims of an established class that was taking pains to promote its own status. No doubt membership of the brahman priestly order was becoming increasingly hereditary, and it occupied the ground which the Buddhists (and other heterodox schools) hoped to make their own – the study and teaching of the way to salvation.

Buddhism did not seek to transform society. The Buddha himself sought recruits among those with cultivated minds, and such people came from relatively privileged backgrounds, including the brahman community itself.[41] The object of criticism was not so much a social order as the perceived failure of the brahman class to live up to its original standards. It was the Buddha's desire to revive these standards, not discredit them. He did not attack the division of society into classes; on the contrary, the canonical scriptures take pride in the purity of his ancestry as a good *ksatriya*, and whenever they mention slavery they fail to criticise it as an institution.[42]

We should not expect to find that Buddhists down the centuries have consistently criticised the institutions of caste (or, outside India, other forms of hereditary class organisation that restrict individual freedom), for Buddhism is not in origin and essence primarily a social movement.[43] Buddhism did not act against existing social hierarchies; sometimes it built itself into them. In Ceylon, where a variant of the caste system patterned social relations, the Buddhist monkhood itself was divided along caste lines, with the dominant Goigama caste monopolising the Siyan Nikaya in the eighteenth century.[44] Modern anthropological study reveals the continued association of caste with subsect in the twentieth century.[45]

Monkhood and the Civic Order

Perhaps a better argument could be made for the Buddhist community as a vehicle of personal liberty when we consider its internal organisation, and not its role within the encompassing society. After all, the ideal of the wandering holy man (*sannyasin*), who lives in complete freedom from the normal claims of society, was fundamental to Indian religious thought. There was an antithesis between the ritual religion of the settled community, which reflected and subserved the structure of the society's world-view, and the unfettered quest for salvation outside society. Buddhism was but one of a number of movements that offered a path to salvation that lay outside the rituals of family and settled community, and in its earliest phase its monks were expected to spend most of their time wandering from place to place, singly or in small groups.

Although the monkhood quite soon became largely coenobitic, concentrated in settled monastic communities, its formative stage and its canonical literature were governed by the values of rootless, wandering mendicants. However quickly Buddhism may have found a place within the structure of rural or urban society, it would be a mistake to overlook the continuing importance of its canonical values as a permanent reminder of the original message, inspiring movements of reform in later centuries. The Buddha's disciples deliberately rejected the claims and duties of life in society and all the restrictions imposed by inherited position; to go forth into such a life was in a sense a radical assertion of personal freedom from the bonds of family and social status.

In the Buddhist monkhood social origins meant little:

> Just, O Bhikkhus, as the great rivers . . . when they have fallen into the great ocean, renounce their name and lineage and are henceforth reckoned as the great ocean, just so, O Bhikkhus, do these four castes [i.e. the *varnas* of society] . . . when they have gone forth from the world under the doctrine and discipline proclaimed by the Tathāgata, renounce their names and lineage and enter into the number of the Sakyaputtiya Samanas.[46]

The original Buddhist message was essentially and specifically a call to forsake *everything* and go forth from one's home in quest of enlightenment. Nothing less would suffice; only the monks, those who had 'gone forth' (*pravrajita*), could realistically hope to attain salvation.

Buddhism built into its way of life an elaborate panoply of death symbolism: its proponents were socially dead, devoid of all the attributes of living members of society. Thus the *Vinaya* (discipline) of their canon prescribed (1) living only on food scraps, (2) wearing clothes taken from a dust-heap, (3) sleeping at the foot of a tree, and (4) using only decomposed urine as medicine.[47] That is, they needed no specially produced resources, and produced none themselves; they were socially blank spaces. They had explicitly surrendered any stake whatsoever in the social order of their natal culture.

It stands to reason that those who heeded the call must often have been asserting personal freedom of choice against the sometimes vigorously expressed interests and inclinations of their families, who needed them. Scriptures do not dwell on such conflicts, but an interesting episode from the *Udana* offers a glimpse of the problems that could be faced by a would-be *pravrajita*. A monk, Sangamaji, is visited by his wife (recalling the story that the Buddha himself had abandoned his wife on the day after the birth of his son when he went forth in quest of enlightenment), who seeks to prise him away from the Buddhist order by showing him his baby son and telling him that he has a duty to look after his family. Sangamaji ignores her.[48] The point of this story was to warn monks about the sort of temptations they could expect. It is significant that the Buddha is represented as criticising the wife, who should have respected her husband's action in deserting her. The message is that the abandonment of the claims of society must be complete.

An influential theory of the concept of freedom divides it into 'freedom to' and 'freedom from';[49] here we see the latter uncompromisingly asserted. Peace of mind lies in freedom from all property and ties:

'He who has sons has delight in sons' – so said the wicked Māra [the evil one, the tempter], – 'he who has cows has delight likewise in cows; for substance [*upadhi*, substratum of existence] is the delight of man, but he who has no *upadhi* has no delight.'

'He who has sons has care with (his) sons,' – so said Bhagavat [the Buddha], – 'he who has cows has likewise care with (his) cows; for *upadhi* (is the cause of) people's cares, but he who has no *upadhi* has no care.'[50]

In solitude, cut off from the burden of his own self just as much as from the burden of society, the monk may find true release:

Separation is bliss for the one who is satisfied, whose Dhamma has been heard, who beholds. Harmlessness is bliss, that control with respect to living beings in this world. Freedom from lust where this world is concerned is bliss, that transcendence of sense-desires.[51]

Having torn the ties, having broken the net as a fish in the water, being like a fire not returning to the burnt place, let one wander alone like a rhinoceros.[52]

But it would be a mistake to see any of this as evidence that the life of a monk is a life of freedom to follow one's own sweet will. On the contrary, every aspect of the monk's daily routine is governed by rules which are to be meticulously observed and form the substance of the 227 rules set out in the *Patimokkha* text. It is clear that the Buddhist monk has always been, at least in theory, disciplined by an elaborate code of thought and conduct more rigorous, in many ways, than ordinary lay life.

Another, much more mundane 'freedom from' was supplied by Buddhism for those less high-flying monks and nuns whose motives in going forth were primarily to escape various forms of poverty, oppression or civic responsibility. It is probable that such recruits, though not the chief targets of the *dharma*'s message, were numerous. An early post-canonical text says that, alongside those who have joined the order to transcend the suffering of life by spiritual cultivation, 'some have left the world in terror of the tyranny of kings, some have joined us to be safe from being robbed, some harassed by debts, and some perhaps to gain a livelihood'.[53]

Eventually, and perhaps as a condition of maintaining good relations with the civil authority, the Buddhist order set formal restrictions on the qualifications for ordination which excluded such people as fleeing prisoners, slaves, army deserters and so forth.[54] But an early text displays the original ideal of totally uncompromising separation from the demands of society: the Buddha is represented as asking King Ajatasattu whether he would demand the return of a slave who had entered the Buddhist order, and the king replies that, on the contrary, he would treat such a person with great honour.[55] There can be no doubt that many joined the order to escape difficulties in their lives (just as happened much later in the Chinese Buddhist order, which became notorious as a resort for deserters, misfits, beggars and criminals fleeing from justice, though it would be wrong to suppose that such people ever constituted the order's dominant membership). A survey of references to 'going forth' in the Pali scriptures brings to light, alongside the approved motive of seeking release from rebirth, the following conditions in which people might be expected to become monks or nuns: finding household life claustrophobic; destitution; idleness; exile or fear of retribution from the government or other agencies; sheer bad luck; debt; exile; loss of employment; the helplessness of old age; seeking to assuage the grief of bereavement; widowhood.[56] People joining the order in all these conditions were looking for quite practical freedom from the griefs of life in society.

Whether the order could offer freedom depended, as we have seen, on its relationship with the civil power. The Buddhist community sought to maintain its independence as a refuge for seekers after salvation; kings sought to maintain their control over all the resources of their kingdoms. Pious rulers might be ready to respect the autonomy of a favoured monastic order, but there was always a potential conflict of interest between the claims of *dharma* and *rajya*. How far has the Buddhist community succeeded in providing freedom from the state for its members?

This is a large subject and it cannot be examined in detail here. A thorough exploration, however, would reveal that, historically, Buddhist communities have been more subject to state control than one might suppose from a knowledge of Buddhist ideals. It is certainly true that pious rulers accorded privilege to the Buddhist order. In China, for example, Kenneth Ch'en points out that monks on joining the *sangha* 'no longer felt bound by the norms of political and social conduct that governed the lives of ordinary people'.[57] Monks did not pay taxes and were not harassed by government agents.

But to whatever extent the *sangha* becomes an influential and respected force in any society, its monasteries become large and prosperous, thereby tending to deprive the state of resources, both in property and in manpower that can be employed or taxed. The government finds itself compelled to define the limits of monastic privilege. Even if privilege remains substantial, everybody recognises that it is the state that makes the rules of the game; monks are free on sufferance. If rulers are pious Buddhists, they endow the *sangha* lavishly. This spells doom to monastic autonomy, for (as has been demonstrated by the relation between modern universities and ministries of education), sooner or later, he who pays the piper calls the tune.

The history of the Buddhist *sangha* in China shows clearly how dependent the order was on the goodwill of rulers, and how it could be gradually made subject to the state bureaucracy. Kenneth Ch'en has charted the process in some detail.[58]

In the early centuries of Buddhist popularity in China, many rulers were ready to respect the claims of the monks to stand outside, and in some respects above, society. In AD 404 Hui-Yüan wrote his *Treatise on the Monk Not Paying Homage to the Ruler*, arguing that monks must reject all social bonds in their quest for emancipation; they represented a quite different order from that of the state. Buddhism received much state patronage during the early Tang dynasty; in AD 622 a proposal to require ritual homage to the emperor from Buddhist monks was defeated after a defence was mounted by Tao-hsuan, who argued: 'Those who leave the household life do not reverence the ruling prince, their parents, or the six relationships.'[59]

However, time was not on the side of Buddhist autonomy. Monks were progressively integrated within the administrative apparatus, and ordination was increasingly subject to government control. In AD 705 the first recorded state-sponsored examinations required monks to be tested on the reading and explanation of scriptures. In 729 rules were promulgated for a regular register of all monks. Anti-Buddhist rulers instituted purges of the order at intervals throughout the centuries; the most famous is that of 842–5, when a mad emperor, who favoured Taoism, was known to fancy the idea of beheading all Buddhist monks. Had he lived longer, Buddhism might almost have been wiped out. The diary of the visiting monk Ennin vividly records the way in which religious affairs were caught in the toils of bureaucracy.[60] Eventually the *sangha* became 'a Chinese religious organization, subject to the jurisdiction of the imperial bureaucracy'.[61]

It is not only in China that the state has asserted controls over the functioning of the *sangha*. In Thailand, for example, centralisation of the administration of the monkhood was enacted by a series of royal initiatives under Chulalongkorn from 1892 onwards. In 1902 the Sangha Administration Act established a unified hierarchical and disciplined organisation for the whole order. Prince Wachirayan, the Supreme Patriarch in 1892, wrote: 'Although monks are already subject to the law contained in the Vinaya [Buddhist monastic discipline], they must also subject themselves to the authority which derives from the specific and general laws of the state.'[62]

However, the Buddhist order's loss of political and social freedom has not been simply a matter of official enactments. It can also be a cultural transformation: to the extent that Buddhism is accepted in any country as a dominant religious influence and cultural orthodoxy, it becomes (like any religious tradition in the same position) a vehicle and a vocabulary for the legitimacy of approved institutions. At the boundary between the ordered state and the marginally assimilated local cultures of various hinterlands, Buddhism above all serves to redefine and validate local customs and beliefs.[63] Even despite the explicitly non-political character of Buddhist teaching, the monkhood can in certain cases become a focus for an ardently patriotic movement with echoes of Moral Rearmament activism.[64]

So Buddhism can play the role of ideology for the establishment, but the circumstances of its origin and the obsessively universalistic tenor of its canonical scriptures have always fitted it as an alternative to the particularistic claims of any local culture or political order. Often enough, and conspicuously in China, Buddhism has lent itself to the articulation of dissent, and has frequently been entwined in the subculture of popular dissidence and rebellion, plundered for the myth and ritual of secret seditious organisations.[65] The figure of Maitreya, the next Buddha who will achieve enlightenment on earth and teach the Buddhist law, is apt as an inspiration for popular millenarian movements, not only in China but even in Theravada countries.[66] There has always been material in the Buddhist teaching capable of validating the aspirations of those who sought freedom from perceived oppression.

It is clear that Buddhist traditions do not return any simple answer to the question of freedom. We can find notions of freedom there if we look for them, or equally we can find the values of particularism, hierarchy and discipline, just as a physicist may find either waves or particles, whichever is sought. We cannot progress very far without proper definitions both of freedom and of Buddhism. Should we be concerned with scriptural theory or with historical practice? And which theory, which practice? Daw Aung San Suu Kyi stands for freedom, and her values are clearly shaped in part by Buddhist ideas traditional in Burma. But this does not of itself mean that freedom is traditional in Burma, because Aung San Suu Kyi and those who support her suffered long denial of the freedom to propagate their values. If this denial is traditional, then freedom is not.

It soon becomes obvious that the concepts of freedom that a modern political scientist might articulate may not be at home in the traditional cultures of Asia. In a prefatory essay tellingly entitled 'Human Rights: A Western Construct with Limited Applicability' Adamantia Pollis and Peter Schwab have this to say:

> It is becoming increasingly evident that the Western political philosophy upon which the [UN] Charter and Declaration [of human rights] are based provides only one particular interpretation of human rights, and that this Western notion may not be successfully applicable to non-Western areas for several reasons ... [These include] cultural differences whereby philosophic underpinnings defining human nature and the relationship of individuals to others and to society are markedly at variance with Western individualism.[67]

Buddhism, we must recall, originated from a set of psychological and ontological assumptions totally unlike those of modern Western thought. The Buddhist teaching about the individual denied the very existence of any permanent and substantial self of which rights to freedom of any sort could be predicated. Buddhist cultivation requires not that individuals should reject the discipline imposed by their condition in life (for the condition of monk imposes discipline just as much as that of lay person) but that, while still accepting the discipline in its entirety, they should come to dispel their ignorance about the nature of all conditions. The demands of discipline, external or internal, are paramount. Life remains subject to restrictions on the self; but the self who lives that life evaporates. *A fortiori* there is no subject of the restrictions. This has fundamental consequences for the individuals' personal relationships and morality; they must constantly monitor their thoughts and feelings with calm alertness; they must transcend all forms of emotional attachment, for these are predicated on the substantial existence of self or objects in the world.

Certainly, it is unlikely that more than a very small proportion of the Buddhist order has ever internalised and lived fully by this doctrine of non-self. For most Buddhists, monkhood and laity alike, it has been a difficult and obscure teaching relevant to real life mainly in reinforcing the status of the monk as an austere figure living by a code that denies and in some ways inverts many of the claims of ordinary life in society. Symbolically, the monk is the permanent outsider, however much the comfortable routines of Buddhist society may obscure his alienness in practice, and this alienness enshrines an implicit call to freedom of a sort – not freedom from all discipline or restraint, but freedom from the limited particularistic values of kin and local community.

Notes

This chapter draws in part upon a research project in progress funded by the Australian Research Council. The database cited at some points below has been prepared by Peter Masefield as part of this project.

1 See for example O. Patterson, *Freedom in the Making of Western Culture* (London: Tauris, 1991), vol. 1, pp. 293–344.

2 H. Welch, *The Practice of Chinese Buddhism 1900–1950* (Cambridge, Mass.: Harvard University Press, 1967), pp. 378f.

3 This is illustrated in I. W. Mabbett and D. P. Chandler, *The Khmers* (Oxford: Blackwell, 1995), fig. 3, p. 11.

4 'Temples these days are crowded with such dogs (*mah wat*), which manage to survive on whatever leftovers may be given them.' Peter Masefield, pers. comm.

5 'There is the story of one old woman who left off reciting the Mantra of Great Compassion just long enough to remind her servant to kill a chicken for supper.' Welch, *The Practice of Chinese Buddhism*, p. 383.

6 *Avihimsa*, variously rendered as 'harmlessness', 'non-violence' or 'absence of cruelty', is one of the precepts to be followed by monks.

7 *Avidya*, Sk; *avijja*, Pali. Here I use the Sanskrit forms of Buddhist terms, since my concern is with Buddhism in general, not just with the Theravada school, which uses the Pali language.

8 Cited by E. Sarkisyanz, 'Buddhist Backgrounds of Burmese Socialism', in B. L. Smith (ed.), *Religion and Legitimation of Power in Thailand, Laos, and Burma* (Chambersburg, Pa.: Anima Books, 1978), pp. 87–99, at p. 92. See also J. Silverstein's contribution to this volume.

9 M. Weber, *The Sociology of Religion*, transl. E. Fischoff (Boston: Beacon Press, 1963), pp. 113f.: 'That these religions [Hinduism and Buddhism] lack virtually any kind of social-revolutionary ethics can be explained by reference to their theodicy of rebirth, according to which the caste system itself is eternal and absolutely just.'

10 See e.g. *Jataka* No. 178, *Kacchapa-jataka*, transl. E. B. Cowell (gen. ed.), *The Jataka, or, Stories of the Buddha's Former Births*, vol. 2 (Cambridge: Cambridge University Press, 1895–1913), pp. 55f.

11 C. F. Keyes, 'Millennialism, Theravada Buddhism and Thai Society', *Journal of Asian Studies*, 36, 2 (1977), pp. 283–302, at pp. 286f.

12 L. M. Hanks, 'Merit and Power in the Thai Social Order', *American Anthropologist*, 64 (1962), pp. 1247–61, at p. 1248.

13 G. Obeyesekere, 'Theodicy, Sin and Salvation in the Sociology of Buddhism', in E. R. Leach (ed.), *Dialectic in Practical Religion* (Cambridge: Cambridge University Press, 1968), pp. 7–40, at p. 21.

14 Padmasiri de Silva, 'The Concept of Equality in the Theravada Buddhist Tradition', in R. Siriwardena (ed.), *Equality in the Religious Traditions of Asia* (London: Pinter, 1987), pp. 74–97, at p. 87.

15 Ibid., p. 78.

16 See, for example, the *Majjhima Nikaya*, *Ariyapariyesanasutta*, transl. I. B. Horner, *The Collection of Middle Length Sayings* (London: PTS, 1976), vol. 1, p. 207.

17 Theravada psychology recognises any cognitive process as lasting for seven *javana* moments, and in certain circumstances actions performed in the first and last of these moments may fail to come to fruition and lapse: Buddhaghosa, *Visuddhimagga* 601; transl. Pe Maung Tin, *The Path of Purity* (London: Pali Text Society, 1975), p. 724.

18 The relationship between enlightenment and past *karma* is problematic. It is discussed by P. Masefield, *Divine Revelation in Pali Buddhism* (Colombo/London: Sri Lanka Institute of Traditional Studies/George Allen & Unwin, 1986), pp. 87–92.

19 *Majjhima Nikaya* 2.104, *Angulimalasutta*; transl. Horner, *Collection of Middle Length Sayings*, vol. 2, pp. 289f.

20 M. Spiro, *Buddhism and Society* (New York: Harper & Row, 1970), p. 118.

21 The coexistence of both traditions (strictly speaking contradictory though they are) in Burma is discussed in ibid., pp. 116–23.

22 Hence the practice of chanting special scriptural passages, *parittas*, by the deathbed. See Obeyesekere, 'Theodicy, Sin and Salvation', pp. 25f.

23 Ibid., pp. 22–5.

24 *Aguttara Nikāya* III.415, cited by M. Carrithers, *The Buddha* (Oxford: Oxford University Press, 1983), p. 67.

25 See particularly N. Chaudhuri, *Hinduism, A Religion to Live By* (Oxford: Oxford University Press, 1979), pp. 103–211, esp. p. 121.

26 *Digha Nikaya (Agganna Suttanta)*, ed. J. E. Carpenter (London: Pali Text Society, 1960), vol. 3, pp. 80–98, at pp. 90–3.

27 J. W. Spellman, *Political Theory of Ancient India* (Oxford: Clarendon Press, 1964), p. 22.

28 *Digha Nikaya* 3.59; transl. T. W. Rhys Davids as *Dialogues of the Buddha*, part 3 (London: Pali Text Society, 1977), p. 60.

29 *Jataka* No. 538, *Muga-pakkha jataka*; transl. E. B. Cowell, *Jataka*, vol. 6, pp. 17f.

30 *ye ca tata vijite adhana assu tesañ ca dhanam anuppadajjeyasi: Digha Nikaya* III, 61.

31 *Jataka*, No. 538, *Muga-pakkha jataka* transl. Cowell, *Jataka*, vol. 6, p. 3. Cf. p. 11: 'In an old birth I played the king, as I remember well / But when I fell from that estate I found myself in hell.'

32 Sarkisyanz, 'Buddhist Backgrounds of Burmese Socialism', p. 89, citing Paul Mus.

33 Ibid., p. 93.

34 *Suttanipata* 648; transl. V. Fausböll, *The Sutta-Nipata: A Collection of Discourses, Sacred Books of the East* (Delhi [reprint] 1965), vol. 10, p. 116.

35 *Dhammapada* 142, 383–423 esp. 388, 393; 'A man becomes not a Brahmin by long hair or family or birth. The man in whom there is truth and holiness, he is in joy and he is a Brahmin' (*Dhammapada* 393; transl. J. Mascaró).

36 *Sutta Nipta* 141; transl. Fausböll, *The Sutta-Nipata*, p. 23.

37 *Digha Nikaya, Aggaññasuttanta*, PTS, ed., vol. 3, pp. 82f.; transl. T. W. Rhys Davids, *Dialogues of the Buddha* (London: Pali Text Society, 1977), pp. 78f.

38 P. de Silva, 'The Concept of Equality', at p. 83.

39 Ibid., p. 83.

40 *Digha Nikaya (Mahaparinibbanasutta)*, T. W. Rhys Davids and J. E. Carpenter, eds (London: Luzac, for the Pali Text Society, 1966), vol. 2, pp. 72–168, at pp. 73-5.

41 On the Buddha and brahman converts see in particular Uma Chakravarti, *The Social Dimensions of Early Buddhism* (Delhi: Oxford University Press, 1987), pp. 122–49, 198–220.

42 On Buddhists and brahmans see particularly Masefield, *Divine Revelation in Pali Buddhism*, pp. 146–61.

43 But for a contrary argument see T. Ling, *The Buddha* (London: Penguin, 1976).

44 Obeyesekere, 'Theodicy, Sin and Salvation', pp. 35f.

45 Hans-Dieter Evers, *Monks, Priests and Peasants: a Study of Buddhism and Social Structure in Central Ceylon* (Leiden: Brill, 1972), p. 7, n. 1: 'The process of fission [of the 'orders' (*nikayas*) of the Ceylonese monkhood] is still going on . . . In fact . . . many of the subgroups have been formed either on caste lines, or on account of power struggles within nikāyas.'
46 *Vinaya, Cullavagga* IX.1.4, transl. Fausböll, *The Sutta-Nipata*, vol. 20, p. 304.
47 E. J. Thomas, *The History of Buddhist Thought* (London: Routledge & Kegan Paul, 1933), p. 23.
48 *Udana* 8 (Sangamaji)
49 C. Wirszubski, *Libertas as a Political Idea at Rome during the Late Republic and Early Principate* (Cambridge: Cambridge University Press, 1960), see esp. pp. 1–3.
50 *Sutta Nipata* 32f.; transl. Fausböll, *The Sutta-Nipta*, vol. 10, p. 5.
51 *Udana* 10; transl. Peter Masefield
52 Ibid., 61; transl. Fausböll, *The Sutta-Nipta*, vol. 10, p. 9.
53 *Milinda Pañha* 2.1.5; transl. T. W. Rhys Davids, *Questions of King Milinda* (Sacred Books of the East) (Oxford: Oxford University Press, 1890), vol. 35, part 1, pp. 49f.
54 Excluded were those suffering from severe chronic illnesses, criminals, soldiers, debtors, slaves, sons lacking their parents' consent, and minors under 20 years old: *Vinaya* 1.76.
55 *Digha Nikaya* 1.60f.; transl. Rhys Davids, *Dialogues of the Buddha*, part 1, pp. 76f.
56 G. Bailey and I. Mabbett, work in progress, database.
57 K. Ch'en, *Buddhism in China: a Historical Survey* (Princeton, NJ: Princeton University Press, 1964), p. 65.
58 Ibid., pp. 65–124.
59 Ibid., pp. 78f.
60 Ennin, transl. E. O. Reischauer, *Ennin's Travels in T'ang China, 838–847* (New York: Ronald Press, 1955).
61 Chen, *Buddhism in China*, p. 124.
62 C. F. Keyes, 'Buddhism and National Integration in Thailand', *Journal of Asian Studies*, 30 (1971), pp. 551–67, at p. 555.
63 See for example F. E. Reynolds, 'Ritual and Social Hierarchy: an Aspect of Traditional Religion in Buddhist Laos', in B. L. Smith (ed.), *Religion and Legitimation of Power in Thailand, Laos and Burma* (Chambersburg, Pa.: Anima Books, 1978), pp. 166–74.
64 C. F. Keyes, 'Political Crisis and Militant Buddhism in Contemporary Thailand', ibid., pp. 147–64.
65 I. W. Mabbett, *Modern China: The Mirage of Modernity* (London: Croom Helm, 1985), pp. 118–38.
66 The future coming of Maitreya is referred to in the canon: *Digha Nikaya* 3.76 *Cakkavatti-sihanada suttanta* (transl. Rhys Davids, *Dialogues of the Buddha*, part 3, pp. 73f.): Maitreya will come to earth in the distant future, in an age of decline when the human lifespan is disastrously short. C. F. Keyes argues, *contra* Conze, for the importance of the Maitreya figure in millennial movements even in Theravada culture: 'Millennialism, Theravāda Buddhism and Thai Society', p. 288. Cf. Sarkisyanz, 'Buddhist Backgrounds', p. 90.
67 Adamantia Pollis and Peter Schwab, 'Human Rights: A Western Construct with Limited Applicability', in P. Schwab and A. Pollis (eds), *Human Rights, Cultural and Ideological Perspectives* (New York: Praeger, 1979), p. 1.

CHAPTER 3

Freedom and Freehold:
Space, People and State Simplification in Southeast Asia

James C. Scott

In this essay I take a few concepts developed in the course of an attempt to understand some of the bases of 'great development failures' and apply them to the Southeast Asian context. That larger inquiry argues that what I would term 'state simplifications' become particularly pernicious when they are joined to 'high modernist' ideologies which use state power to utterly transform the lives of citizens, usually according to a presumed utopian plan. Such plans, designed to improve the human condition, have had melancholy results, in part because they have destroyed long-standing social patterns of community, work, and interaction with nature that have proven satisfactory and have replaced them with a 'one-size-fits-all' formula that negates local adaptive knowledge.

The concept of freedom invoked in this context is more closely related to the anarchist concept of 'mutuality' (i.e. co-operation without hierarchy – or at least without state-structured hierarchies) than to liberal notions of freedom. That is, I am particularly interested in the degree of relative freedom from state control enjoyed by non-state social units such as the household, the kinship group, the village or settlement as distinct from the individual freedom of the citizen. A word about the distinction is in order.

Freedom, in classical liberal thought, is an attribute of the individual citizen. In this sense, inasmuch as the concept of the individual citizen is unthinkable without the concept of the state, the individual citizen's freedom is created and secured by the state. Behind this simple assertion lies, of course, a long and violent history of struggle to secure individual freedom against tyrannical states. The purpose of that struggle was precisely to create a state that would enshrine individual freedom in law as its first principle and that would afford citizens the kind of institutions that would protect that freedom. There is relatively little of this kind of freedom to be found in Southeast Asia, even within the most modern and open economies of the region.

There is in fact a historical logic that connects the codified individual freedoms of liberal thought to the growth of the state. One of the remarkable things about the history of freedom of individual citizens vis-à-vis the state is that the expansion of liberty was accompanied by a concomitant growth in the size and weight of the state. This growth could be measured in terms of personnel, budget, and the instruments of coercion. It could also be measured by the vast expansion of the state's knowledge about each of its citizens. The state came to 'certify' birth, death and marriage, to create universal conscription and voter lists, to conduct cadastral surveys in which every scrap of land was accounted for and attached to an owner and, typically, a taxpayer.

What astonished anarchists, and not only anarchists, was the juxtaposition of great revolutions which promised both new freedoms and the unprecedented growth of the state. Thus, in France, the revolutions of 1789, 1830 and 1848 (where universal manhood suffrage was enacted in forty-eight hours) each brought about a larger state that was more intrusive, more costly and more hegemonic, in part because it was more popularly elected. The new post-revolutionary state that legislated individual freedoms was also a state which, for the first time, dealt systematically with individuals rather than groups. The absolutist state, though it frequently aspired to deal with the French one by one as conscripts and taxpayers, was typically forced to work through existing social groups – communities, guilds, municipalities, heads of households, local notables and their retainers. One powerful effect of the revolutions was to sweep away, first in law and increasingly in practice, most of the 'private' individuals and social units who had functioned as intermediaries between the state and the individual. With the acquisition of certain freedoms, the individual also became bearer of obligations to pay taxes, to register for conscription, and to comply with an expanding array of regulations designed to enhance 'the general welfare'.

Having yet to secure the individual freedoms of the modern liberal state, the practical or operative freedom of most Southeast Asians depends, to a considerable degree, on the relative autonomy of the social units within which they live.[1] It is with this autonomy that I shall be largely concerned. In particular, I am interested in the *relative* freedom of non-state social units to determine their own residence, their own forms of community, and their own forms of property and production as opposed to the imposition of state-mandated forms of these.

My emphasis throughout is on 'state simplifications', a term that will be elaborated below. This orientation directs our attention to the efforts of the modern state to arrange its subjects/citizens in a manner that is increasingly 'legible', uniform, and hence more amenable to manipulation and control from above.

State Simplifications

Certain forms of knowledge and control require a narrowing of vision. The great advantage of such tunnel vision is that it brings into very sharp focus certain limited aspects of an otherwise far more complex and unwieldy reality. This very simplification, in turn, makes the phenomenon at the centre of the field of vision far more legible, and hence far more susceptible to careful measurement, calculation and manipulation.

The invention of scientific forestry in late eighteenth-century Prussia and Saxony serves as something of a model of this process.[2] While the story of scientific forestry is important in its own right, I use it here as a metaphor for the forms of knowledge and manipulation characteristic of large institutions with sharply defined interests, of which the state is perhaps the outstanding example. Once we have seen how simplification, legibility and manipulation operate in forest management, we can then explore how a similar optic is applied by the modern state to urban planning, rural settlement, land administration and agriculture.

A Parable of the State and Scientific Forestry

The early modern European state, even before the development of scientific forestry, viewed its forests primarily through the fiscal lens of revenue needs. To be sure, other concerns such as timber for masts, shipbuilding, state construction and sufficient fuelwood for the economic security of its subjects were not absent from official management. These added concerns also had heavy implications for state revenue and security.[3] Exaggerating only slightly, one might claim that the Crown's interest in forests was resolved through its fiscal lens into a single number: the revenue yield of the timber which might be extracted annually.

The best way to appreciate exactly how heroic this constriction of vision is, is to notice what is left out of its purview. Lying behind the number indicating revenue yield are not so much trees as 'commercial wood', representing so many thousands of board feet of saleable timber and so many cords of firewood fetching a certain price. Missing, of course, are all those trees, bushes and plants that hold little or no potential for state revenue. Also missing are all those aspects of trees – even 'revenue-bearing' trees – that may be useful to the population but whose value cannot be converted into fiscal receipts. Here I have in mind the uses of foliage as fodder and thatch, fruits as food for domestic animals and people, twigs and branches as bedding, fencing, hop poles and kindling, bark and roots for medicine and tanning, sap for resins and so forth. The actual tree with its vast number of possible uses is replaced by an 'abstract' tree representing a volume of lumber or firewood.

From a naturalist's perspective, nearly everything is missing from the state's picture. Gone are the vast majority of flora, the grasses, flowers, lichens, ferns, mosses, shrubs and vines. Gone, too, are reptiles, birds, amphibians and innumerable species of insects. Gone is the vast majority of fauna except, perhaps, those of interest to the Crown's gamekeepers.

From an anthropologist's perspective, nearly everything touching on human interaction with the forest is also missing from the state's tunnel vision. Except for its attention to poaching, which does impinge on either the state's claim to revenue in wood or its claim to royal game, the state typically ignores the vast and complex negotiated social uses of the forest for hunting and gathering, pasturage, digging valuable minerals, fishing, charcoal-making, trapping, and food collection as well as its significance for magic, worship, refuge and so on.[4]

If the utilitarian state cannot see the real existing forest for the (commercial) trees, if its view of its forests is abstract and partial, it is hardly unique in this respect. A certain level of abstraction is necessary for certain forms of analysis, and it is not at all surprising that the abstractions of state officials should reflect the paramount fiscal interests of their employer. The vocabulary used to organise nature typically betrays the overriding interests of its human users. In fact, the term 'nature' is, in utilitarian discourse, replaced by the term 'natural resources' in which the focus is on those aspects of nature that can be appropriated for human use. A comparable logic extracts from a more generalised natural world those flora or fauna that are of utilitarian value (usually marketable commodities) and in turn reclassifies those species that compete with, prey on, or otherwise diminish the yields of the valued species. Thus *plants* that are valued become *crops*; the species that compete with them are reclassified as *weeds*, and the insects that ingest them are reclassified as *pests*. Thus *trees* that are valued become *timber*, while species that compete with them become 'trash' trees or underbrush. The same logic applies to fauna. Those *animals* which are highly valued become *game* or *livestock*, while those animals which compete with or prey on them become *predators* or '*varmints*' (vermin).

The kind of abstracting, utilitarian logic that the state, through its officials, applies to the forest is thus not entirely distinctive. What is distinctive is the narrowness of its field of vision, the degree of elaboration to which it can be subjected, and above all, as we shall see, the unique capacity of the state to impose (in part) its optic on the very reality it is observing.[5]

Scientific forestry was developed from about 1765 to 1800, largely in Prussia and Saxony. Eventually it would become the basis of forest management techniques in France, England, the United States, and throughout the Third World. Its emergence can hardly be understood outside the larger context of centralised state-making initiatives of the period. In fact the new forestry science was a sub-discipline of 'cameral science' – an effort to reduce the fiscal management of a kingdom to scientific principles that would allow systematic planning. Traditional domainal forestry had hitherto simply divided the forest into roughly equal plots – the number of plots coinciding with the number of years in the assumed growth cycle.[6] One plot was cut each year on the assumption of equal yields (and value) from plots of equal size. Owing to poor maps, the uneven distribution of the most valuable large trees (*Hochwald*) and very approximate cordwood (*Bruststärke*) measures, the results were unsatisfactory for fiscal planning.

The first attempt at more precise measurement was made by Johann Gottlieb Beckmann on a carefully surveyed sample plot. Walking abreast, several assistants carried compartmentalised boxes with colour-coded nails corresponding to five agreed-on size-categories of trees. Each tree was tagged with the appropriate nail until the whole sample plot was covered. Having begun with a specified number of nails, it was a simple matter to subtract those remaining from the initial total and arrive at an inventory of trees by size-class for the entire plot. The sample plot had been carefully chosen for its representativeness, allowing the foresters to calculate the timber and, given certain price assumptions, the revenue yield of the whole forest. For the forest scientists (*Forstwissenschaftler*) the goal was always to 'deliver the greatest possible *constant* volume of wood'.[7]

The effort at precision was pushed further as mathematicians worked from the cone/volume principle to specify the volume of saleable wood contained by a standardised tree (*Normalbaum*). Their calculations were checked empirically against the actual volume of wood in sample trees.[8] The final result of such calculations was the development of elaborate tables with data organised by classes of trees by size and age under specified conditions of normal growth and maturation. References to these tables coupled with field tests allowed the forester to estimate closely the inventory, growth and yield of a given forest. In the regulated, abstract forest of the *Forstwissenschaftler*, calculation and measurement prevailed and the three watchwords were 'minimum diversity', 'the balance sheet', and 'sustained yield'.

The achievement of German forestry science in standardising techniques to calculate the sustainable yield of commercial timber, and hence revenue, was impressive enough. What is decisive for our purposes, however, is the next logical step in forest management. This was to attempt to create, through careful seeding, planting and cutting, a forest that was easier for state foresters to count, manipulate, measure and assess. Forest science and geometry, backed by state power, had the capacity to transform the real, disorderly, chaotic forest so that it more closely resembled the administrative grid of forestry techniques. To this end the underbrush was cleared, the number of species was reduced (often to monoculture), planting was done simultaneously and in straight rows for large tracts. These management practices, as Lowood observes,

> produced the monocultural, even-age forests that eventually transformed the *Normalbaum* from abstraction to reality. The German forest became the archetype for imposing on disorderly nature the neatly arranged constructs of science. Practical goals had encouraged mathematical utilitarianism, which seemed, in turn, to promote geometric perfection as the outward sign of the well-managed forest; in turn the rationally ordered arrangements of trees offered new possibilities for controlling nature.[9]

The tendency was towards 'regimentation' in the strict sense of the word. The forest trees were drawn up into serried ranks, as it were, to be measured, counted off, felled, and replaced by a new rank and file of look-alike conscripts. In the end, the forest itself would not have to be seen; it could be 'read' accurately from the tables and maps in the forester's office.

This utopian dream of scientific forestry was, of course, only the *immanent* logic of its techniques. It was not, and could not, ever be realised in practice. Both nature and 'the human factor' intervened. The existing topography of the landscape and the vagaries of fire, storms, blights, climatic changes, insect populations and disease conspired to thwart foresters and to shape the actual forest. Given the insurmountable difficulties of policing large forests, the adjacent human populations typically continued to graze animals, poach firewood and kindling, make charcoal, and generally make use of the forest in ways that prevented the foresters' management plan from being fully realised.[10] Although, like all utopian schemes, it fell well short of attaining its goal, the crucial fact is that forest science did partly succeed in stamping the actual forest with the imprint of its designs.

Facts-on-paper, facts-on-the-ground

The administrators' forest cannot be the naturalists' forest. Even if the ecological interactions at play in the forest were known, they would constitute a reality so complex and variegated as to defy easy short-hand description. The intellectual filter necessary to reduce the complexity to manageable dimensions was provided by the state's interest in commercial timber and revenue.

If the natural world, however shaped by human use, is too unwieldy in its 'raw' form for administrative manipulation, so too are the actual social patterns of human interaction with nature bureaucratically indigestible in their raw form. A hypothetical, but realistic, case of land tenure arrangements may help to demonstrate why this is so. The land tenure practices I describe here are all ones that I have encountered in the literature or in the course of fieldwork.

Let us imagine a community in which families have usufruct rights to parcels of cropland during the main growing season. Only certain crops, however, may be planted and every seven years the usufruct land is redistributed among families according to family size and the number of able-bodied adults. After the harvest of the main season crop, all cropland reverts to commons where any family may glean, graze their fowl and livestock, and even plant quickly maturing, dry-season crops. Edible wild plants growing on the margins of fields, along watercourses, and on bunds are available to those who gather them. Trees which are known to have been planted are, together with their fruit, the property of the family that planted them, no matter where they are now growing. Fruit fallen from such trees, however, is the property of anyone who gathers it. When a family fells one of its trees or it is felled by wind, the trunk of the tree belongs to the family, branches to the immediate neighbours, and the 'tops' (leaves, twigs, fronds) to any poorer villager who carries them off. Land is set aside, exceptionally, for use or leasing out by widows with children or dependants of conscripted males. Usufruct rights to land and trees may be 'let' to anyone within the village but not to anyone outside the village unless no one in the community wishes to use it.

Let us also imagine that fishing rights are distributed so that anyone may take fish (by net, weir, or hook and line) from canals and streams. In flooded usufruct fields, however, while anyone may fish with hook and line for small fish, the larger fish – taken usually when the field is drained – belong to the owner of the crop growing in that field.

After a crop failure leading to severe food shortage, many of these arrangements are adjusted. Better-off villagers are expected to assume some responsibility for poorer relatives – by sharing their land, by employing them, or simply by feeding them. Should the shortage persist, the council of lineage heads may inventory food supply and begin daily rationing. In case of an outright famine, the women who have married into the village but have not yet borne children will not be fed and are expected to return to their natal village.

This description is a simplification, but it does convey some of the actual complexity of property relations in contexts where customary local arrangements have tended to prevail. To describe the usual practices in this fashion, as if they were laws, is a serious distortion. They are better understood as a living, negotiated tissue of practices which are continually being adapted to new ecological and social circumstances – including, of course, power relations. Their very plasticity is the source of micro-adjustments which may or may not lead to shifts in prevailing practice.

Imagine, if you will, a written system of positive law that attempted to represent this complex skein of property relations and land tenure. The mind fairly boggles at the clauses, subclauses, and sub-subclauses which would be required to reduce these practices to a set of regulations that an administrator might understand, let alone enforce. If, in principle, they could nevertheless be codified, the resulting code would necessarily sacrifice much of the plasticity and subtle adaptability of practice. The circumstances that might provoke a new wrinkle in practices are too numerous to foresee, let alone to specify in a regulatory code. That code would, in effect, freeze a living process. Changes in the positive code designed to reflect evolving practice would at best represent a jerky and mechanical adaptation. One of the finest and most elaborate attempts to describe the involutions of earlier Southeast Asian land tenure practices may be found in Pierre Gourou's meticulous account in *L'Utilisation du sol en Indochine Francaise*.[11]

And what of the *next* village, and the village after that? Our hypothetical code-giver, however devilishly clever and conscientious, would find that the code devised to fit one set of local practices would not travel well. Each village, with its own particular history, ecology, particular cropping patterns, kinship alignments and economic activity would require a substantially new set of regulations. In the end there would be at least as many legal codes as there were communities.

Administratively, such a cacophony of local property regulations would be a nightmare – not one experienced by those whose particular customs are being represented but rather by state officials and those who aspire to a uniform, homogeneous, national administrative code. Local practice is perfectly legible to those inhabitants who 'live' it each day. Its details may be often contested and far from satisfactory to all of its local practitioners, but there is no doubting its familiarity; local residents have no difficulty in grasping its subtleties and using its flexible provisions for their own purposes. State officials, on the other hand, cannot be expected to decipher and then apply a new set of property hieroglyphs for each jurisdiction. The very concept of the modern state is inconceivable without a vastly simplified and uniform property regime that is legible, and hence manipulable from the centre.

Use of the term 'simple' to describe modern property law, whose intricacies provide employment to armies of legal professionals, seems grossly misplaced. It is surely the case that property law has in many ways become an impenetrable thicket for ordinary citizens. The use of 'simple' in this context is thus both *relative* and *perspectival*. Modern freehold tenure is tenure that is mediated through the state and therefore readily legible only to those who have sufficient training and grasp of the state statutes to allow them to decipher it. Its relative simplicity is lost on those who cannot break the code, just as the relative clarity of customary tenure to the villagers who live it is lost on the mystified outsider.

The major, but not the only, driving force behind a simple and legible system of property is the need for a reliable format for taxation. There are some instructive parallels here between the development of modern, fiscal forestry and modern forms of taxable property in land. Premodern states were no less concerned with tax receipts than modern states, but, like premodern state forestry, the techniques and reach of the state left much to be desired.

This is where the rough analogy between forest management and taxation breaks down. In the absence of reliable information about sustainable timber yield, the state might either inadvertently overexploit its resources and threaten future supply, or else fail to realise the level of proceeds it might sustain.[12] The trees themselves, however, were not political actors, while the taxable subjects of the Crown were most certainly political actors. They signalled their dissatisfaction by flight, by various forms of quiet resistance and evasion, and, *in extremis*, by open revolt. A reliable format for taxation of subjects thus depended not just on discovering what their economic condition was but also on trying to judge what exactions they would vigorously resist.

The next step, one to which all modern states aspire, is to measure, codify, and simplify land tenure in much the same way as scientific forestry reconceived the forest. In no way could the state begin to incorporate the luxuriant variety of customary land tenure. The historical solution, at least for the liberal state, has typically been the heroic simplification of individual, freehold tenure. Land is owned by a legal individual who disposes of wide powers of use, inheritance or sale, and whose ownership is represented by a uniform title deed

enforced through the judicial and police institutions of the state. Just as
the flora of the forest were reduced to *Normalbaum*, so were the complex tenure arrangements of customary practice reduced to freehold,
transferable title. In an agrarian setting, the administrative landscape
was blanketed with a uniform grid of homogeneous land, each parcel
of which has a legal person as owner and hence taxpayer. How much
easier it becomes to assess such property and its owner on the basis of
its acreage, its soil class, the crops it *normally* bears, and its assumed
yield, than to untangle the thicket of common property and mixed
forms of tenure. The cadastral survey, the 'permanent revenue settlement' and the Torrens system of land-titling in British colonies were
precisely the techniques by which a simplified fiscal space could be
defined.[13] As in the case of the forest, it provided the means to extract a
presumably sustainable fiscal yield. The modern land register and its
tax roll was the equivalent, for land tenure, of the scientific foresters'
table of timber growth and yield.

If the web of customary land tenure was a mystifying hieroglyph to
outsiders and state officials, the new forms of individual, freehold
tenure were now a mystifying hieroglyph to those whose terrain was
being recast. The new forms of tenure, however simplified and uniform they might seem to an administrator, flung villagers willy-nilly
into a world of unfamiliar objects and institutions: title deeds, land
offices, law, courts, fees, assessments, applications, cadastral surveys.
They faced powerful new specialists in the form of district officials,
surveyors, lawyers and judges whose procedures and decisions were
unfamiliar. A central consequence of the new tenure system – one
might more accurately say its very purpose – was to map a terrain
of taxable real property that was perfectly legible to any clerk or
trained state official. At the same time it radically devalued local knowledge and autonomy. Such forms of specialised knowledge backed by
state authority profoundly changed the balance of power between the
locality and the state. Where the new tenure system was a colonial
imposition, that is, totally unfamiliar, imposed by alien conquerors
using a radically different language and institutional context, the
transformation conferred unique opportunities for those who first
plumbed the mysteries of tenure administration. Thus the Vietnamese
secrétaires and *interprètes* who served as intermediaries between the
French officials in the Mekong Delta and their Vietnamese subjects
were in a position to make great fortunes. By concentrating on getting
the paperwork for the title deeds and appropriate fees in order, they
occasionally became, overnight, landlords to whole villages of cultivators who had imagined they were opening common land free for the
taking. They might, of course, occasionally use their knowledge to see

their compatriots safely through the new legal thicket. Whatever their conduct, their fluency in a language of tenure specifically designed to be legible and transparent to administrators, coupled with the illiteracy of the rural population under them to whom the new tenure was undecipherable, was a momentous shift in power relations.

The actual practices of land tenure – the facts-on-the-ground – did not yield quickly, passively, or entirely to the new tenure regime. Owing to the vagaries of enforcement and the practical interests and values of villagers, a wide variety of unsanctioned and/or illegal tenure practices persisted. Forms of common property survived in popular practice, though they might now be legally defined as poaching or trespass. Customary restrictions on sale might continue to be observed for fear of informal local sanctions, although not recognised in law. If the real forest never quite came to resemble the simple homogeneity of the scientific forest's tables, even less did real tenure practices quite come to resemble simple transferable, freehold property so long as the people on whom it was being imposed had vital interests which led them to resist it. The new scheme, thanks to the powers behind it, did, however, as in the case of scientific forestry, shape actual tenure practices increasingly in its mould.

'Vos Papiers, Monsieur'

This stock phrase, by which a gendarme addresses a man he wishes to question, illustrates the degree to which even face-to-face encounters in the modern state are mediated by standardised documents. Just as paper currency, as an abstract and uniform unit of value, permits many-tiered exchanges between economic actors who are not known to one another, so do the citizens of the modern state come to be symbolised by paper representations: birth certificates, identity cards, title deeds, tax returns, death certificates and so on.

The first thing to appreciate about the modern state is that most of its officials are, of necessity, usually at least one step removed from direct contact with citizens. They observe and assess the life of their society by a series of simplifications and shorthand fictions that are always some distance from the full reality these abstractions are meant to capture. Thus the forester's charts and tables, despite their power to distil many individual facts into a larger pattern, do not capture (nor are they meant to) the real forest in its full diversity. Thus the cadastral survey, the title deed and tenure contracts are a very rough, and sometimes misleading, representation of actual existing rights to land use and disposal. Functionaries of any large organisation actually 'see' the human activity of interest to them largely through the simplified approximations of documents and statistics: tax proceeds, lists of taxpayers, land records, average income, unemployment numbers, mortality rates, trade and productivity figures, the cases of cholera in a certain district. These stylised facts are a powerful form of state knowledge, making it possible to discover and intervene early in epidemics, to understand economic trends that greatly affect public welfare and/or state power, and generally to form policy with many of the crucial facts at hand.[14]

State simplifications, by their very nature, have a particular character. Most obviously, they are observations of those aspects, and only those aspects, of social life that are of official interest. They are nearly always written or numerical facts recorded in documents. Third, they are *static* facts. Even when they appear dynamic, they are typically the result of multiple static observations through time. Observation of, say, land records or income figures over two or more points in time may reveal a greater inequality in landownership or an increase in income, but it will not reveal how this new state of affairs came about or whether it will persist. Finally, most stylised state facts are aggregate facts. Aggregate facts may be impersonal (e.g. the density of transportation networks) or simply a collection of facts about individuals (e.g. employment rates, literacy rates, residence patterns). For most purposes, state officials need to group citizens in a way that permits them to make a collective assessment.

Facts that can be aggregated and presented as averages or distributions *must* perforce be *standardised* facts. However unique the actual circumstances of the various individuals who make up the aggregate, it is their sameness, or more precisely their differences, along a standardised scale or continuum that are of interest. The working lives of many people, for example, are exceptionally complex and may change from day to day. For the purposes of official statistics, however, 'gainfully employed' is a stylised fact; one is or is not gainfully employed. The problem of how to categorise many rather exotic working lives is, in the final analysis, covered over by the categories reflected in the aggregate statistics.[15] Those who gather and interpret such aggregate data understand that there is a certain fictional and arbitrary quality to each of the categories they must employ – that they hide a wealth of problematic variation. Once set, however, these thin categories operate unavoidably *as if* all cases similarly classified are in fact homogeneous and uniform. All *Normalbäume* in a given size range are the same; all auto-workers (if we are classifying by industry) are the same, all Catholics (if we are classifying by religious faith) are the same.

So far I have been making a rather straightforward, even banal, point about the simplification, abstraction and standardisation necessary for the observation by state officials of the circumstances of some or all of the population. I want, however, to make a further claim, analogous to that made for scientific forestry, that the modern state through its officials attempts, with varying success, to create a population with precisely those standardised characteristics which will be easiest to monitor, count, assess and manage. The utopian (immanent) tendency of the modern state, continually frustrated, is to reduce the chaotic, disorderly, social reality beneath it to something more closely resembling the administrative grid of its observations.

This tendency is perhaps one shared by almost all large hierarchical organisations. As Chisholm, reviewing the literature on administrative co-ordination, concludes: 'Central coordinating schemes do work effectively under conditions where the task environment is known and unchanging, where it can be treated as a closed system.'[16] The more static, standardised and uniform a population or social space is, the more legible it is to the techniques of state officials. I am suggesting that state officials endeavour to transform the population, space and nature under their jurisdiction into the closed system without surprises that they can best observe and control. The reason that they can, to some considerable degree, make their categories stick and impose their simplifications is because the state, of all institutions, is best equipped to *insist* on treating people according to its schemata. If you want to defend your claim to real property you are normally obliged to defend it with a document called a property deed, and in the courts and tribunals created for that purpose. If you wish any standing in law, you must have the documents (birth certificate, passport, identity card, etc.) that officials accept as a claim of citizenship. The categories used by state agents are not merely a means of making their environment legible; they are an authoritative tune to which much of the population must dance.

Some of the most taken-for-granted categories with which we now routinely apprehend social reality had their origin, I believe, in just such state projects of standardisation and legibility. Consider something so fundamental as naming practices. Until at least the fourteenth century, the great majority of Europeans did not have permanent patronyms. A male child's name was typically an amalgam of his given name and his father's given name. Universal last names were achieved quite late, particularly among the propertyless, and were a great step forward in the legibility of the entire population to state officials, especially tax officials. It is a process still occurring in much of Southeast Asia.

A great part of state-making consists in the comprehensive mapping of a nation's population, its physical space and its natural resources.

Without such mapping – and without the simplifications, standardisation, naming and classification that make it possible – most of the activities of the modern state would be inconceivable.

State Simplifications and Legibility in Southeast Asia

Flight and 'non-state spaces'

The historical basis of freedom in precolonial, and much of colonial, Southeast Asia was physical mobility – the capacity to flee the reach of the state. Inasmuch as the power of the precolonial state was predicated largely on the control of population rather than territory, a decline in population marked a weakening kingdom, and an increase in population a kingdom growing more powerful. Wars were more for the conquest of populations to be settled within the immediate radius of the court than for the conquest of territory alone. Given the relative ease of flight, the precolonial kingdom trod a narrow path between a level of taxes and corvée exactions that could sustain a monarch's ambitions and those that could precipitate wholesale flight.

The precolonial state was thus interested in the *sedentarisation* of its population, in the creation of fixed, permanent settlements. The greater the *concentration* of population, providing they produced an economic surplus, the greater the ease of appropriating grain, labour and military service. The colonial state had similar aspirations and, frequently, superior means of realising these aspirations in practice. The administrative ideal of both regimes was the creation of a permanent, fixed, concentrated population under their jurisdiction. Such a population not only provided the reliable tax base that would help secure the continuity of the kingdom's dynasty; it also facilitated administrative and political control, including conscription.

One could write, I think, a very illuminating history of Southeast Asian statecraft and popular resistance along these lines. It would contrast the efforts of states and kingdoms to constrain the freedom of movement of their subject populations and the struggles of those populations to avail themselves of the physical mobility that was one of their few resources for freedom.[17] I offer a few brief examples to indicate the directions such a history might take.

The importance of physical mobility to statecraft is evident in Chandra Muzaffar's book *Protector?*[18] My reading, I should stress, is very much against the grain of Chandra's own reading of the evidence. He examined the major texts (*sejarah* and *hikayat*) of precolonial Malay history and found them pervaded by a denunciation of disloyalty and treason (*durhaka*). On the basis of this evidence he concluded that

Malays were deferential to a fault, and that the avoidance of treason or disloyalty was the hallmark of their political culture. One of his purposes was to develop a critique of contemporary Malay political culture within the ruling Malay party. My own reading of the evidence would be nearly the opposite. Why should the court chronicles take as one of their major themes the condemnation of treason? My assumption is that it was precisely because it was the key problem of Malay statecraft. With a sparse population and a scattering of many petty kingdoms jockeying for clients, the would-be follower was in a fairly enviable position. The objective of an ambitious ruler was to prevent his Malay retainers from running off individually or in groups to settle under the protection of another, competing *datok* or sultan. Thus the frequency with which *durhaka* was censored in the chronicles is an excellent indication of how frequently it actually jeopardised the survival of Malay kingdoms. It is a case of 'Methinks the Lady doth protest too much'; the chroniclers are trying, by their exhortations, to contain the physical freedom that is the central limitation on the ruler's power. Nor is it out of place to note that the same fragility of political loyalty has continued to characterise much of contemporary Malay politics.

Traditional Thai statecraft was also preoccupied with minimising flight and firmly attaching commoners to the state or to their noble lords. A system of tattoos was devised to 'mark' commoners so that it was clear to which noble family they belonged. The tattooing was itself evidence that exceptional measures were required to identify and fix a subject population which was inclined to vote with its feet. So common was physical flight that a body of bounty hunters made a living by coursing the forests in search of runaways to return to their 'lawful owners'.[19]

Precolonial Burmese statecraft follows much the same pattern. In *The Glass Palace Chronicle* King Narathihapate was admonished by Queen Saw for having oppressed his subjects with onerous taxes and corvée:

> Consider the state of the realm. Thou hast no folk or people, no host of countrymen and countrywomen around thee ... Thy countrymen and countrywomen tarry and will not enter thy kingdom. They fear thy domination; for thou, O King Alaung, art a hard master. Therefore, I, thy servant, spake to thee of old; but thou wouldst not hearken. I said, bore not thy country's belly ... cut not thy country's feet and hands![20]

The result, the chronicler wrote, is that his people have abandoned him to flee to the forest and now he is left without defence against his enemies. The series of wars between precolonial Burma and Thailand followed the same logic. The winner took as many captives as possible, who were then settled near their captor's court – hopefully growing wet rice – so as to add both to the economic strength of the kingdom and to the fund of available manpower.[21]

Flight was one of the major problems besetting the friar estates in the Spanish Philippines. Those Tagalogs who were resettled and organised for supervised production in the clerical *ecomiendas* frequently fled the harsh labour regime. They were known as *remontados*, that is, peasants who had gone back to the hills where they enjoyed more freedom. There were strong parallel tendencies in Spanish America.

The importance of flight is of interest not only to historians of colonial and precolonial Southeast Asia. It is worth noting that in the early 1960s in Vietnam, when the Diem government was in a position to reassert itself in the countryside, many peasants took to the hills to escape conscription, taxes and rent-collecting landlords. Much of this occurred *well before* many of them were incorporated into the rival state organised by the National Liberation Front. While the Diemist state followed the counter-insurgency doctrines developed in Malaya and the Philippines, which favoured the construction of controlled, fortified villages (variously termed 'new villages', 'strategic hamlets', etc.), much of the population resisted such incorporation. Once the countryside became unsafe for government forces, officials and landlords took to residing in the provincial towns (at least at night) where their physical safety was most secure. Civil society had, as it were, become 'unglued'. Much of the peasantry 'retreated' to the small hamlets and hills outside the easy reach of state power and the property-owning élites, and officials 'retreated' to the towns where state coercive power was strongest.[22]

In more general terms for precolonial and colonial Southeast Asia, it might be helpful to think in terms of '*state spaces*' and '*non-state spaces*'. In the former, the subject population is settled rather densely into permanent communities, producing a surplus – usually of wet rice – which is fairly easily appropriated by the state.[23] In the latter, the population is sparsely settled, typically practises slash-and-burn forms of cultivation, maintains a mixed economy (polyculture, reliance on forest products), and is highly mobile, thereby severely limiting the possibilities of reliable state appropriation.

Edmund Leach's path-breaking article 'The Frontiers of Burma' implicitly follows this logic in understanding the traditional Burmese polity.[24] He suggests that we look at the precolonial Burman state *not* as a physically contiguous territory as we would in the context of modern state sovereignty, but as a patchwork which follows a quite different logic. This requires us to conceive of the landscape of traditional kingship in terms of horizontal slices through the topography. Following this logic, 'Burma' was, in practice, a collection of all those sedentary, valley, wet-rice producers settled within a plausible ambit of the court centre. The next horizontal stratum of the landscape, from, say, 500 feet to 1000 feet, would, given its different ecology, contain inhabitants who practised shifting cultivation and were more widely scattered, who were not promising objects of appropriation, and who were hence not part of the kingdom, though they might be in a tributary relationship to it. The higher elevations would constitute yet another ecological, cultural and political zone. What Leach proposes, in effect, is that we consider all relatively dense, wet-rice settlements near the capital as 'state spaces' and zones inhabited by scattered, shifting cultivators as 'non-state spaces'.

This logic had an irreducible geographic and ecological foundation. Locations that are geographically strategic because they are 'choke-points' or bottlenecks for commerce and/or migration are potential *state spaces*. The mouth of a river, a narrows or straits, a key mountain pass, a goldmine, favoured positions along any trade route, in addition to highly fertile lands with a reliable surplus, all fit this description. They offer privileged locations, 'natural monopolies', for the accumulation of surplus. They frequently become the nodes of kingdoms and social settings where wealth, stratification, and legislated inequalities abound.[25] Where states were organised along different ecological principles as in coastal settlements, the distinctions between state spaces and non-state spaces would take a different form. Thus in the Malay world, the *hulu-hilir* contrast followed a comparable logic, with the *hulu* or upstream area constituting a non-state space and the *hilir* or downstream area being typically organised into a petty kingdom. Once again, the two zones would be closely bound by links of complementary trade and exchange, and perhaps by tribute, but they would rarely be politically unified.

Although Southeast Asian patterns are distinctive in many respects, one can find analogous polarities elsewhere. Marshes (e.g. the now beleaguered 'Marsh Arabs' on the Iraqi–Iranian border), mountains ('Montagnard' groups in Vietnam), deserts (nomadic Berbers and Bedouins), the sea (the so-called 'sea gypsies' of Burma), and mangrove swamps (the Sundarbuns of Bengal), and the frontier more generally, have all been 'non-state spaces' in the sense I have been using the term. They share one or more of the following characteristics: they are relatively impenetrable (wild, rugged, trackless, labyrinthine, inhospitable), their population is dispersed, they are unpromising sites for surplus appropriation, and their population is often migratory.

State strategies for control, appropriation and legibility

'Non-state spaces' have always been liminal and subversive, both in a symbolic and practical sense. Such spaces and their inhabitants have served as the exemplars of nature, barbarity, rudeness, disorder, immorality and irreligion against which the culture, civility, sophistication, order, morality and orthodoxy of the centre could be measured. Those who dwell in such spaces saw the matter differently, of course, contrasting their freedom, mobility, honour and so on to the bondage of those under the thumb of the court.[26] Such spaces have served as refuges for rebels, bandits and princely pretenders, in part because they have represented nearly intractable problems of control. It is for this reason that ambitious rulers, whether precolonial, colonial or independent, have attempted to gain control over such areas or, failing that, reduce their independence. The guiding principles of this effort have been *sedentarisation*, *concentration*, *order* and *legibility*. Perhaps the most extreme version of this policy could be seen during the Vietnam War in the US military policy of permanently settling nomadic peoples, creating planned strategic hamlets, and finally by using 'agent orange' to defoliate the forests so that the terrain would be legible from the air. It was an ambitious high-tech version of more modest efforts along the same lines by the French and the Vietnamese court earlier.

In what follows I hope to suggest some of the ways in which such a perspective could throw some light on the history of settlement patterns in Southeast Asia and on state efforts to recast them according to its formulae. The cases I examine are plantation agriculture versus smallholder agriculture generally, the FELDA (Federal Land Development Administration) schemes in Malaysia, and Singapore's housing program.

Plantations versus smallholders

How do we explain the decided colonial preference for plantation agriculture over smallholder production? The one explanation that is ruled out by hard economic facts is efficiency. In almost any crop you can name, with the possible exception of sugar,[27] smallholders have historically been able to out-compete large units of production. Time and time again the colonial states found that smallholders, owing to their low fixed costs and flexible use of family labour, could undersell state-managed or private-sector estates.

The great advantage of estate production, I believe, was that it was vastly superior to smallholding as a unit of control and appropriation. At the beginning of the rubber boom, British officials and investors firmly believed that estate-produced rubber would prove more efficient and profitable than smallholder rubber because of better planting stock, better scientific management, and labour use. When they discovered that they were wrong, they persisted in systematically favouring estates, at some considerable cost to the overall economy of the colony. The infamous Stevenson Scheme in Malaya in the 1930s was a particularly blatant attempt to preserve the estate sector of the rubber economy by limiting smallholder production. Without this scheme most estates would have perished.

The estates benefited from the fact that the colonial officials were more likely to place their interests (i.e. the interests of their compatriots and metropolitan investors) ahead of those of Malay and Chinese smallholders. But the advantages of the estates scarcely ended there. While they may have been less cost-effective as rubber producers than the peasantry, they were far more convenient as units of taxation. It was *relatively* easier to monitor and tax large publicly owned businesses than a vast swarm of small growers who were here today and gone tomorrow, and whose financial affairs were illegible to the state. Their very specialisation on a single crop meant that their production and profits were legible to the state; the efficiency of plantations as producers was less relevant to the state than the efficiency with which the state could effectively tax whatever they did produce. A second advantage of estate rubber production for the government was that it typically provided centralised forms of residence supervision and labour use that were more amenable to political and administrative control. They were, in a word, far more 'legible communities' than the Malay kampung with its own history, leadership and mixed economy.

The logic of legibility, surveillance and appropriation has prevailed over criteria of efficiency in other settings. Collectivised agriculture in the former Soviet Union was a striking case in point. The collectivisation ordered by Stalin originated *not* in a failure of production but in a crisis of state appropriation. Under the aegis of the New Economic Policy (NEP) inaugurated in 1921 – itself a retreat from the command economy methods of the post-revolutionary civil war period – production had expanded. Despite the expanded production the failure of the Soviet economy to provide the industrial or consumer goods for which rural producers would exchange livestock and foodgrains resulted in a crisis of appropriation. Stalin's decision to collectivise, at whatever cost, was not aimed at enhancing production so much as making certain that the state could seize whatever production it needed for a program of crash industrialisation. In the absence of positive incentives to sell their grain, the small farmers of the NEP period had become adept at hiding their actual production, avoiding ruinous

requisitions, and developing a parallel economy. The great advantage
of collectivisation was that it created large administrative farming units
whose investments, cropping patterns and wages could be set by fiat
and monitored, and whose production could be directly seized and
distributed. Production, as one might have predicted, plummeted.
But the state had nonetheless created new, legible, agricultural units it
could control, and its share of a diminished harvest was greatly
increased.

A comparable logic can, I believe, be applied to establishment of
federal land schemes in Malaysia. Why did the Malaysian state elect to
establish large, costly, bureaucratically monitored settlement schemes
in the 1960s and 1970s when the frontier was already being actively
pioneered by large-scale voluntary movement? Pioneer settlement
cost the state virtually nothing and had historically produced viable
household enterprises growing and marketing cash crops. During the
colonial period, as we have seen, it was just such smallholders whose
low-cost production threatened to bankrupt the private estate sector.
As an economic proposition, the huge rubber and oil palm schemes
made little sense: they were enormously costly to establish, the capital
expenditure per settler being far beyond what a rational businessman
would invest.

Politically and administratively, however, the advantages of large,
centrally planned and administered government schemes were manifold. At a time when the attempted revolution of the Malayan
Communist Party was still fresh in the minds of the country's Malay
rulers, planned settlements had some of the advantages of strategic
hamlets. They were laid out according to a simple grid pattern and
were immediately legible to an outside administrator. The house lots
were numbered consecutively and the inhabitants all registered and
monitored far more closely than in open-frontier areas. The settlers
could be, and were, carefully selected for age, skills and political relia-
bility. In the late 1970s, when I was working in the state of Kedah, from
which many settlers were recruited, all prospective 'pioneers' understood that it was advantageous to be recommended by a local politician
closely affiliated with the ruling party.

The administrative and economic situation of the settlers was
comparable to that of the 'company towns' of early industrialisation
where all worked at comparable jobs, were paid by the same boss and
shopped at the same company store. Until the plantation crops were
mature, the settlers were paid a wage, their produce was marketed
through state channels, and they could be dismissed for any one of
a number of infractions against the rules established by the scheme's
officials. The economic dependency and direct political control meant

that such schemes could regularly be made to produce large electoral majorities for the ruling party. Collective protest was rare and could usually be snuffed out by the sanctions available to the administrators. It goes without saying that FELDA settlements allowed the state to control the mix of export crops, to monitor production and processing, and to set producer prices so as to generate revenue.

The public rationale for planned settlement schemes was almost always couched in the rhetoric of orderly development and the provision of social services such as education, health clinics, sanitation, adequate housing, clear water, and infrastructure. This public rhetoric was not insincere; it was, rather, misleadingly silent about the manifold ways in which 'orderly development' of this kind served crucial ends of surveillance and control that could not have been met through autonomous frontier settlement. FELDA schemes were, in short, a 'soft' version of the 'new villages' established by the British as a part of their counter-insurgency policy during the Malayan Emergency. Model villages in socialist Ethiopia and Ujamaa villages in Tanzania might be analysed along the same lines. In strictly economic terms they were rarely successful; in the case of Ethiopia and Tanzania they were fiscal and production disasters of such massive proportions that they have largely been abandoned. The 'return' they provided to the regimes which established them was less an economic return than a dividend of political and administrative control. Ben Kiernan gives a similar example from Cambodia.

A remarkable geometrical meticulousness was followed in Pol Pot's Cambodia. Walls of earth were thrown up to make long, straight canals, eliminating irregular paddy fields, and creating 1 hectare squares of 100 such units. Concentration of population, forced labor, the prohibition of foraging or departure, the control of food rations, and executions were carried to an extreme rarely seen elsewhere.[28]

State plans of sedentarisation and planned settlement and production have rarely gone as anticipated. Like the scientific forest or the planned grid city, such settlements have often escaped their inventors' aspirations to fine-tuned control. The ways in which the autonomous activities of the subjects of development subvert the grids of planners is well worth careful study. What such a study must never overlook is the social order that planned development schemes, however inflected by local practice, supersede. The political importance of planned development lies at least as much in what it replaces as in how meticulously it lives up to its own rhetoric.

The concentration of population in planned settlements may not create exactly what state planners had in mind, but it has almost always disrupted or destroyed prior communities whose cohesion derived from non-state sources. The communities thus superseded had their own unique, and often deep, history, together with the social ties, mythology, and capacity for joint action that history might provide. The community in question might embody several historically embedded social bases of action: kinship, ritual ties, dialect, ethnicity, religion, etc. The state-designed settlement must start from the beginning to build its own sources of cohesion and joint action. A new community is thus, by definition, a community *demobilised* and hence a community more easily amenable to control from above and outside.[29]

This logic of social demobilisation is incidentally the key element in the commonly observed fact that at the beginning of industrialisation the declining rural community is more likely to be a source of collective protest than the newly constituted proletariat – the standard Marxist reasoning to the contrary notwithstanding. Resettlement, whether forced or unforced, often eliminates a prior community that might have served as a point of cohesion and resistance, and replaces it with a temporarily disaggregated mass of new arrivals. It is ironically just such population that may, for the time being, more closely resemble 'potatoes in a sack' than the peasantry of the *bocage* that Marx characterised in *The Eighteenth Brumaire*.

To recapitulate briefly the advantages of planned settlements, the new community is typically laid out on new terrain where an overall administrative logic stipulates the order of the residential pattern. Where the economy or the crop regimen (as in monocropping) is radically simplified, the scope for planning from above is greatly facilitated. At the limit, property relations, work, and residence patterns are made legible by fiat. The planners, as in Brasilia or in an Ujamaa village, do not have to make many compromises with an existing set of living arrangements or social practices. The new residents are, at least at the beginning, far more dependent on the planning authorities for their subsistence and housing.[30] They may in fact have been handpicked to make certain that central control was easier. Above all, the population in question has been *removed* from communities whose history and interests are relatively autonomous of current state policy and reassembled in new settlements where the state's resources are often decisive.

The highly touted achievement of the Singaporean government under Lee Kuan Yew in rehousing most of that city-state's population ought to be examined in this context as well. As a feat of engineering and administrative mobilisation, it remains an impressive accomplishment. Nor is there any doubt that the rehoused population now enjoys improved sanitation, social amenities, education, health and infrastructure. To stop there, however, is to take the self-promoting rhetoric of the city-state for granted and to miss the feat of political and social engineering accomplished simultaneously. One purpose of the vast scheme of housing flats launched by the People's Action Party (PAP) under Lee Kuan Yew was precisely to *supersede* the older forms of settlement that were the most politically opaque and resistant to PAP control. Thus local Malay kampung areas of the city as well as the poorer Chinese areas dominated by local clan associations were explicitly targeted for dispersal. The object was not simply to rehouse these communities *in situ* but rather to break them up, to scatter them throughout the housing projects so that they could not reconstitute themselves. All of the social nodes of opposition to the PAP were erased, and their populations reshuffled throughout the new high-rise flats.

The obliteration of the old neighbourhoods and the re-creation of a newly designed urban space were tailor-made to make the disaggregated population beholden to the PAP. In each housing flat it was the PAP activists who were able to take charge of aspects of life that had previously been outside direct state control, such as recreation, local welfare and sports, not to mention housing itself. Without a doubt the population was better off in most respects after the transformation. There is also no doubt that they were resettled in a way designed to maximise the surveillance and monopolistic political control of the PAP. The ruling party rehoused Singapore and in so doing designed a more directly legible and more easily dominated population.

The history of government-sponsored transmigration (*transmigrasi*) in Indonesia could be analysed in this fashion as well. As in the case of Malaysian frontier settlement, transmigration has been taking place spontaneously for centuries. What is new is the massive effort of the independent Indonesian state to settle hundreds of thousands of Javanese in planned settlements in the Outer Islands. In addition to the advantages to Jakarta of creating planned settlements under relatively close supervision at the periphery, there is a not-so-subtle strategy of ethnic-based internal colonisation being pursued as well.

It is worth noting in this last connection that communities which are designed to reflect the needs of the state for control and surveillance seldom succeed very well as human communities from the vantage point of their inhabitants. Thus spontaneous transmigration has been notably more successful than government schemes, from which a large percentage of recruits return home – without leave. There is a perverse logic here. State settlements are typically laid out in square or rectangular grids for the convenience and speed of the surveyors. The housing is also standardised for the same reason. The rules that govern cropping, credit and the governance of the schemes follow a 'one-size-fits-all' format; they are by now the product of settled bureaucratic routines. It is hardly surprising that the administrative grids thus devised have violated the ecological realities of local places, the needs of different families, and the particularities of each new settlement.

The logic in question is not confined to Indonesia; it follows wherever states attempt directly to devise and impose standard formulae for living. Whether the aim is political control or utopian plans for human happiness, such schemes nearly always substitute geometrical rigour, standardisation, and simplicity for the complexities of local knowledge and adaptation.[31] The result, more often than not, is that the planned communities fail their residents in some fundamental ways. The history of Ujamaa villages, collectivisation, Brasilia, Chandigarh, and strategic hamlets is a history of alienation and/or resistance. The results are often the opposite of what the state planners intended. For example, Charles Jenks dated the symbolic end of 'modernism' at 3:32 p.m., 15 July 1972, when the prize-winning Pruitt-Igoe Housing Development in St Louis, now unlivable, was dynamited.[32] It is claimed that the vast high-rise apartment flats built on the outskirts of Algiers and other major cities by the revolutionary state of Algeria – having failed utterly as human communities – have become the base areas of the most intractable Islamic fundamentalists. To return to Southeast Asia, in Burma the democratic movement against General Ne Win and the State Law and Order Council (SLORC) in the late 1980s was particularly tenacious in Okalapa, on the outskirts of Rangoon. The irony is that Okalapa was a planned settlement begun in 1959 by the first Ne Win government to rehouse the squatter population in Rangoon itself. The regime's failed slum clearance project came back to haunt it thirty years later.

A historically grounded concept of freedom in the Southeast Asian context requires a consideration of *social* autonomy as well as of individual liberty. The relative freedom of state-subjects in Southeast Asia has depended greatly on their autonomy in matters of social organisation, residence patterns, cultural life, economic activity and, above all, physical movement. These zones of autonomy provide the nodes of cohesion that give a local society the means of creating its own self-understanding and means of social action.

The tendency of the state has historically been to narrow this margin of autonomy. It has done this by attempting to restrict physical mobility, both by forced settlement and by the apparatus of identity cards, cadastral surveys and censuses that allow it to monitor and control movement. It accomplishes this also by closing off the 'forest commons' and the 'free-access frontier' (the modern equivalent of the enclosure movement in European history) and by encouraging and implementing planned communities practising planned agriculture. Such new communities are usually laid out in legible forms, administered from above, practise a simple (e.g. monocropping) as opposed to composite economic life, in which appropriation is easier and the population is dependent in fundamental ways on the agents of the state and the ruling party. Above all, these new communities replace existing communities (villages, slums, pioneer hamlets) over which the state had far less control.[33]

Notes

1 Many of these social units themselves are hierarchical and arbitrary, and greatly constrain the freedom of the individual. The crucial difference perhaps is that, as a historical matter, most of these social groups have not held an imposing degree of coercive power and have thus been *relatively* easier to evade or flee than the modern state.

2 Henry E. Lowood, 'The Calculating Forester: Quantification, Cameral Science, and the Emergence of Scientific Forestry Management in Germany', in Tore Frangsmyr, J. L. Heinbron, and Robin E. Rider (eds), *The Quantifying Spirit in the 18th Century* (Berkeley: University of California Press, 1991), pp. 315–42. The following account is largely drawn from Lowood's fine analysis.

3 The most striking exception was the royal attention to the supply of 'noble game' (e.g. deer, boar, fox) for the hunt and hence to the protection of its habitat. Lest one imagine this to be a quaint premodern affectation, it is worth recalling the enormous social importance of the hunt to such recent 'monarchs' as Erich Honneker and Tito.

4 For an evocative and wide-ranging attempt to explore the changing cultural meaning of the forest in the west, see William Pogue Harrison, *Forests: The Shadow of Civilization* (Chicago: University of Chicago Press, 1992).

5 This last is a kind of reverse Heisenberg principle. Instead of altering the phenomenon observed through the act of observation, so that the pre-observation state of the phenomenon is unknowable in principle, the effect of (interested) observation in this case is to alter the phenomenon in question over time so that it in fact more closely resembles the stripped-down, abstract image the lens had revealed.

6 In the late seventeenth century Colbert had extensive plans to 'rationalise' forest administration both to prevent poaching and to generate a more reliable revenue yield. To this end, Etienne Dralet's *Traité du Régime Forestier* proposal regulated plots (*tire-aire*) 'so that the growth is regular and easy to guard'. Despite these initiatives, nothing much came of it in France until 1820 when the new German techniques were imported. Peter Sahlins, Forest Rites: The 'War of the Demoiselles' in Ariège, France (1829–1831), unpublished paper presented to the Program in Agrarian Studies, Yale University, January 1992.

7 Lowood, 'The Calculating Forester', p. 338.

8 Various techniques were tried: cutting an actual tree into tiny bits and then compressing it to find its volume; putting wood in a barrel of known

volume and adding measured amounts of water to calculate the volume of the barrel *not* occupied by the wood, etc. Ibid., p. 328.

9   Ibid., p. 341. See also, Harrison, *Forests*, pp. 122–3.

10 See, for example, Honoré de Balzac, *Les Paysans* (Paris: Pleiades, 1949); E. P. Thompson, *Whigs and Hunters: The Origin of the Black Act* (New York: Pantheon, 1975), Douglas Hay, 'Poaching on Cannock Chase', in Douglas Hay et al. (eds), *Albion's Fatal Tree* (New York: Pantheon, 1975) and Steven Hahn, 'Hunting, Fishing, and Foraging: Common Rights and Class Relations in the Postbellum South', *Radical History Review* 26 (1982), pp. 37–64. For a directly opposite German case, see one of Karl Marx's first published articles linking the theft of wood to the business cycle and unemployment in the Rhineland: reported in Peter Linebaugh, 'Karl Marx, the Theft of Wood, and Working-class Composition: A Contribution to the Current Debate', *Crime and Social Justice* (Fall–Winter, 1976), pp. 5–16.

11 Centre d'études de politique étrangère, Travaux des groupes d'études, Publication No. 14 (Paris: Paul Hartmann, 1940).

12 This assumes that the Crown wants to maximise its long-term proceeds. It was and is common, of course, for regimes in political or military crises to mortgage their future by squeezing as much as possible from their forests and/or their subjects.

13 It goes without saying that the homogenisation that serves fiscal ends also is crucial for commodities entering the market. A modern market in land is virtually inconceivable where every property bears all the particular traces of the land rights and customary arrangements from which it arises.

14 See Ian Hacking, *The Emergence of Probability: A Philosophical Study of Early Ideas About Probability, Induction and Statistical Inference* (Cambridge: Cambridge University Press, 1975).

15 There are at least three problems here. The first is the hegemony of the categories. How does one classify someone who works largely for relatives who may sometimes feed him, sometimes let him use some land as his own, and sometimes pay him in crops or cash? The decisions, sometimes quite arbitrary, about how to classify such cases are obscured by the final result in which only the prevailing categories appear. The second problem, and one to which we shall return, is how the categories – more particularly the state power behind the categories – shape the data. For example, during the recession of the 1970s in the United States there was some concern that the official unemployment rate, which had reached 13 per cent, was greatly exaggerated. A major reason, it was claimed, was that many nominally unemployed were working in the informal economy 'off the books' and would not report their income or employment for fear of being taxed. One could say then and today that the fiscal system had provoked an 'off-stage' reality that was designed to stay out of the data bank. The third problem is that those who collect and assemble the information may have very special interests in what the data show. During the Vietnam War the importance of 'body-counts' and 'pacified villages' as a measure of counter-insurgency success led commanders to produce inflated figures which pleased their superiors – in the short run – but increasingly bore little relation to the facts-on-the-ground.

16 Donald Chisholm, *Coordination without Hierarchy: Informal Structures in Multiorganizational Systems* (Berkeley: University of California Press, 1989), p. 10.

17 See Michael Adas, 'From Avoidance to Confrontation: Peasant Protest in Precolonial and Colonial Southeast Asia', *Comparative Studies in Society and History*, 23, 2 (1981), pp. 217–47.

18 Chandra Muzaffar, *Protector? An Analysis of the Concept and Practice of Loyalty in Leader–led Relationships within Malay Society* (Penang: Aliran, 1979).

19 This was far from exclusively a Southeast Asian pattern. In the late fourteenth and fifteenth centuries, after the Black Plague had reduced the western European population by nearly a third, the problem of attracting serfs by favourable terms, now that flight to unoccupied land was so easy, became a major one for the nobility. Slave systems with an open land frontier have always been vulnerable on this score. In Russia the subject of most Tsarist decrees was runaway serfs. One might say in general that unfree forms of labour are untenable where there is an open frontier, unless, of course, sufficient coercion can be mobilised to contain the population.

20 *The Glass Palace Chronicle of the Kings of Burma*, transl. Pe Maung Tin and G. H. Luce (London: Oxford University Press, 1923), p. 177.

21 Victors also captured and led back valued artisans, dancers, concubines, and precious objects.

22 Much the same pattern can be detected in parts of Southeast Asia during the Japanese occupation of World War II. With certain exceptions such as the Chinese, who had special reason to fear the Japanese authorities, élites often concentrated in the cities – at the centres of state power – while much of the peasantry scattered to the periphery. The importance of food supply meant that, for a change, direct producers of food goods enjoyed relatively favourable terms of trade with the towns.

23 There is a fairly straightforward logistical geography involved here. Collecting taxes, other things equal, from a densely settled population close to the centres of state power is far more efficient than collecting a surplus (in either kind or labour) from a widely scattered population far from the centre of state power. Transportation technology is a sharply limiting factor. In pre-industrial Europe, the carting of grain more than 20 or so miles was a losing proposition. At about that distance the oxen or horses carting the grain would have had to have been fed (over and above their maintenance ration) roughly the same amount of grain as was in their cargo. Water buffalo cannot have been much more efficient, although they could certainly forage for some of their food requirements. The point is that the cost of appropriation increases exponentially as the distance from the centre increases. This helps explain the scale of inland (*kraton*) kingdoms, the importance of water-borne transport, the tendency for long-distance trade to carry relatively 'precious' goods, the relative absence of stable kingdoms in slash-and-burn areas where population is scattered, and the importance of a wet-rice base with its dense, productive population for state-building.

24 Edmund Leach, 'The Frontiers of Burma', *Comparative Studies in Society and History* (1960), pp. 49–68.

25 Changes in technology greatly modify these patterns. Thus rail and road junctions often replace the mouths of rivers or natural harbours; locations of coal, bauxite, or iron ore may supersede locations of precious gems, silver and gold as decisive geographical strongholds.

26 One thinks of the more even-handed Afghan proverb in this context: 'Taxes ate the valleys; honour ate the hills.'

27   Sugarcane must be crushed quickly once it is cut to avoid losses through evaporation and fermentation. The large crushing mill, problems of transportation, and bulk reduction through processing provide a kind of natural bottleneck that allows the owner of the crushing mill to control production directly or through tied tenancy contracts. Compared to coffee, tobacco, tea, rubber, palm oil, etc., this advantage to centralised production is unique to sugarcane.

28   Ben Kiernan, *The Pol Pot Regime: Race, Power, and Genocide in Cambodia under the Khmer Rouge, 1975–79* (New Haven: Yale University Press, 1996), Ch. 5.

29   Thus the morally obtuse but sociologically correct observation by Samuel Huntington during the Vietnam War that the massive bombing of the countryside and the subsequent creation of huge refugee settlements on the outskirts of the major cities provided many advantages to those who wanted to influence and mobilise the electorate. Those in the camps, he reasoned, were more easily manipulable than those still living in their rural communities. The implicit but macabre logic was impeccable; the more bombs rained on the countryside the greater the opportunities for the United States and its allies in Saigon to dominate any peaceful political competition which followed. 'Getting Ready for Political Competition in South Vietnam' (*c*.1970), Southeast Asia Development Advisory Group of the Asia Society.

30   The danger for the state is that virtually all questions in such settlements become, by definition, political struggles between the residents and the authorities. Issues such as wages, house rents and land rights which might otherwise have been between private parties, with the state standing aside, become, in this new context, almost immediately politicised struggles between the state and the settlers.

31   The literature relevant to this topic is vast. Two particularly distinguished contributions are Jane Jacobs, *The Death and Life of Great American Cities* (New York: Vintage, 1964) and Paul Richards, *Indigenous Agricultural Revolution: Ecology and Food Production in West Africa* (London: Hutchinson, 1985).

32   Quoted in David Harvey, *The Condition of Post-Modernity: An Enquiry into the Origins of Cultural Change* (Oxford: Basil Blackwell, 1989), p. 40.

33   Perhaps the most significant limiting factor has been fiscal. The economic inefficiencies of most such schemes and their failure to provide an economic return sharply restrict the ambitions of the state. Where the fiscal means have been most limited, as in Burma, the pretence of a planned economy and society under Burmese socialism is paper-thin. Where the terrain and the means are more substantial, as in Singapore, the intrusion is far more pronounced and effective.

CHAPTER 4

China and Freedom

W. J. F. Jenner

Do concepts of political freedom have any relevance to the long history of Chinese cultures before Western notions of freedom were introduced in the nineteenth century? They have certainly been relevant since then.

Only with the armed intervention of the West did ideas of political freedom come into the Chinese world. Once these alien concepts were known about they appealed to some Chinese thinkers, even though the general preference has been to see freedoms as collective rather than individual.[1] The very limited but genuine gentry democracy of the last years of the Qing dynasty (AD 1644–1911), which granted Western-style political freedoms to some educated, property-owning males, helped to destroy the whole Qing order.[2] Dangerous foreign notions of a right to political freedom continued to appeal to a few independent-minded thinkers through the years of the Republic and then the People's Republic, and there has been talk of democracy by military dictatorships throughout the twentieth century. But there are still few places in the Chinese world where political and civic freedoms are generally accepted as good things in themselves. Few, but not none.

This openness to the concept of freedom has mainly been in cities strongly affected by the West. The new kinds of cities that were created in foreign-run enclaves in the nineteenth and early twentieth centuries were not under the control of the imperial or the republican mandarinate. Colonial rule gave many opportunities for new social, economic and political values and institutions to emerge. Shanghai's International Settlement became the intellectual centre of the Chinese world in the 1920s and 1930s. But while Chinese residents of the settlement had opportunities lacking elsewhere in China, there was no politics that was democratic in actuality rather than merely in name. Shanghai residents' freedoms in their daily lives did not turn into political ones, and though a few bold spirits campaigned for human rights and democracy they did not get far.[3]

The vigorous development of political freedoms and the mass demands for them that have marked Taiwan and Hong Kong since the 1980s have been without precedent in the Chinese world and are a good illustration of the principle that profound and rapid changes to long-established traditions can happen. In Hong Kong this owes nothing to big business, which continues an old tradition of kowtowing to the power of the imperial state, whether British or Chinese. It would rather buy the permission of the mandarinate to make money undisturbed than fight for political rights. Big business is at odds with the large professional middle class, which started in the fading twilight of a profoundly undemocratic colonial rule to demand the kinds of freedoms that their counterparts around the developed world expect.

In Taiwan, by contrast, where part of the business class sees itself as having a Taiwanese identity rather than (in the political sense) a Chinese one, some private businesses have provided financial support to the would-be pro-independence Democratic Progress Party. This could be seen as another way in which Taiwan is not part of China as a political entity. Interestingly enough, Peking has been using the leverage it now has on much Taiwan business to try to bribe and bully the island into submission.[4]

The spread of ideas of political freedom in the Chinese world since the late nineteenth century, a subject explored by David Kelly in Chapter 5, contrasts strongly with the near-total absence of any such concepts in earlier Chinas. By concepts of political freedom I refer especially to the odd notions of freedom as a value (or, in the case of individuals, a status) to be prized for its own sake that have survived at the western end of Eurasia from tribal societies to our own times and been spread from there to some other parts of the world. Odd because they are not found everywhere, and are neither natural nor self-evident. These odd notions can be group freedoms, as when groups within a larger society are held to have the right to make some choices about their own lives without having to take into account the wishes and interests of the state and its rulers. Another odd notion of freedom can vest a freedom in the individual that may be held against the state, the larger society, and even the family or other smaller groups to which the individual belongs. A related group of odd freedoms are rights to be involved in making decisions about one's society.

Though in the modern West we take such freedoms for granted, their 'odd', socially constructed character becomes clear when we consider that they only matter when someone wants to do or not do something that others dislike. They legitimate resistance to the will of rulers or to consensus views in a society. These are not the same as much more common and unremarkable wishes to be delivered from such unavoidable ills of our mortal condition as pain, sickness and death. Poverty and hunger are rarely welcome. Though the solutions or escapes offered in various cultures show fascinating differences and similarities, the longings are universal. These longings do not need separate explanations each time they are found.

China's pre-Western cultures, like so many others in the world, can provide plenty of examples of such longings which, whether attainable or illusory, are essentially escapes. Zhuang Zhou and the other authors of the Daoist book *Zhuang zi* in the fourth and third centuries BC give exhilarating lessons on how to go along with the forces of nature which, if resisted, would destroy humanity. They celebrate the desirability of keeping out of politics and avoiding the burdens of office. Their way of achieving freedom from the misery of death is simply to accept our mortality. Zhuang Zhou and his followers celebrate uselessness and ways of achieving inner freedom. They do not address anything that could be regarded as political freedom, though they have excellent suggestions about how to escape from the state and its demands. *Zhuang zi* remains a wonderful handbook on how to live and preserve one's inner freedom under tyrannical government. Later Daoism offered the prospect of avoiding, or at any rate postponing, death. The methods included exercise, diet, the taking of elixirs, and other techniques of physical longevity and, so it was claimed, immortality.[5]

Buddhist philosophy went even further than offering escapes from death. It taught one how to find freedom from suffering through escape from life itself. From the Indian world it brought a whole new set of fears that had been part of that culture since before Buddhism, fears from which Buddhism had originally offered deliverance: the torments of hell and the endless cycle of reincarnation into all sorts of life-forms, nearly all undesirable. Buddhism thus gave China new needs for freedom and new ways of attaining it. Neither the Daoist nor the Buddhist notions of freedom as deliverance from suffering carry any implication of, or connection with, notions of political or social freedom.

The Primacy of Authority

While ideas about what constitutes oppressive rule and what is normal government will vary with time and place, it seems safe enough to assume that anywhere state structures are found there will be those who long for or celebrate the freedom-as-deliverance of no longer being under a bad ruler. Since the first millennium BC political thinkers in China have offered the prince who will listen ways of freeing his country from the dangers of famine, invasion or rebellion. Rulers who behaved badly could be criticised harshly by a principled official and denounced by later historians. Even by the authoritarian standards of the so-called Confucian tradition, some originally legitimate rulers are seen as being so appalling that getting rid of them is in certain circumstances justifiable.

This is, however, far from being a notion of political freedom or political rights. The need to remove an extremely bad ruler or, even more drastically, to overthrow an incurably decadent dynasty is one about which Confucian thinkers from Mencius onwards have felt very uncomfortable. It challenges the profound commitment to obeying established authority that is central to the traditions of Chinese political thinking that have been dominant from the first century BC and are conventionally (and not inappropriately) labelled Confucian. Nor does it take much imagination to be aware of the awkwardness felt by the pre-Confucian propagandists who wrote the harangues justifying the violent overthrow of their Shang overlords by the Zhou chiefs in the twelfth or eleventh centuries BC that are among the most plausibly authentic parts of the canonical *Shu Jing* (*Book of History*). This awk- wardness is palpable in, for example, the 'Duo shi' and the 'Jun shi', sections of the *Shu Jing* in which the Duke of Zhou, the Zhou regent, insists to survivors of the fallen Shang dynasty that Zhou was right to rebel against it.

For mainstream Chinese political thinkers such things had to be done from time to time, but they threatened the very structures in the best interests of which they are supposedly carried out. Removing a bad ruler is not seen as an exercise of the rights of a subordinate nor as one of the freedoms of a sovereign people, though the people's suf- fering can be used to justify it. It is a little like using the mistreatment of animals as a reason for changing the ownership or management of a farm, a process that does not put the animals in charge of their own fate.

Even when a monarch was irredeemable, his officials could not, with good Confucian conscience, help to overthrow him. They could rem- onstrate with him, just as a son could deferentially try to persuade a father of the error of his ways. They could retire from the ruler's service to live in quiet obscurity, which was sometimes done rather conspicuously. They could even make the ultimate protest by killing themselves. But they could not honourably depose him, join in a rebel- lion, or take office under a successor regime unless the previous ruler had abdicated in a way that transferred the obligations they owed him to the new sovereign. Here again, a comparison with the authoritarian Confucian family helps to make clear the unfree nature of the Confucian gentleman's place in the political order. He was not a free agent with the right to vote on matters of state or to help choose who should hold the highest public offices. An official could no more switch his allegiance to another regime with propriety than a married woman could respectably leave home. The exceptions in both cases are comparable: the husband could transfer control of his wife to another by sale or other means, and the ruler could transfer his officials to a successor regime.

It is as unusual to come across challenges to the principle of authoritarian rule (as opposed to misrule) in Chinese written records as it is to find the institution of the family being questioned. In an apparently non-Daoist part of the collection *Zhuang zi*, the legendary brigand – or, according to Maoist historiography, popular rebel – Zhi is shown giving Confucius a ferocious diatribe against respectable notions of social order as he feasts on human livers. But this is writing deliberately meant to shock by putting the case that the established authorities are no better than brigands. It is not an argument for political freedoms as a desirable good.[6]

Respectable Subjects

In European and related traditions the abominable institution of slavery has long provided one way of defining freedom by contrast.[7] Curiously enough, slavery in China did not throw up a contrasting notion of freedom. It was clearly an undesirable state. Hardly anyone will be a slave by choice, unless this is seen as an evil lesser than such alternatives as allowing others to whom one owes an obligation to be enslaved, or facing the death and destruction of one's family. In Chinese cultures it was long acceptable, even praiseworthy, to make the sacrifice of your own non-slavery in order to buy your parents' well-being. But this was great altruism, admirable precisely because it was not what people would normally choose for themselves.

The nature and scale of slavery, serfdom and other forms of semi-slavery in different parts of the Chinese world and in different periods are topics on which one might have hoped that Chinese historians would have done some useful general surveys in the last half-century. Unfortunately the question of slavery has not been adequately discussed. This is almost certainly because the party-state used the power of dictatorship to enforce the Engels paradigm of human social development in the interpretation of China's history, which compelled Chinese historians to subscribe to the highly questionable notion that

China had gone through the stages of 'slave society' then 'feudalism'. This led to many decades of essentially meaningless discussions about the dating of a transition between two social formations whose existence in China Maoist historiography has asserted but never convincingly demonstrated.

The Maoist story has it that 'slave society' emerged in north China in the second millennium BC and gave place to 'feudalism' somewhere around the era of the Qin conquest in the third century BC. The problem is that while most producers in the Shang, Western Zhou and Spring and Autumn periods do not seem to have been economically free, their dependence appears to have been more like that of serfs tied to the land and obliged to spend some of their time working for their masters than that of chattel slaves who could be bought and sold as commodities. War captives, especially those from other ethnic groups such as the Qiang, were sometimes enslaved and presented to the living or sacrificed to the dead. But the evidence of such ritual slaughter, grisly as it is, does not point to chattel slavery as the dominant form of production.

Good evidence of slavery in production is found just at the period when 'slave society' was supposedly giving way to 'feudalism'. From the Warring States period (fifth to third centuries BC) onwards some private entrepreneurs used large numbers of slaves. One such was Diao Jian of Qi in Western Han times, who made a fortune worth several tens of millions of cash by trusting his slaves, even insubordinate ones, and letting them trade for him.[8] The short-lived Qin empire ran its own huge state slave economy. The Qin legal code of the third century BC included detailed regulations on how state slaves were to be managed, and even set tariffs for redeeming people from state slavery by replacing them with substitutes of greater value to the government. Thus an adult male state slave could be redeemed with two equivalent substitutes. Presumably this was intended to allow some to obtain the freedom of members of their family. If an elderly mother was unlucky enough to be an embroiderer or a seamstress, however, she was too useful to the authorities to be let go, even in exchange for a strapping youngster.[9] The laws of the Qin state, which according to Maoist theory was fundamentally opposed to the slave-holding order, actually provided for officials to support the property rights of private slave-owners by disciplining their unruly slaves for them.[10]

By the sixth century AD we find chattel slavery taken for granted in the north Chinese estate-owner's manual *Qi min yao shu* ('Essential arts for the common people'). In the chapter on the commercial cultivation of *Brassica rapa* (rape turnip) the reader is told that three cartloads of the leaves of this vegetable can be sold for one male slave, and twenty loads for a female slave.[11] Elsewhere in the book prices for commodities are given in cash, silver, grain and plain silk. At around the same time the *juntian* system of land allocation by the state granted the lifetime use of arable land to householders. Householders received an amount of land calculated on a per capita basis that took into account not only themselves and their immediate adult kin but also their male and female slaves and their oxen as long as they owned them.[12]

The early Tang social order of the seventh and eighth centuries AD was built on sharp distinctions of status. At the bottom were slaves. As the Commentary to the Tang Code explains it bluntly, 'slaves are the same as chattels (*zicai*), which means that their owner can dispose of them'.[13] Next came the semi-servile *buqu*, serfs or other dependants. Then came the bulk of the population, the 'good subjects' (*liang ren*),[14] then gentry, then aristocracy, and so on up to the emperor. It would be hard to describe any of them, except possibly the monarch, as free, even in the limited Athenian, Roman or antebellum American sense.

For the next 1000 years semi-slaves continued to make up a significant (but by now unquantifiable) part of the workforce, while chattel slavery seems to have declined as a source of productive labour. The serf risings of the middle of the seventeenth century and the thoroughgoing reforms of agrarian relationships that the Manchu conquerors imposed in the decades that followed spelled the end of serfdom as a major mode of production. By the eighteenth and nineteenth centuries slavery and serfdom were much less important than they had been, though they were still to be found in China. The number of people in these categories was much smaller than it had been between Qin and Tang. Field serfs survived mainly in areas whose geography kept them isolated, such as the mountain-girt valleys of Huizhou, which at the same time as preserving a kind of serfdom well into the twentieth century were also for centuries the home of some of China's most dedicated and successful merchants. In nearly all of the rest of rural China the serf was replaced by the hired hand or the small tenant farmer after the great social revolution that followed the Manchu conquest of the seventeenth century.[15] In the Han-Chinese parts of the Qing empire slavery was almost extinct except as a criminal sanction – some offenders were enslaved to soldiers on the frontier – by the time it was formally abolished in 1909 amid the many other modernising measures of the last years of the Qing.

Selling or giving one's own junior family members into formal or *de facto* slavery was both legally and morally acceptable within certain limits in China from remote antiquity until recent times. The father who sold his child was simply disposing of his property. But for a child to sell a parent was an abomination to be severely punished. The child was not free within the family, and did not win the right to run his or her own life by becoming an adult. A woman never did, and a man could only do it by becoming the senior living male in the family. Once that happened he was in his own small way an emperor, whose limited freedoms entailed restricting the freedoms of others.

Chattel slavery fitted easily into such family power structures. Dynastic legal codes differentiated very sharply between the heinousness of, for example, hitting various members of one's family according to the relative status of striker and struck. Similarly the law gave the slave or semi-servile dependant less protection against assault than the non-servile and punished them more severely if they beat non-slaves. The penalties for slaves and semi-slaves beating their own masters or mistresses were even more severe than those for assaulting other non-slaves. Within the family the concubine was a legally recognised inferior sub-wife and a semi-servile dependant. As with other half-slaves, the law discriminated against her. The maidservant, in earlier centuries a slave, often had a status even lower than the concubine; she had only minimal legal protection against her master or mistress.[16]

Slavery, though marginal, survived into the nineteenth century, and various forms of semi-slavery that allowed women and children to be sold lasted well into the twentieth. Even in the 1980s and 1990s the Chinese authorities have to wage constant campaigns against those who abduct women and children for sale to others, and against those who buy them. It is apparently still necessary to make propaganda to persuade rural people that buying women and children is wrong. In 1989, 10,032 women were abducted and sold in the province of Sichuan alone. These were only the cases that were reported to the authorities, and they do not include a probably much larger number of women who were sold against their will by their families.[17] While forced labour in China's prison system can be paralleled in many other countries, the Chinese state is one of the few that sends its subjects for forced labour ('re-education through labour') by administrative decision alone without requiring a court trial and sentence.

What is remarkable for our present investigation is that well over 3000 years of slavery and semi-slavery seems not to have produced a contrasting concept of personal freedom. This is very different from, say, Europe, where to be non-slave or non-serf was to be free or freed, *liber* or *libertus*.

In China the opposite of 'slave' was not 'free' or 'freed' but 'respectable'. Someone could be 'respectable' instead of 'base' (the generic epithet for slaves and dependants) and enjoy certain privileges over their inferiors. To be released from slavery or semi-slavery and become a *liang min*, a respectable subject, was to rise in status and lose some legal disabilities. But one acquired nothing that was thought of as a freedom one could hold against the state or anyone else by right. Whatever actual 'little freedoms' (to use a later political jargon notion to which we will return) one had were never turned into a consciously held concept of being free. Freedom is irrelevant as a concept in looking at relationships between slavery and non-slavery in China.

Bureaucratic Absolutism

If slavery did not give rise to ideas of freedom, what about political life in China? Before nineteenth-century pressures from the imperialisms of Europe and America, there was nothing remotely like the notions of positive political freedom or political rights within the public life of society that have developed at the western end of Eurasia over the last 2500 years. The European ideologies of rights and freedoms that first grew on the dunghills of slavery and conquest in Athens and Rome and reached their heights as European, then American, empires dominated much of the world were the products of happenstance, the fortunate consequences of many factors.

One of the most important of these was the political backwardness of Europe, which by comparison with China hardly had a state worth speaking of before the eighteenth century. Europe's luck was to be so primitive in its state structures that it preserved features of its ancient tribal societies such as the communal assembly. The assemblies that survived were often no more than a symbolic vestige, or represented only a small, privileged minority, as did the Senate under the Roman principate. Yet they embodied the notion that the ruler was obliged to win the agreement of some of his subjects for some of his actions. Thus it was that the medieval English parliaments were obstacles that prevented royal power coming anywhere near what the Chinese world would have regarded as the proper and civilised norm for a true monarchy. The close state control established in England just after the Norman conquest was an exceptional phase that did not last. Though far from democratic, assemblies of the nobility did keep alive a limited concept of government by consent. They marked, even if only symbolically, a limit to the king's absolute power and embodied the notion that some of his subjects had freedoms and rights.

One only has to compare the tiny and essentially tribal city-states of ancient Greece with the efficient, powerful, rational bureaucracies of China's Warring States that struggled for life and death during the fourth and third centuries BC to see the difference between embryonic and highly developed states. Even Athens at the height of its glory as the bully-boy of the Aegean and the Hellenistic monarchies that followed were primitive, backward polities compared with the absolutist Chinese kingdoms which ruled through all-embracing officialdoms that had the whole population on their books and tried to control all important aspects of the lives of every man, woman and child in peace and war. The most centralised of the Warring States did not tolerate such relics of earlier hereditary aristocratic societies as the customary right that the leading families in the capital, the *guorén* (the people of the capital) or the *roushizhe* (meat-eaters) had once had to comment on affairs of state.[18] One of these states, Qin, went so far as to punish even those who praised the government.[19]

Set alongside the power of the Western Han empire with its huge bureaucracy and enormous military establishment, the Roman Empire, its contemporary at the other end of Eurasia, looks primitive and archaic, an improvisation kept working by a small group of professional soldiers, notably the centurions who made a few legions into the force that held it all together. The Han civil service was bigger, more all-pervasive and better organised than anything Europe had before the eighteenth century. Though the Han state and its successors tended over time to relax direct control over some aspects of their subjects' lives, they never permitted any such pernicious notion as that of political freedom to emerge. Even if ancient societies in what is now China had recognised rights that could be held against the monarch, such notions had been eradicated by the late third century BC. The weakness of medieval European monarchies that allowed cities to select their own governments and bargain with kings would have shocked a Song official's sense of a well-ordered world. But then anything like real feudalism had disappeared from the Chinese political mainstream for well over 1000 years.

One of the most fundamental reasons why 'feudal' is so inappropriate an adjective with which to characterise the dominant Chinese political systems of the last 2000 years and more is that feudalism is not compatible with a strong state structure. Relationships between lords and vassals, whether those of medieval Western Europe that gave rise to the Anglo-French word 'feudal', or those of the western Zhou political order to which the Chinese word *fengjian* (also used to represent 'feudal' and its equivalents in many European languages) originally referred, imply all sorts of limits to the power of the sovereign, who transfers some areas of authority to his vassals. Feudal or *fengjian* relationships involve rights on both sides and limit each side's range of options. It was only after some of the leading states in the Chinese world restricted or eliminated the powers of their own hereditary *fengjian* or feudal aristocracies that the powerful bureaucratic monarchies so characteristic of mature Chinese political culture could develop.

The Chinese state that has evolved since then has nearly always been jealous of its claims to absolute power, power administered through officials who can be appointed or dismissed at will and who are subject to strict discipline. Relationships that could be labelled 'feudal' in a political sense were generally confined to marginal ones between the rulers of all or part of China (as defined culturally) and non-Chinese tribal leaders and others who were not under direct Chinese-style bureaucratic rule. The use of *fengjian* or feudal to characterise the dominant political structures in China since then is nearly always fundamentally wrong-headed and misleading. Had China been feudal for the last 2000 years, concepts of freedom would surely not have been as irrelevant as they were.

For concepts of freedom and rights to survive the rise of the state in Europe, weak governments were essential. European states before the rise of Prussia were primitive by Chinese standards; so far from knowing how to establish and run a large and well-disciplined bureaucracy, they were not even aware of the need for one. They often allowed some of their subjects openly to defy the will of the monarch. The ability of the ruler to control the peasant directly was limited. Centrally held records of who lived where were normally pathetically sparse. By medieval European standards the Domesday Book was an astonishing achievement possible only in a small country during the first flush of acquisitive enthusiasm of a newly arrived set of gangsters.

The barbaric notions that subjects had rights and freedoms were so incompatible with 'true' values that the language of civilisation, Chinese, could barely express them. Europe's good fortune was that it only learned how to create effective states long after some western Europeans had become attached to keeping hold of rights and freedoms that, however limited and flawed, made at least some of them citizens rather than subjects. The combination of young and vigorous states with notions of individual and corporate rights proved to be extraordinarily dynamic and aggressive. These states conquered most of the world in the eighteenth and nineteenth centuries, carrying with them the liberating ideas that were to bring down the very empires they established.

Chinese states by the fourth century BC at latest were often remarkably successful in keeping records of their whole populations so that they could be taxed and conscripted. The state had the surname (that most useful bureaucratic label), personal name, age and home place of every subject, and was also able to ensure that nobody could move far from home without proper authorisation.

In the late third century BC the Qin state's officials noted the rainfall and the state of the crops field by field throughout the empire and measured the girth of every ox every year, giving out rewards and punishments depending on how many inches each beast gained or lost. All the members of all the households were liable to be held criminally responsible for any offence committed by any of them that was not reported by the neighbours before it was discovered by the authorities.[20] These records were compiled by officials who were themselves subject to strict discipline and who held their jobs by licence and not by right. The essentially feudal notion of job tenure for life had no place in the Chinese civil service.

Officials had not rights and freedoms but privileges, which could be withdrawn without notice, and duties. High officials could discuss matters in their area of responsibility at court conferences, or submit memorials, but only at the monarch's pleasure. Ill-chosen words could lead to disgrace or death. This noble tradition of principled protest was still alive in the second half of the twentieth century, and some of Mao's subordinates paid the price for it – but it was nothing to do with freedom.

The earlier dynastic state admitted no free choice about where one lived or moved. It punished those who absconded from where officialdom had them on its books for tax, corvée and military service. A clear illustration of this can be found in a collection of specimen difficult legal cases found in Han tomb 247 at Zhangjiashan in Jiangling, Hubei, and published in 1993. In a case dating from about 200–196 BC, a time when the new Han rulers were supposedly applying gentler laws than their Qin predecessors, a Man-Yi tribesman Wuyou 'absconds'. His defence is that as a Man-Yi he has paid a commutation charge to be let off forced labour. The case is referred to higher authority for decision. The ruling is unambiguous. Wuyou is to be cut in half.[21]

In the Tang code from about 850 years later we find the state still taking a very dim view of subjects who abscond (*wang*) from their place of registration, and not only of them. It is even a flogging offence to 'drift' (*fulang*) somewhere else for ten days or more without such good cause as trade or study.[22] Even the ward heads in villages or towns who allow absconders or drifters to stay in their wards will be flogged.[23] There was thus clearly no legally recognised freedom or right to choose where you went or where you lived. In early imperial China people lived where they were registered and stayed there unless given permission to the contrary. This suspicion of mobility, with its dangerous potential for freedom, is part of Chinese official thinking even now, at a time when Chinese people are more mobile than ever.

Over the 2000 years and more that followed the end of the Qin dynasty in 206 BC, the state machine achieved a huge reduction in the scale of its activities while preventing the emergence of social forces that might challenge its monopoly of power. By the eighteenth century the state normally appointed officials directly only down to the level of the *xian* or county, an administrative unit that usually had a population of several hundred thousand. Below that level it operated through village heads, local gentry and other notables who were part of their own communities, letting them get on with things as long as they did not threaten the political and moral order.[24]

There are strong arguments for seeing this reduction in the role of the state as making for greater freedom and more autonomy for the component parts of society. It is clear that the Qing state took a much smaller part of its subjects' wealth and working time through tax and conscript labour than had most early ones. Apart from where the later state saw itself as having a duty to its subjects to monitor and if necessary influence the price of grain through strategic intervention, it no longer concerned itself with controlling the market economy, which by the nineteenth century had long involved the overwhelming majority of the population. Serfdom had, as we have seen, ended in nearly the whole of the empire. There was a growth in *de facto* small freedoms, so that for practical purposes individuals and families had more control over their own lives than their ancestors had enjoyed. Yet the state did nothing to acknowledge the kinds of public political rights discussed here. It continued to do all it could to prevent the emergence of organised social forces outside its control that might challenge its monopoly of legitimate authority.

Religion Dwarfed

Potentially subversive religious cults were suppressed from the beginning to the end of dynastic times, a tradition that continues in the ongoing persecution of unauthorised Islamic, Christian and other groups that try to operate outside state-sanctioned religious organisations. In controlling religion the later dynastic state was applying lessons learned much earlier. Between the fifth and eighth centuries AD some Buddhist monasteries had shown their potential to become rich, powerful and permanent institutions. When the faithful gave them property the property stayed theirs. Many peasants preferred becoming semi-servile dependants of monasteries to being taxed and conscripted by the government, with the result that the monasteries acquired large numbers of their own serfs.[25] This was unlike secular wealth, which was normally divided fairly equally between the male heirs in each generation or, if it was arable land held from the state only on lifetime tenure, was liable to be reassigned to others by the government.

Had this tendency been allowed to go on for much longer China might have seen a Buddhist church with the independence, wealth, power and influence that some Buddhist monasteries had in Tibet before the Chinese invasion or the Catholic church had in medieval western Europe. The medieval European church set limits to the power of the secular state. In Tibet monks actually replaced secular monarchs as heads of government. The proto-states of medieval Europe could not match the church's ideological authority or touch its wealth with impunity. Such an uncontrollable force within a state's territory created spaces in which notions of freedom could emerge or develop. It also created the need for political doctrines that justified and rationalised limits to state power. The success with which the Chinese state prevented any religion from becoming a potential rival source of authority across the empire was one of many factors preventing the emergence of a doctrine that the monarch's rights were limited by the rights of groups and individuals.

Were we looking here at how the concepts of individual rights that the state cannot easily challenge survived in western Eurasia, and in the Islamic world as much as in Christendom, it would be necessary to consider the political implications of concepts of the soul and its relationship to a monotheistic god. Cultures that take this relationship seriously – and not all cultures do – sometimes have to make the state's or the monarch's claims take second place to those of a deity. The emphasis on the soul as a moral actor and the prospect of posthumous rewards and punishments found in Jewish, Christian and Islamic traditions is not found in the traditions of China's ruling political culture. Though something of this came into China with Buddhism and became an important part of some popular religions, it remained somehow vulgar. No official would have been taken seriously had he argued the peril to his – or to his imperial master's – immortal soul of a given action. (By contrast, an appeal to how future history might see it was a much more potent threat.)

Localism Stifled

The Buddhist church was a potentially strong rival to the absolute state that was brought under control before it could nurture dangerous notions of freedom. The Chinese aristocracy was another potential hotbed of freedom in which nothing grew.

Magnates in western Europe could pass on most of their estates to a single male heir in each generation who inherited his predecessor's title and privileges, irrespective of whether he had done anything to earn them. In medieval Europe aristocrats could sometimes defy kings and get away with it, especially when they acted together. They had military power through their private armies and economic power through their great estates. They produced doctrines of their rights and freedoms and were willing in some circumstances to fight for them. In many European monarchies the state did not succeed before recent centuries in controlling the nobility and the freedoms they claimed for themselves but denied others, with consequences that were crippling for some states or, as in the case of Poland, fatal. Aristocrats were a plague to king and commoner, but in their selfish way they set precedents for freedoms that others could strive for.

In the second to eighth centuries AD some leading Chinese clans did manage a remarkable continuity of local power and wider influence, while many dynasties, among them non-Chinese ones in the north, rose then fell. This continuity was ensured not by the European method under which a single all-powerful individual in each generation controlled the family's wealth and military might but by the collective coherence of big clans that held together through troubled times and kept their local pre-eminence. Though they were strong enough from the late second till the fourth century to band together to threaten and even bring down dynasties, by the end of the fifth century regimes in both northern and southern China had cut them down to size militarily.

While some leading non-Chinese clans were to pose threats to governments after that, this virtually marked the end of the Chinese aristocracy as an independent and effective political force. Their claim to high office as if by right lingered on into the early reigns of the Tang dynasty, but their importance was by then declining rapidly as regular civil servants, recruited through competitive exams, replaced them at court. Though some families or clans were locally dominant right into our own times, that influence was generally kept at the level of the county or below. In the last 1000 years the Chinese monarchy has thus not had to contend with the challenge of aristocrats defending their own liberties or acting as patrons of unorthodox thinking. This absence made it easier to keep the principles of absolutism almost unchallenged.

The state proved to be very effective in keeping power strictly local, and in making arrangements with the dominant families or clans in a county that gave some *de facto* recognition to their influence and also kept it under control. Under the later dynasties the rule that members of the regular civil service could not hold office in their own province was, except in times of dire crisis, strictly followed. So too was the principle that officials were not posted in any one province for too long. These measures ensured that the regular civil servant who represented the power of the imperial bureaucracy was not allowed to form permanent alliances with local landed power. This eliminated the possibility of locally defined rights and freedoms being defended by an alliance of local magnates and disgruntled Crown officials.

One of the ways in which the reforms of the dying years of the Qing dynasty at the beginning of the twentieth century fatally weakened the dynasty's chances of survival was allowing the local gentry to organise themselves politically right across a province through provincial assemblies. Even that very limited measure of political freedom for property-owning, educated males was to prove devastating for the autocracy. Within a few years of the assemblies' first meetings they were to be some of the most important theatres in which the secession of many provinces from the Manchu empire was brought about and the Republic came into being.

Had the sprouts of democracy of the last years of the Qing and the first few years of the Republic been allowed to grow, the political history of twentieth-century China would have been very different. We might speculate about what would have given the best chance of democracy and the necessary supporting concepts of rights and freedoms establishing themselves in China. If after the death of the Empress Dowager Cixi in 1908 the Qing dynasty had been under the control of a monarch or regent competent enough to handle the transition to constitutional monarchy, the dynasty might just have been able to use limited democracy as a way of renewing its legitimacy. Institutions enjoying some degree of independence from the state might have developed, and China might have been spared nearly ninety years of misrule by a succession of army or party/army regimes. As it happened, democracy and freedom never stood a chance except in rhetoric.

Commerce Encircled

What about economic foundations of freedom and the role of cities? Though the volume of commerce was huge and we might guess that China's economy was the biggest in the world up to the nineteenth century, economic activity was carried out by millions of small individual performers. In recent centuries the market functioned with minimal intervention by the state, apart from occasional attempts to flatten out fluctuations in grain prices. Capital existed and was recognised. Chinese languages are full of metaphors about capital, interest, profit and loss. But despite the remarkable extent to which Chinese economies have been commercialised in the last 1000 years, and especially since the eighteenth century, neither the state nor custom allowed large and permanent private companies to emerge. Capital did not become a force in its own right, independent of the people who owned it, or provide the resources for intellectual or political challenges to absolutism. Indeed, it is open to question whether a concept of absolute property rights ever developed in China.

It is only possible to argue that late traditional China had a 'civil society' if one gives that overworked term a very weak meaning, one with Chinese characteristics. In China capital did not become capitalism. Traders and city-dwellers did not become a bourgeoisie.

City air did not make one free in China, though those who breathed it sometimes had forms of practical independence not available to villagers. Cities were centres of state power. For the first 2500 to 3000 years of urban history in what is now China, most cities were essentially extensions of the palaces of monarchs, princes, or the local delegates of the emperor. The cities were there to meet the material, religious and military needs of the rulers, and were laid out, in north China at least, on grid patterns that speak not of the organic growth of the medieval European city with its crowded rabbit-warren plan but of structures designed and imposed from above for the greater glory and security of the regime.

The prehistory of the city in what is now China is much richer and more complicated than was generally recognised only a decade ago. In the Yangtze Valley and its tributaries, Neolithic walled settlements distinctly larger than villages are found as far upstream as the Chengdu region, and groups of towns have been identified in Shandong. Leaving aside the very small walled compounds in some late Neolithic settlements, such as those at Dengcheng and Pingliangtai, as well as the small town at Longshan, none of which seem big enough to be worth calling cities, the earliest settlements of undoubtedly city size in the Yellow River area are the pre-Shang city and the more recently discovered early Shang city in Yanshi county to the east of modern Luoyang. As this is the area where the ancestors of the later Chinese state developed, these cities are probably more relevant than most to understanding relations between city and state in ancient pre-China.

While the layout of the pre-Shang city at Yanshi, which has not yet been shown to have a substantial wall, has not been well enough established to permit a clear view of how it was organised, the early Shang city built before 1500 BC was very obviously an example of the walled, palace-dominated city intersected by a grid of roads. This pattern was one that was to be followed literally for millennia.

When the newly established Western Han dynasty built its capital at Chang'an about 1300 years later, the large walled city was mostly filled with enormous palaces, each set in a huge compound. Two thousand years later the remains of the foundations of some of the main palace buildings, each the product of astronomical amounts of forced labour, still dominate the surrounding plain as substantial hills. Chang'an, built about 800 years later on a neighbouring site under what is now Xi'an, was still a palace city, though by now the other inhabitants were allowed within the walls. The state continued to try to regulate everything in the city, requiring the city-dwellers to live in walled and policed wards from which they were not allowed to emerge during the hours of curfew, and confining trade to enclosed markets under government supervision.[26] The great capitals of early imperial China had much to offer, but freedom, citizenship and urban rights were not among them.

The closeness of state control over urban life was relaxed under the dynasties of later imperial times from the Song onwards, letting merchants set up their shops and stalls along city streets instead of being confined to the strictly regulated market.[27] But cities were not allowed to become autonomous. They never acquired rights or charters, never elected their self-governing corporations or chose their own mayors. Merchants could win some *de facto* control over some urban activities, as William Rowe has shown in his studies of nineteenth-century Hankou.[28] They might riot or protest in other ways against officials who were seen to be behaving unreasonably, even put local officials to flight, but they could not in the long term defy or even bargain with the emperor and hope to get away with it.[29] The Chinese city had no forum, no assembly in which public affairs could be decided. Though trade had broken out of closed markets by AD 1000 and every kind of urban pleasure flourished – restaurants, commercial entertainment, the sex industry – the Chinese city did not have citizens, only city-dwellers.

Manchu Peking was a permanent armed camp in its northern part, the city proper, with its parts assigned to different units of the hereditary alien army of occupation. City government was run by imperial officials, and to make it doubly certain that Peking should be denied anything approaching a corporate political identity in its own right, the city was not even given its own local government, but divided between the two administrative counties of Wanping and Daxing. Commercial activity existed on sufferance in the southern, 'Chinese' city.[30]

Even in other cities where trade played a much more important part in the city's life, merchants did not become a bourgeoisie. The great pottery centre of Jingdezhen, the world's biggest industrial city before the European industrial revolution, was so low in status that it was not even the seat of a county magistrate.

In China itself doctrines of freedom do not emerge in cities. What urban life does offer under the later dynasties from around the tenth century AD is room for what we can call by the label used in the Mao era, 'petty freedoms' (*xiao ziyou*). As long as you could afford to live there and had the ability and connections to enable you to earn a living, it seems to have been fairly easy to move to a city and set up a business. The impression of the urban world of the lower Yangtze in later imperial times that one gets from reading the commercial printed fiction it produced and consumed is of one in which petty business people get on with their lives in their neighbourhoods. They have little to do with the state unless they kill each other or commit other crimes.

In the first half of the second millennium some craftsmen are still dependants of the court or of princes, which limits their freedoms in some ways, but not as much as one might expect. This is illustrated in a printed vernacular story that is thought to date back to Southern Song or Yuan times. Xiuxiu, a young bondswoman in the Southern Song capital (modern Hangzhou), takes advantage of the general panic of a fire to run away from the palace of the prince her master to spend the night with her fiancé, Cui Ning, an expert jade-grinder, in the part of the city where he lives. She has been sold by her parents to the prince's household to serve as a bonded and highly skilled embroideress for a set term of years. Young Cui is also a dependant of the prince, with the expectation that he will be available when the prince wants a piece of jade worked, and has also secured the promise of Xiuxiu as a bride when the bondswoman has served the time for which she has been sold.

Their premature marriage is unauthorised and thus illegal, so they have to flee from the capital. After their flight to another city far away (Tanzhou, today's Changsha) he is able to set up in his trade under his own name as a craftsman from the capital without needing anyone's authorisation or patronage, doing jobs for senior officials posted to the region, until a servant of the prince comes across him by chance, returns to the capital and reports his and Xiuxiu's presence to his master. The prince obtains a warrant for their arrest and return to the capital for absconding. He kills Xiuxiu and has Cui Ning relatively lightly punished by the local government. Though Cui is exiled to Nanjing for a while as part of his punishment he is able to return to the capital when he successfully repairs a jade statuette for the emperor.[31] Though Cui is not free to marry someone else's semi-slave he is able to practise his trade in a distant city without needing anyone's patronage. Such practical freedoms should not be underestimated. By Qing times they were considerably greater than they had been under the Song. Tradespeople's relations with clients were purely commercial. It could well be that common people in eighteenth-century China enjoyed at least as much practical freedom as most of their counterparts in western Europe, the great majority of whom had virtually no political freedoms. But these 'freedoms' in China remained personal rather than political.

Unfreedom of Expression

Schools in China rarely mounted any fundamental challenge to ideological orthodoxy before the twentieth century but, especially in the
last 500 years of dynastic rule, generally trained students for the official
exams by making them learn canonical texts and approved interpretations by heart, or else provided the sons of many urban families with
basic literacy for practical needs. Upper-class education, combined
with an examination system that at each stage failed the overwhelming
majority of candidates, kept intellectuals docile, albeit frustrated. It
also discouraged – but could not eliminate – systematic thinking on big
issues. There were no rewards for questioning in any fundamental way
orthodox views from outside Confucian values. Bold textual scholarship and the exploration of alternative Confucian traditions were
about the limit of the permissible when considering issues affecting
state and society. Other values, such as those of Buddhism and Daoism,
could be held on private matters, but only as long as they did not
threaten the absolute supremacy of the Confucian approach to state
and society.

In Europe printed books in many languages undermined the
attempts of some governments to impose intellectual orthodoxies
within their territories. Books could be banned or their production
controlled in one territory, but they crossed frontiers. The book was a
vital medium through which the rivalry of ideas could be played out.
Books also gave many vernacular languages the status of print and
thus helped promote the rise of the chaotic diversity of European
nationalisms. In China, where books had been printed for many centuries before Europe finally borrowed the technology, they were
hardly ever associated with freedom of expression. Instead they were
used to inculcate standardised thinking in a single language.

It was not that original thinking did not happen, but that it was not
encouraged. In particular, it is virtually impossible to find Chinese
intellectuals before the twentieth century concerning themselves with
issues of active political freedom as opposed to escape freedoms such as
those offered by liquor, poetry, Buddhism or Daoism. This is not to be
explained by lack of interest in politics. They sometimes concerned
themselves with politics and other public issues of the day even if they
were not holding office; and their comments might leave them open to
punishment.

A few bold spirits down the ages challenged some aspects of absolute
monarchy. When one of the boldest of them, Huang Zongxi, attacked
the very moral basis of monarchy itself in the seventeenth century he
did not advocate anything approaching democracy, but instead argued

for an even more authoritarian kind of oligarchy. He put in an extreme form the claims of the Confucian-educated, morally superior scholars to run society for society's good, knowing best because they were the best indoctrinated. He demanded the banning of all religious activity not provided for in the Confucian ritual texts. Pubs, restaurants, the professional theatre and all but the simplest clothes were also to be suppressed. The local school superintendent was to be a commissar enforcing orthodox living with an absolute ruthlessness that went beyond normal Maoist excess and was curiously reminiscent of Red Guards in action.[32] So far from advocating freedom, Huang Zongxi, more Savanarola than Montesquieu, wanted a much harsher and more intolerant dictatorship.

It took the 'spiritual pollution' of Western bourgeois liberalism to turn Chinese students into political troublemakers from the late nine-teenth century onwards. When some former student radicals were among those who seized power in 1949 they did all they could to restore authoritarian education.

The very word used to represent 'freedom', *ziyou*, still has more bad associations than good ones. As 'self-origination' (see Chapter 10 in this book), it was quite unattractive to the Confucian intelligentsia, implying something like 'licence', doing what you like and to hell with everyone else. Thus when Erzhu Shilong was briefly dictator from AD 530 in Luoyang, the Northern Wei capital, he 'controlled power at court, and granted life or death as he wished [*ziyou*]'.[33] The word continues to mean doing what one likes until it is borrowed from Japanese usage as a translation for words for freedom or liberty in European languages in the nineteenth century. But it kept its other meanings as well. Those who advocate *ziyou*/freedom have to be prepared to face accusations of selfishness and letting down the finest traditions of Chinese culture. Mao or one of his ghost writers wrote a very hostile essay, 'Against freedom-ism' (the latter word is a free rendering of the Chinese term for liberalism);[34] and Deng Xiaoping took the line that all liberalisation (*ziyouhua*) is bad. While 'democracy' in its various Chinese equivalents has been a value, or rather a word, to which almost every group eager for power for almost a hundred years has laid claim, freedom as a good in itself has yet to win universal acceptance in China. So too has the sense of disinterested civic responsibility that, however imperfectly we live up to it, makes free societies – civil societies – work.

Although freedom had not been seen as a positive political value in mainstream Chinese traditions before the nineteenth century, the concept has greatly attracted or alarmed Chinese thinkers since it was introduced by the West about a hundred years ago. It may be that if faced with a choice between freedom and poverty or tyranny and wealth many in China would accept unfreedom. We cannot tell as they have not been allowed to choose for themselves. Outside observers do not have the right to make that choice for them.

People in Taiwan, where for about forty years after the Japanese surrender the talk of 'free China' barely disguised the reality of military dictatorship, seem to value their newly won political freedoms, to the horror of Peking. Fifteen years ago one would have needed to be totally unrealistic to foresee the possibility of Taiwan evolving peacefully in the direction of a multiparty democracy in which the main difference over the question of Taiwan's status between the two biggest political groupings is over whether the island should be independent of China *de facto* or *de jure*, and only a small minority is still serious about political reunification with the mainland. Yet already it seems unimaginable that Taiwan would surrender its fledgling democracy except in the face of irresistible military blackmail from China. In Hong Kong too, the partial democracy given in the fifty-ninth minute of the eleventh hour by the colonial authorities appeared to be valued by a sizeable proportion of the territory's electorate despite the certainty that they were soon to be handed over to another imperial power impatient to eliminate their brief sampling of limited self-government.

A problem in China is how political rights and freedoms can grow without creating havoc in a country whose people have been so ill prepared by their past and present rulers for self-government. This is not to argue that political freedoms are impossible in China, only that the prospects are for a long and difficult process. Despite the arguments I have set out that political freedom was not a concept to be found in Chinese cultures before the nineteenth century, its appeal has been powerful among those to whom the concept has been introduced. In 1859 Hong Rengan, the kinsman of the deranged Taiping emperor Hong Xiuquan, wrote the *Zi zheng xin pian* (A New Resource for Government), an unrealistic and unrealised program for that most illiberal rebellion in which he praised the rule of law and American democracy (without actually advocating it for China) and called for the abolition of slavery (on the grounds that it laid China open to the ridicule of foreigners) and of infanticide. This is perhaps the earliest (albeit cautious) Chinese statement of the case for somewhat Western and slightly liberal institutions in that country.[35] It is not, however, an argument for political freedom.

Rights and freedoms have been strongly resisted by Chinese governments and ideologists right up to the present, even when waging propaganda campaigns arguing that China is deeply committed to human rights. But none of this proves that they will never win acceptance. Indeed, the very fear that such concepts of political rights and freedoms arouse among China's rulers, as with other authoritarian regimes in Northeast and Southeast Asia, is a good indication that they realise just how appealing such notions are.

Throughout the decades of Communist Party rule there have been campaigns run with widely differing degrees of ferocity against supposedly bourgeois ideas held by the educated, among them freedom and democracy. The popularity of limited freedoms in Hong Kong and Taiwan shows that their value can quickly be appreciated in the Chinese world when they are on offer. No wonder Peking is so eager to eliminate even the narrowly restricted political pluralism of Hong Kong before the contamination spreads to other cities. Taiwan's rapid progress towards real democracy is perhaps even more alarming as it has already reached the stage of full elections and permitting such basic issues as the future status of the island to be debated and decided by the people.

Concepts of freedom have had very little to do with China until the last hundred years, and even in this recent period citizens have had to fight very hard to survive. This is not to suggest that there is for that reason something inherently wrong with the Chinese traditions and values to which freedom is irrelevant. A case could be made to show that the absence of divisive and selfish notions of freedoms and rights was one of the causes of the triumphs of Chinese civilisation before, say, the eighteenth century, and of ethnically Chinese territories that have done well in recent decades. Indeed, one could argue perversely that in raising freedom to an issue of principle western Eurasia went wrong, ensuring that conflict, division, chaos and lack of certainty would be characteristics of Western cultures for the last two and a half millennia.

There are other freedoms, fundamental by modern Western standards, about which there is very little to say when discussing the Chinas of the past because the concepts simply are not found. Notions that freedom of thought, belief and expression are in themselves desirable are almost completely absent from pre-Western Chinese ideologies and would be irrelevant to them. I am not arguing that nobody ever thought, spoke or wrote freely, only that such freedoms were never conceptualised and turned into abstract goods. Indeed, over 2400 years ago even so strong a critic of the value system advocated by Confucius and other pundits of the Ru school as Mo Zi explicitly condemned diversity of opinion as inherently bad.[36]

And yet the alien concepts of rights and freedoms have, like all sorts of Western fashions, caught on in recent times. If we look back over the whole course of Chinese history it is hard to find a more creative and exciting period than the Warring States (481–221 BC). In these centuries there were no doctrines of positive freedoms of which records have been preserved. But neither was there a dominant ideology imposed across the Chinese world by political authority. The rival would-be absolutist monarchies could not prevent a practical freedom of expression greater than anything that preceded or followed. Even such believers in suppressing other views as Confucians and Mohists had to resort to strength of argument rather than state power or the authority of tradition if they were to prevail in court debates. It is a period heavy with historical might-have-been relevances.

In the end it was Confucian intellectual and political authoritarianism that was to win in the reign of the Han Emperor Wu (141–87 BC) and to survive the rise and fall of dozens of monarchies thereafter. Doctrines of freedom of thought or religion, like doctrines of political and personal rights, never grew on Chinese soil till they came in as exotics. Since then these doctrines have come to be of immense importance in shaping the course of Chinese history. But even though doctrines of freedom were essentially non-existent before recent times, there was a growth between the tenth and the early twentieth centuries of *de facto*, unconceptualised freedoms as the state withdrew from trying to control all aspects of its subjects' lives while continuing to suppress any organisations that were not under its control. When exotic notions of freedoms and rights were brought in by the West in the nineteenth and twentieth centuries they in time took root. The issue is not one of whether these transplanted concepts will spread more widely in China, but of when, how, and with what consequences.

Notes

1 A useful set of essays on freedom and democracy in China over the last century is to be found in Andrew J. Nathan, *Chinese Democracy* (London: I. B. Tauris, 1986).

2 These elections have been much discussed by Western historians. See, for example, several of the contributions in Mary C. Wright (ed.), *China in Revolution: the First Phase, 1900–13* (New Haven and London: Yale University Press, 1968).

3 One such effort was the short-lived China League for Civil Rights of 1932–3 that tried to protect the interests of political prisoners and was effectively suppressed with the murder of its leader Yang Xingfo on 18 June 1933. See the note on pages 144–5 of Lu Xun, *Selected Poems*, translated and annotated by W. J. F. Jenner (Beijing: Foreign Languages Press, 1982). On the defeat of liberalism in the 1940s see Suzanne Pepper, *Civil War in China: the Political Struggle 1945–49* (Berkeley: University of California Press, 1978) and Dai Qing, *Liang Shuming Wang Shiwei Chu Anping* [Liang Shuming, Wang Shiwei and Chu Anping] (Nanjing: Jiangsu wenyi chubanshe, 1989).

4 See, for example, the report by Andrew Higgins in the *Guardian*, of 28 November 1995, p. 10.

5 The fullest study of Taoist techniques of immortality is volumes 2–5 of Joseph Needham, *Science and Civilisation in China* (Cambridge: Cambridge University Press, 1974, 1976, 1980, 1983). Earlier studies by Henri Maspero remain enlightening. See the essays collected in his *Mélanges Posthumes sur les Religions et l'Histoire de la Chine*, vol. 2, *Le taoïsme* (Paris: Civilisations du sud, 1950). These and some other pieces are translated by Frank A. Kierman Jr in Henri Maspero, *Taoism and Chinese Religion* (Amherst: University of Massachusetts Press, 1981).

6 The conversation between Confucius and Brigand Zhi is found in the first part of ch. 29 of *Zhuang zi*. In the *Zhuang zi ji shi* edited by Guo Qingfan that is included in vol. 3 of the series *Zhu zi ji cheng* (Beijing: Zhonghua shuju reprint of Shijie shuju edition, 1954 and 1959) it will be found on pp. 426–32. Translations of this passage may be consulted in A. C. Graham, *Chuang-tzu: the Seven Inner Chapters and Other Writings from the Book Chuang-tzu* (London: Allen & Unwin, 1981), Burton Watson, *The Complete Works of Chuang Tzu* (New York: Columbia University Press, 1968), or in the French version by Liou Kia-hway as revised by Paul Demiéville, *Philosophes taoistes: Lao-tseu, Tchouang-tseu, Lie-tseu*, a volume in the Bibliothèque de la Pléiade (Paris: Gallimard, 1980), pp. 318–24.

7 Here I am glad to acknowledge the stimulus provided by the work of Orlando Patterson.

8 See *Shi ji* [Records of the historian], ch. 69 (Beijing: Zhonghua shuju, 1959, p. 3279) and *Han shu* [History of Han], ch. 91 (Beijing: Zhonghua shuju, 1962, pp. 3691–92).

9 *Shuihudi Qin mu zhujian zhengli xiaozu* [Editorial team for the bamboo strips from the Qin tomb at Shuihudi], *Shuihudi Qin mu zhujian* [Bamboo strips from the Qin tomb at Shuihudi] (Beijing: Wenwu chubanshe, 1978), pp. 53–4. For an English translation see A. F. P. Hulsewé, *Remnants of Ch'in Law: an Annotated Translation of the Ch'in Legal and Administrative Rules of the 3rd Century B.C. Discovered in Yün-meng Prefecture, Hu-pei Province, in 1975* (Leiden: E. J. Brill, 1985), p. 45. These two works are a good place at which to begin exploring the regulations on how the Qin gulag was supposed to work.

10 See, for example, specimen cases E15 and E16 in Hulsewé, pp. 193–5 and *Shuihudi Qin mu zhujian*, pp. 259–61.

11 Shi Shenghan (ed.), *Qi min yao shu jin shi* [Modern commentary on the *Qi min yao shu*] (Beijing: Kexue chubanshe, 1958), vol. 2, p. 158 (sections 18.5.2 and 18.5.3 in Shi's division of the text).

12 The main surviving *juntian* regulations issued in AD 485 by the Northern Wei are found in *Wei shu juan* [The history of the Wei] 110 (Beijing: Zhonghua shuju, 1974), pp. 2853–5, and Du You, *Tong dian juan* [Universal compendium] 1 (Beijing: Zhonghua shuju, 1988), pp. 17–19, and discussed in many works, notably Hori Toshikazu, *Kindensei no kenkyū* [Researches on the *juntian* system] (Tokyo: Iwanami, 1975), Part II, and Nishimura Genyū, *Chūgoku keizaishi kenkyū* [Researches in the history of the Chinese economy] (Kyoto: Tōyōshi kenkyūkai, 1968), Part II, ch. 1.

13 See p. 270 of the *Tang lü shu yi* in the edition by Liu Junwen (Beijing: Zhonghua shuju, 1983, reprinted 1993), *juan* 14.

14 Under other dynasties the term was *liang min*, but the Tang avoided the syllable *min* out of respect for the taboo on the personal name of the dynasty's founder Li Shimin.

15 A very important study of this social revolution is Li Wenzhi, 'Lun Qingdai qianqi di tudi zhanyou guanxi' [On land tenure relationships in the early Qing period], *Lishi yanjiu*, 1963, no. 5, pp. 75–108. See also his *Ming Qing shidai fengjian tudi guanxi de songjie* [The loosening of feudal land relationships in the Ming-Qing period] (Beijing: Zhongguo shehui kexue chubanshe, 1993).

16 Such discriminations can be seen 1000 years apart in the Tang and Qing codes. See *juan* 22 of the *Tang lü shu yi* in the edition edited by Liu Junwen (Beijing: Zhonghua shuju, 1983, reprinted 1993); and *juan* 28 of *Da Qing lü li* [The Great Qing code], pp. 484f. of the edition punctuated by Zhang Rongzheng and others (Tianjin: Tianjin guji chubanshe, 1993–95).

17 A good introduction is the volume *Guaimai renkou zui* [The crime of abduction and sale of people] edited by Cui Nanshan and others that was published by the Zhongguo jiancha chubanshe [China procuratorial publishing house] in the *Xingshi fanzui anli congshu* [Model criminal case series] and compiled by the Supreme People's Procuratorate (Beijing, 1991).

18 On the meat-eaters see *Zuo zhuan*, tenth year of Duke Zhuang, and its story of one Cao Gui who though not a meat-eater himself had a low opinion of meat-eaters' vision and dared to advise his ruler, the Duke of Lu, on how to resist a Qi invasion in 684 BC. See Yang Bojun (ed.), *Chun qiu zuo zhuan zhu* [Annotated Spring and Autumn annals and Zuo zhuan] (Beijing: Zhonghua shuju, 1990), pp. 182–3. The *guoren* are mentioned quite often in texts on Spring and Autumn period history.

19 The classic anecdote is included by Sima Qian in *Shi ji* [Records of the historian], *juan* 68, 'Shang jun lie zhuan' (Beijing: Zhonghua shuju, 1959), p. 2231.

20 The best evidence on Qin state control is to be found in the Shuihudi tomb documents cited in note 9 above.

21 This is the first in a selection of the legal texts found in 1984 in Han tomb no. 247 at Zhangjiashan that were transcribed and published in *Wen wu*, 1993, no. 8, pp. 22–5, together with articles by Li Xueqin and by Peng Hao. They are documents of a kind known as *zouyanshu* or *zouxianshu*, specimen hard cases reported to higher authority – ultimately the imperial court – for a ruling that was later circulated within the legal bureaucracy as guidance in handling similar cases that might occur again later.

22 A whole section of the Tang code, *juan* 28, is devoted to the capture of absconders. See pp. 4/57–4/70 of the *Tang lü shu yi* in the Guoxue jiben congshu edition (Shanghai: Commercial Press, 1933 and later reprints) or pp. 525–44 of the better edition by Liu Junwen (Beijing: Zhonghua shuju, 1983, reprinted 1993). The article on drifters, no. 12 in the section, is on p. 4/65 of the Guoxue jiben congshu edition of the code, on p. 536 of the Liu Junwen edition, and on p. 958 of *Tang lü shu yi yi zhu*, ed. by Cao Manzhi (Changchun: 1989).

23 *Tang lü shu yi*, pp. 4/69–70 (Guoxue edition), or pp. 539–40 (Liu edition).

24 In the extensive literature on Qing local government two works are still of fundamental value: Ch'ü T'ung-tsu, *Local Government in China under the Ch'ing* (Cambridge, Mass.: Harvard University Press, 1962, and later printings as a Stanford paperback); and Hsiao Kung-chuan, *Rural China: Imperial Control in the Nineteenth Century* (Seattle and London: Washington University Press, 1960).

25 The classic study in a Western language of the wealth of Buddhist institutions in early medieval China remains Jacques Gernet, *Les Aspects*

Économiques du Bouddhisme dans la Société Chinoise du Ve au Xe siècle (Saigon: École française d'Extrême-Orient, 1956).

26 The best description of life in a capital city of the first thousand years after the Qin conquest is Yang Xuanzhi's account of sixth-century Luoyang, *Luoyang qielan ji*. It is translated in Part II of W. J. F. Jenner, *Memories of Loyang: Yang Hsüan-chih and the Lost Capital (493–534)* (Oxford: Clarendon Press, 1981).

27 On urban life in the Song capitals see Jacques Gernet, *La Vie Quotidienne en Chine à la Veille de l'Invasion Mongole 1250–1276* (Paris: Hachette, 1959).

28 *Hankow: Commerce and Society in a Chinese City, 1796–1889* (Stanford: Stanford University Press, 1984) and *Hankow: Conflict and Community in a Chinese City, 1796–1895* (Stanford: Stanford University Press, 1989):

29 On urban protest see, for example, the chapters by Fuma Susumu, 'Late Ming Urban Reform and the Popular Uprising in Hangzhou', and by Paolo Santangelo, 'Urban Society in Late Imperial Suzhou' on pp. 47–79 and 81–116 of Linda Cooke Johnson (ed.), *Cities of Jiangnan in Late Imperial China* (Albany, NY: State University of New York Press, 1993) and by Tsing Yuan, 'Urban riots and disturbances' in Jonathan D. Spence and John E. Wills Jr (eds), *From Ming to Ch'ing: Conquest, Region and Continuity in Seventeenth-Century China* (New Haven and London: Yale University Press, 1979), pp. 280–320. There is also an extensive literature in Chinese and Japanese to which these chapters refer.

30 The literature on Peking under Manchu rule is vast. A good recent introduction to Manchu Peking can be found in vol. 7 (by Wu Jianyong) and vol. 8 (by Wei Kaizhao and Zhao Huirong) of the ten-volume *Beijing tongshi* [General history of Beijing] under the general editorship of Cao Zixi (Beijing: Zhongguo shudian, 1994).

31 The story was first printed as 'Cui daizhao sheng si yuanjia' [Master craftsman Cui's foe in life and death], the eighth tale in the collection edited by Feng Menglong as *Jing shi tong yan* [Universal words to wake up the world] in 1624. It can be found on pp. 90–105 of Yan Dunyi's edition (Beijing: Renmin wenxue chubanshe, 1956, reprinted 1962) and in English translation as 'The jade worker' in *The Courtesan's Jewel Box*, translated by Yang Hsienyi and Gladys Yang (Beijing: Foreign Languages Press, 1957). Specialists in the dating of vernacular fiction generally regard this story as being of Song or Yuan date, which would make it at least 300 years earlier. A useful study is that of Patrick Hanan, *The Chinese Short Story: Studies in Dating, Authorship and Composition* (Cambridge, Mass.: Harvard University Press, 1973).

32 On Huang Zongxi and his *Ming yi dai fang lu* see the recent study and annotated translation by William Theodore de Bary, *Waiting for the Dawn: a Plan for the Prince. Huang Tsung-hsi's Ming-i-tai-fang lu* (New York: Columbia University Press, 1993).

33 *Bei shi* [History of the Northern Dynasties], *juan* 48, p. 1771 (Beijing: Zhonghua shuju, 1974). This reference is lifted from the entry for *ziyou* on p. 1308 of vol. 8 of the excellent *Hanyu da cidian* [Great Chinese dictionary] (Shanghai: Hanyu da cidian chubanshe, 1991, reprinted 1994), which brings together well-chosen citations from texts dating from or referring to the Northern and Southern Dynasties period (fourth–sixth centuries AD).

34 Mao Zedong, 'Fan ziyouzhuyi' [Against liberalism], translated as 'Combat Liberalism', *Selected Works of Mao Tse-tung*, vol. 2 (Peking: Foreign Languages Press, 1965), pp. 31–3.

35 The Chinese text has been reprinted in many collections of Taiping documents. See, for example, pp. 27–47 of Jin Yufu, Tian Yuqing and others (eds), *Taiping tianguo shiliao* [Historical materials on the Taiping Heavenly Kingdom] (Beijing: Zhonghua shuju, 1955). An English translation by Chang Chung-li can be found on pp. 748–76 of Franz Michael in collaboration with Chang Chung-li (ed.), *The Taiping Rebellion: History and Documents*, vol. 3 (Seattle and London: University of Washington Press, 1971).

36 This condemnation is set out with inescapable clarity in all three versions of the chapter 'Shang tong' ['Exalting uniformity', a translation to be preferred to the more commonly offered ones such as 'Honouring superiors'] of the *Mo zi*. See *Mo zi xian gu*, ed. by Sun Yirang, Chs 11, 12 and 13, on pp. 44–61 of vol. 4 of the *Zhu zi ji cheng* collection reissued by the Zhonghua shuju in Peking in 1959.

CHAPTER 5

The Chinese Search for Freedom as a Universal Value

David Kelly

The simplest and most adequate way of describing the history of China would be to distinguish between two types of periods: (1) the periods when people wished in vain to enjoy a simple slave condition; and (2) the periods when people managed to enjoy a simple slave condition. The alternation of these two states is what our old scholars called 'the cycle of chaos and order.'

Lu Xun[1]

China provides an apparent case in point of Orlando Patterson's thesis of a 'stillbirth of freedom in the non-Western world' (see Chapter 1 of this volume). For despite the existence of developed institutions of slavery and serfdom, and of a politically centralised community with governmental institutions, freedom failed to emerge as a socially significant shared vision of life. That is to say, no positive evaluation of the free state in the socially constructed form so crucial for Patterson – featuring a 'triadic fusion' of personal, civil and sovereignal freedoms – was to emerge in China until the modern era. Moreover, the impact of the modern era was traumatic for China as for few other countries. Thus the construction of freedom, while unquestionably a major item on the political agenda in recent history, has been attended by tensions and schisms of major intensity. Mainland China has, more than anywhere in the Asian region, been imprinted by Marxism and its ideal of a social order emancipated from class oppression. Chinese Marxism speaks of freedom and bondage, to be sure, but especially after coming to political power has dismissed the liberal democratic language of rights, liberties and immunities as fraudulent. Even after the falling away of faith in Marx, Stalin or Mao, the Chinese imagery of collectivism lingers and reinforces new anti-liberal notions that appeal to the imperatives of development and to the 'illiberal' cultural specifics of the East Asian region. However, even when we take into account the daunting weight of the factors militating against a political culture of freedom in China, China's resilience, spiritual strength and capacity to grow are in the end impressive.

Bill Jenner, analysing in Chapter 4 why there has been so little room in China for freedom to grow, uses a severely defined (and thus telling) view of freedom. The following account attempts to amplify the other side of the story. Using a looser and more multidimensional notion of freedom, I argue that it is possible to identify, first, a range of values and visions of life which can stand as precursors to freedom; and second, a range of ways in which the modern system of concepts was unpacked and reworked in the Chinese context. In particular, notions of civilisation, modernity and development have proven both irresistible and almost impossible to decouple from the liberal ideology of political freedom they are said to entail. These perspectives give us some understanding of why modern freedom, while far from securely rooted in China's historical experience, cannot be rejected as an intrinsically alien ideology.

Precursors to Freedom

Today, were one writing an intellectual history of contemporary China, freedom would have to receive more than a scattering of index references. The Constitution of 1982 mentions freedom twelve times, proudly stating in the *Preamble* that

> China is one of the countries with the longest histories in the world. The people of all nationalities in China have jointly created a splendid culture and have a glorious revolutionary tradition. Feudal China was gradually reduced after 1840 to a semi-colonial and semi-feudal country. The Chinese people waged wave upon wave of heroic struggles for national independence and liberation (*jiefang*) and for democracy and freedom (*ziyou*).[2]

The *Preamble* is not wrong as far as it goes. Its use of *ziyou* (freedom) is implicitly universal: what the Chinese had struggled for was something any people might struggle for. Few would dispute that the freedoms actually enjoyed by citizens of the People's Republic are severely limited in comparison to any Western country – even those like Australia, whose constitutions barely mention freedom. This is no paradox, granted that the *Preamble* is talking only about Patterson's 'organic sovereignal freedom', the freedom of the entire community from external oppression (and granted again that, in a former British colony like Australia, freedoms of various kinds are assumed to be guaranteed by common law and similar institutions).

What of China's personal and civic freedoms? Patterson would incline one to the view that these were 'stillborn' because of the failure of a developed slave system, including a broad class of freedmen, to coincide with a developed political community based on citizen participation such as happened 'a long time ago in the West'.

A simple slave condition

Large-scale slavery was important for much of Chinese dynastic history. It was a developed institution in China through Han times, and was replaced piecemeal by a comparably long-lasting and evolved manorial system where large populations of hereditary bonded serfs were a major component. The great Buddhist monastic estates in the Tang were largely slave-operated. A number of critical sequences failed to connect to produce the triadic fusion of elementary freedoms. Yet what was in existence was far from insignificant, and has played a major role in conditioning the reception of post-Enlightenment ideologies like socialism and liberalism.

Patterson argues that a value will be placed on *personal* freedom under virtually all circumstances where man is placed in the servitude of man, and this holds for China. A class of freedmen (*liang min, liang ren*) formed as a byproduct of serfdom. With them was produced a large literature of manumission. Elvin argues that this literature extols the desirability of something close enough to that known in the West as freedom.[3] This view is supported on the mainland, where scholars have spent decades unearthing what purports to be a history of resistance to servitude and oppression constituting a Chinese tradition of human rights, freedom and even democracy.[4]

Jenner sets out in some detail the opposite point of view, and points up the need for further historical study. The full meaning of slavery in China (and even more so, Korea) is yet to be recovered. It is unlikely, however, that further study will show that the *liang min* ever evolved, above and beyond the value of personal freedom, the distinct, crucial dimension of *political* or civic freedom. Where, one might ask, were the serf revolts bearing aloft banners inscribed with calls for freedom *per se*?

Hereditary serfdom came to an end in the Ming–Qing transition of the seventeenth century. The transition had both economic and political factors. The Qing (Manchu) state (1644–1911) recognised that disaffected serfs were a potent source of the insurrections which had assisted their own seizure of power from the Ming. The Yongzheng emperor (1723–35) abolished hereditary serfdom in the early eighteenth century. Economic changes had in any case led to a flow of

capital out of the secure but inefficient and unprofitable forms of
bondsman-operated agriculture, into new avenues such as commerce,
pawnbroking and urban real estate. The remaining populations of
slaves had been increasingly able to buy their freedom.[5]

Once again, however, none of these developments signal the rise of
freedom as a shared vision of life. Rather, we have some confirmation
of the thesis that the failure of slavery to come to a head in the same
institutional forms as the West militated against the crystallisation of
freedom as a political value. Thus the Qing abolition of manorial serfdom failed to produce an interest group dedicated to the extension of
freedom more widely in society. This is demonstrated by the preva-
lence of vestigial forms of slavery in certain territories, for example
Hong Kong, virtually up to the present. Watson showed that slavery of
a broadly symbolic kind, largely confined to females except for a few
exceptionally wealthy families able to afford male slaves, survived in
Southern China into recent living memory.[6] Traffic in humans, particularly in females, has never been completely suppressed in China and
has re-emerged on an alarming scale in the reform period.

Lao-Zhuang thought

The existence of certain democratic and libertarian threads in Confucianism, that vast tapestry of doctrine and practice, has been argued
in a number of recent scholarly works.[7] It is an item of faith among
modern Confucian revivalists from Liang Shuming to Tang Chün-i
and Tu Wei-ming. In the non-partisan view of Shih Chih-yu, in contrast
to Japanese feudalism,

> Confucianism actually encourages eremitism if state authority deviates from
> the spirit of the *dao*, the essence of which can be sensed only by the individ-
> ual. In other words, the freedom from overall obligation to people holding
> office may have given the Chinese a higher degree of liberty in making
> judgements independent of their social status.[8]

Many of the libertarian threads identified in Confucianism, however,
have been rejected by orthodoxy and should in fact be credited to its
ancient rival, Taoism. The book known as the *Zhuang zi* (sometimes
Chuang Tzu), or book of Master Zhuang, is the classical source of a doctrine of inner spiritual freedom which has influenced much of Chinese
thought. Leading scholars consistently identify this freedom as the
core theme. In Chen Guying's account,

> the main thrust of Zhuang Zi's philosophy is the pursuit of spiritual free-
> dom. It was Zhuang Zi's conviction that while human beings are naturally

inclined toward freedom, they constantly get entangled in every kind of artifice and self-contrived restraint . . . How is man to live in a world dominated by chaos, suffering and absurdity? Zhuang Zi's answer to the question is: free yourself from the world.[9]

This branched out in imperial times into various countercultures including an anarchist critique of rulers and the ruling Confucian ideology. Bao Jingyan (early fourth century AD) is, for example, often cited as a proponent of freedom in this sense. Somewhat reminiscent of anarchism, his views are known from quotations recorded in Ge Hong's (AD 283–363) *Bao pu zi*.[10] Bao argued that 'antiquity, having no rulers, was superior to the present age'. In the first place, the establishment of the ruler was not in response to a Heavenly Mandate. Rather, the strong had coerced the weak, and the intelligent had deceived the simple-minded. The resulting servitude of the people 'had nothing to do with a vast and distant heaven'. Second, Bao argued that freedom was the natural condition of man. 'At the dawn of time, the nameless was valued, and the various living beings found their pleasures in being let alone to go their own ways.' This appears to strengthen the element of personal freedom expressed by Zhuang Zi, who, while holding in highest value the ideal of *xiaoyao* ('wandering in unfettered bliss'), still observed the duty of servitor to ruler.[11] Intriguingly, when Bao was restored to grace for the first time this century, it was by the intellectuals of the *guocui* ('national essence') school, who as Yü Ying-shih points out were, for all their ultra-conservative reputation, quite radical in their own way.[12]

Buddhist liberation

As other contributions to this volume note, Buddhism offers a range of values and practices which bear important relation to the eventually dominant Western schemata of freedom. China was of course one of the major conduits of Buddhism to the East Asian region and developed powerful intellectual variations of its own on the classical doctrines. Kung-chuan Hsiao wrote that after the shock encounter with legalism in the third century BC,

> there were never more than two alternatives for the educated Chinese: he could either affirm this world which appeared to be based on eternal Confucian laws, or he had to retreat into a different, spiritual and frequently religious world, but which was cut off from the world of reality . . . All anti-Confucian ideals which envisaged the replacement of the hierarchical social order based on the model of the family by absolute freedom and equality arose in a religious environment.[13]

Buddhism improved greatly on Taoism in that it projected this sense of personal freedom as liberation from slavery to desire onto an expanded inner stage, extending it into infinite kalpas of transmigration. On the other hand it imposed, as the price of entrance to this transpersonal subjectivity, cessation of the individual – and, it would seem to follow, the political self. Buddhism has been criticised throughout Chinese history for unworldliness, for its tendency to political indifference. The growth of monastic estates in the Sui and Tang dynasties led to a reduction of the class of free peasants; the work of these estates was mainly done by slaves.[14] On the other hand, chiliastic insurrections and revolutionary movements have explicitly drawn on these doctrines. Buddhism and Taoism have fed into antinomian currents which have challenged the Confucian-dominated social order up to modern times.

Heroic rebellion as sovereignal freedom

Over many centuries the outlaw heroes known as *hao han* have been another source of anti-systemic values in Chinese popular culture.[15] The great range of literary forms in which they figure is perhaps best represented by the novel *The Water Margin* (also translated as *All Men are Brothers*). The *hao han* glories in antinomianism, in reversing the moral code of a mainstream Confucian society which is regarded as debased and hypocritical. This is a folk ideology of sovereignal freedom; freedom is often freedom to violence over others, who if they are found to fail the *hao han*'s code of honour may be killed or brutalised without compunction. The *hao han* will do anything for a mate, including slaughtering his wife and children to ensure his devotion to the higher cause of rebellion. There are female *hao han* who are admirably daring and high-minded, but usually as bloody-minded as the men. All are unmistakably adherents of an ethic of personal and sovereignal freedom. Civic freedom is virtually absent. The outlaw gang is organised despotically, with mass execution a normal mode of asserting authority. This ancient popular culture has strong echoes in the *gemen'r* ('mateship') culture of contemporary urban youth, but above all perhaps in the secret societies which are re-emerging strongly and with no great propensity to support civic virtues. The *hao han* drive to antinomianism, to reverse the moral code of a mainstream society which is regarded as debased and hypocritical, has a poor record of combining with other elements of a modern ethic of freedom.

Freedom and Civilised Modernity

This is undoubtedly why many sinologists would maintain with Wolfgang Franke that

> the concept of freedom never played a great role in Chinese civilization. The modern word (*ziyou*) is relatively young, and the term *ziran* (which one could translate as 'self-determination') has a distinctively individualist if not anti-social and even anarchic ring.[16]

The rapid acceptance of liberal notions of personal and civic freedom in the late Qing period is thus all the more remarkable; it raises as a serious hypothesis the question of whether these ideas had local functional equivalents needing only to be given explicit formulation to come to life. Tendencies to urban self-government undoubtedly provided a catalyst. For all the reservations about its liberalism entered by Vera Mackie in Chapter 6, the demonstration effect of Japan's transformation into a modern power at the same time was clearly important, just as it provided the very word for freedom.[17]

Republican liberalism

By the end of the nineteenth century, classical Western notions of freedom were being widely disseminated in China. Reformists like Yan Fu (1854–1921), Tan Sitong (1865–98), and Liang Qichao (1873–1929) registered the impact of nineteenth-century liberalism, then at its height.[18] Yan Fu, a famous translator and exegete, consciously used elements of Lao-Zhuang thought to interpret Western doctrines of Rousseau and Mill. He proposed the formula *yi ziyou wei ti, yi minzhu wei yong* (freedom is the essential principle, of which democracy is the application).[19] Liang Qichao, who began as a fiery reformist and iconoclast, in 1902 wrote a pioneering article on freedom, which he clearly saw as the defining value of the powerful West of his day. He defined freedom as liberty to do as one pleases provided one does not encroach on the liberty of others. Liang viewed freedom as opposed to slavery and in particular slavery of the mind.[20] Reflecting perhaps the Chinese expression *quanli*, where *quan* indicates 'power over' as well as 'rights',[21] Liang saw rights as the outcome of superior strength. China lacked a culture of rights, and while people felt they had a right to good government, when misruled felt it a virtue to accept this as inevitable and something to be endured. However, the freedom of the organic community, while resting on that of its component individuals, superseded it. 'As soon as he moved from theory to practise, his value orientation moved from freedom to autocracy (*jiquan*).'[22]

At the most general level, it is apparent that the discourse of freedom was part of a discourse of civilisation. Very few disputed that freedom was the key to the cultural mastery of the West. But the West's possession of this mastery could be and was often seen as quite fortuitous or conditional. The West had an unquestionable superiority in social organisation and control of material resources, but failed to exemplify the highest of civilised ideals, especially when it came to competing for colonial empires. Many Western thinkers seemed to doubt that their own civilisation was able to sustain the demands placed on it: Nietzsche, Spengler and others taught that it must succumb to decadence. It was not unnatural to think that China could realise its own form of modernity by adapting freedom and the other key modern values to its own style of civilisation.

The encapsulating discourse of civilisation has continued down to the present, and has deeply conditioned the ways in which freedom has been constructed as a value. Wang Gungwu has suggested that three main viewpoints have dominated since the late nineteenth century: those who

> urged the Chinese people to defend civilization from barbarism by turning inwards . . . those who [urged defending] Chinese civilization by changing it and by trying to strengthen it and enrich it with new ideas . . . and those who [after debates in the 1920s] went so far as to suggest that, for China to remain civilized, *it was necessary for China to change in stages to a new civilization.*[23] (emphasis added)

Thus the anarchists who dominated radical social thought of the pre-Marxist period saw themselves as embracing the highest available ideals of freedom, higher than those currently realised in the West or China. The goal of the anarchist revolution was to liberate the individual, not from society but from coercive institutions which distorted the essential sociability of human beings. In their insistence that the revolution could not achieve its goals through means contrary to its aspirations, they differed from the Marxist socialists who were to replace them (and who had often passed through a period of anarchist tutelage).[24]

Similarly, Zhang Taiyan (1868–1936), a leader of the struggle to depose the Manchu Qing dynasty, opposed subordination of the individual to society and demanded absolute freedom and personal emancipation. In his case, adherence to Buddhism as the source of the moral ideal of equality for all was combined with virulent anti-capitalism and opposition to parliamentary democracy. As with Yan Fu and Liang Qichao, disillusionment with the West in his later career was coupled with a return to authoritarian political models. In most of these cases Daoism and Buddhism, the ancient antinomian doctrines opposed to the social ethic of Confucianism, were an important resource in framing libertarian values.

Probably most significant of the early proponents of freedom was Sun Yat-sen (1866–1925), founder of the Nationalist regime which still continues on Taiwan. Sun's tridemism or 'Three Principles of the People' reflected a belief that traditional China had actually allowed too much in the way of personal licence, resulting in the weak state of the late Qing dynasty which he sought to overthrow. The Nationalist regime was never liberal in his time, and certainly not under his successor, Chiang Kai-shek. Nonetheless Sun's provisions for free enterprise in the economy and the division of power in political authority provided a basis for later liberal reforms.[25]

May Fourth radical idealism

The careers of the early republican liberals proved the resulting eclectic forms of liberalism too weak to meet the needs of their times. With the New Culture Movement (c.1915–25), intellectuals began to dissociate individual freedom from the wealth and power of the state and confer independent value on it, but the intimate relations between the two were never totally eliminable.[26] In 1919 Li Dazhao wrote, 'Contemporary life is a life in prison. Our world, our nation, our society, our family, are different levels of prison which confine us, locks that deprive us of freedom . . .' He was joined in this sentiment, which was formulated to a more acute and generalised degree than that of the preceding generation, by a broad church including the liberal Hu Shi, the Nietzschean Lu Xun, and soon-to-be-Marxist Mao Zedong. Early in their careers, later communist leaders like Chen Duxiu, Li Dazhao, Qu Qiubai and Mao Zedong himself shared much of the anarchist outlook. Socialism too was regarded as a progressive form of democracy. Class division was incongruent, in the first place, with liberty and equality.[27] Ip Hung-yok recently revised the common view that early twentieth-century Chinese intellectuals were 'nation-oriented utilitarians', instrumentalist in their adherence to democracy and freedom. Chen Duxiu and Li Dazhao, in particular, went far beyond this at times, embracing democracy from the perspective of an autonomous value. This, he argues, conditioned their eventual commitments to socialism. Nonetheless, Ip concedes that nation-oriented utilitarianism lay at the base of their commitments and tended to win out.[28]

As in the preceding period, the discourse on freedom was subordinated to one on civilisation (often phrased as a discourse on modernity). While it was now clear that Chinese civilisation had first to be thoroughly purged of backward elements, even those making use of the slogan of 'complete Westernisation' did so instrumentally. They knew they were not absolved from momentous fatal choices, and indeed wavered on which of the variant forms should take priority in China given the interests of national salvation. The contemporary intellectual historian Li Ming sums up this mode of thought:

> Mankind's recent history shows that establishing an autonomous, national, democratic state is one of the fundamental prerequisites for the modernization of human societies . . . Thus, Chiang Kai-shek never dared declare himself emperor, rather he upheld Sun Yat-sen's 'Three principles of the people' . . . Most essential to the modernization of society is the modernization of the self-organizing capacity of the social system.[29]

Hegelian and Marxist thought

The radical idealists of the New Culture and May Fourth movements occupied a wide spectrum of ideological positions. This spectrum was dramatically narrowed in the 1920s and 1930s. Following the Nationalists' defeat and the founding of the People's Republic, Marxism-Leninism, as interpreted by Stalin and Mao, took over, claiming to be the sole viable bearer of May Fourth ideals.

Hegelian and Marxist-Leninist teachings strongly support the organic sovereignal formulation of freedom; in another terminology they constitute the prime example of ideological reliance on positive rather than negative freedom. They provide a key underpinning of official doctrines which define rights in terms of 'subsistence' in contrast to 'bourgeois liberal' human rights. In the Cultural Revolution, encouraged by an ageing Mao, the increasingly bureaucratic state was radicalised in the complete absence of and contempt for civic, political institutional norms. While the Cultural Revolution clearly presented itself to many individuals as a heady taste of personal freedom,[30] it was rarely formulated as such. Of course there were exceptions. In 1965 an underground journal produced by the poet Zhang Langlang 'showed iron bars, with the Chinese word meaning freedom (*ziyou*) shining through in red'.[31] Such *cris de coeur* emerged from the educated élite, in this case from 'salons' held at the homes of high-level cadres' children.

The reformist Marxist synthesis of epistemic and social freedom

Generally though, the earliest forms of struggle against the Party's ideological stranglehold accepted the previously established Marxist-Leninist framework, attempting to rectify or purify it of putative revisionist distortions.[32] The acceptance of Marxism in its Stalinist-Maoist form resulted in a dogmatic, formal doctrine of freedom which has been stable over many decades. An update of this catechism for the reform period is presented as the culmination of a volume on contemporary Chinese social philosophy, which appeared in the pivotal year of 1990.[33] The authors rehearse the Hegelian dialectic of freedom and necessity ('freedom is the knowledge of necessity'). Freedom in social terms is defined as the opposite of enslavement to alien social forces (*Ziyou' shi yu shou yijide shehui liliang de nuyi xiang duiyingde*). Under capitalism, as under archaic social orders, freedom in the ultimate sense is impossible.[34] Only with the abolition of class relations can the contradiction between socially necessary labour time and free time (when human potential is fully expressed) be overcome. However, the authors admit, the new technological revolution (the postwar waves of secondary and tertiary modernisation) has allowed humanity to approach much closer the kingdom of genuine freedom – though still only asymptotically, with an appreciable gap still to overcome.[35] China has used an alternative strategy, seeking first to overcome the antinomy of individual and social freedom. After all, in Marx's ideal society 'the free development of each is the condition of the free development of all'.[36]

Interestingly, the authors consider at some length the deficiencies in China's realisation of individual freedom.[37] In a following systematic subsection, 'Conditions for the realization of human freedom in contemporary Chinese society', stress is laid on the limitations imposed by China's economic backwardness. China must satisfy its people's needs by advancing commodity production, but the aim should be higher – Marx's goal of genuine freedom.[38] Similarly, there are political preconditions to be met. The lesson of the Cultural Revolution was that a 'democratic, harmonious' atmosphere is necessary if science and culture are to thrive. China is in need of ongoing reform of the political system. Previous reforms of the education and employment systems need to be followed through into reform of the civil service, among other domains, to complete the destruction of the 'traditional personnel system' – the universal occupational ascription which has thwarted the talents of so many since 1949. The authors are notably reticent about the need for legal and electoral system reforms. Instead they turn to a consideration of spiritual conditions of freedom. This means in the first place implanting a 'scientific' conception of freedom itself.[39]

Humanist-Marxist liberalism.

Factual and critically aware as the authors attempt to be, in the above account Chinese political reality is treated with circumlocution. The political reform and democratisation called for go little if at all beyond the official pronouncements of Deng Xiaoping. The intellectual counter-élite had long been disabused concerning these formulae. Building a series of halfway houses in the post–Cultural Revolution collapse of Marxist belief, they stress legal and democratic reforms as prerequisites of meaningful freedom. Both the dissident human rights movement and the slightly more official humanist Marxism of the post-Mao era did, however, retain much of the discourse of Hegelian Marxism.[40] Su Shaozhi, Wang Ruoshui, Gao Ertai, Li Zehou and many others created a groundswell of argument for constitutional liberalism in Marxist dress. Establishment intellectuals all, they unambiguously committed themselves to developing a democratic politics, often at the cost of careers, of imprisonment and exile.

Li Zehou was one of the key figures in this development. A pre-1949 convert to Marxism, he concentrated in the 1950s on aesthetics, one of the few areas where party ideology left some room for contention. Li and Gao Ertai, another aesthetician, developed philosophies which, while admitting the central role of the social matrix in human development, still allowed a modest role for the individual subject. The young Marx generally supports a classical idealist account of 'Beauty as the symbol of Freedom', the title of a characteristic work by Gao.[41] Freedom in this Hegelian idiom is a datum of the essential humanity or 'species nature'. When the writings of the young Marx and associated Western Marxist texts of Lukàcs became available, Li, Gao and others used the issue of 'subjectivity' to create a counter-discourse within Marxism. These thinkers argue from this datum to the need for reformed political institutions in a socialist regime. Li's account of 'subjectivity' (*zhutixing*), while repeatedly under official attack, was able to function in the 1980s as a surrogate for the still unsavoury terms freedom and democracy. Li was to write:

A great quantity of Western liberal writings [i.e. Popper, Hayek] show that freedom and democracy do not mean unlimited arbitrary license, nor some wonderful ideals. They essentially involve clear demarcations and legal norms regarding one's own, as opposed to others', sphere of rights [*quanxian*]. What is distinctive of democracy and freedom is that they prevent the worst from happening, such as military dictatorship, fascism, anarchy, 'expanding the elimination of counter revolutionaries,' etc.

. . . In the case of freedom, there had been imprecisely defined, general unlimited freedoms in Chinese tradition, but there had been a lack of legal, restricted freedoms, so that these were always 'freedoms' of non-interference in the style of [Sun Yat-sen's simile of] 'a plate of loose sand,' or [Marx's metaphor of] 'a sack of potatoes,' while at the same time the strong oppressed the weak, the many took advantage of the few, and the high oppressed the low. This was not genuine freedom, and could only lead to the despotism of a minority. Only by setting up a rigorous rule of law, clearly separating the various powers so that they check and supervise each other, and thoroughly ending things like 'the monk puts up his umbrella, there is neither law nor Heaven,' [as Mao described his own autocratic behaviour] party committees being superior to the Constitution, or Party secretaries standing in place of the nation's laws, can modern, concrete socialist democracy and freedom be realized.[42]

One commentator writes that for intellectuals like Wang Ruoshui, Su Shaozhi and Yan Jiaqi, 'all roads lead to democracy'.[43] These three and others like them were once well placed in the establishment, were sincerely committed to Marxism, and made every effort to reformulate it to support key liberal concepts of individual rights, legality, pluralism, and proceduralism. The heretical 'humanism' they espoused in the early Deng period can be understood as a refusal to define Marxism as non-liberal.

This came to a head in a 1986 debate over freedom instigated by Wang Ruoshui in an article entitled 'Freedom of literature and the literature of freedom'.[44] Hu Qiaomu, Wang's conservative opponent and a high-ranking party 'authority', had invoked Hegelian and Marxist definitions of 'freedom as the knowledge of necessity' to propound the line that since the party knows what is necessary, it is the sole dispenser of freedom. Wang demanded that these philosophical usages be kept distinct from the socio-political sense of freedom. Otherwise the Marxian notion of freedom as working within objective laws would simply be a cover for political repression. An infuriated Hu Qiaomu arranged for the appearance of a conservative article entitled 'Reflections on the Question of "Freedom"' to attack Wang and other 'bourgeois liberal' humanists. It hinted that the wave of free thinking of that time was causing turbulence in the leadership. Indeed, it was to lead to the student demonstrations of late 1986 and the subsequent fall of party secretary Hu Yaobang. Crystallising the humanist viewpoint, Yu Haocheng, a legal specialist, roundly refuted the ideological burden of the article:

If socialist society cannot offer the individual more and greater freedom, how can it display its superiority? Even in capitalist society there is similar law and discipline in the interests of maintaining social order and stability. For a long time we held a simplistic viewpoint, calling those who created anarchy, or thoughts or actions calling for absolute freedom without restrictions, 'bourgeois liberalizers.' Actually this is quite wrong. When this happens, democracy and freedom very easily become derogatory terms associated with the bourgeoisie, as if our proletarians and communists did not want democracy or freedom, only dictatorship or discipline. This can only distort our image among our own people and in the world. According to Wu, on the one hand we set a high level of democracy as one of the objectives of our struggle, while on the other we proclaim that socialist society cannot offer the individual more and greater freedom. Is there not a contradiction here?[45]

When orthodox ideologists insisted on driving a new wedge between liberalism and Marxism, Su Shaozhi and Wang Ruoshui accepted expulsion from the Party rather than fall in line. Yan Jiaqi made a break with Marxism after going into exile in the wake of the 1989 Beijing massacre. The differences between these three mainly reflect different rates of intellectual evolution. While Su and Wang still adhered to socialism, they insisted that it must be preceded by a period of capitalist development, and all three envisioned that the form of China's future democracy would have at least a family resemblance to 'Western-style' liberal democracy, in that it must include civic freedoms allowing participation in politics.[46]

1989 and After

Writing in the very 'open' period before the 1989 upheaval, Li Zehou portrayed the May Fourth movement of seventy years before as a musical 'double variation' in which the primary theme of enlightenment came to be overwhelmed by that of national salvation.[47] 'Enlightenment' consciously invoked the eighteenth-century Western movement of that name as an intellectual ancestor. 'National salvation' encapsulates the fundamental claims of the Chinese Communist Party (CCP) to legitimacy. No wonder that Li Zehou and the loose association of intellectuals referred to as the New Enlightenment school attracted unfriendly official attention.

In terms of the intellectual history outlined above, the 1989 movement represents an uneasy blending of May Fourth idealism and humanist/Hegelian Marxism with hastily assimilated contemporary political ideologies from the developing world and the Eastern bloc, but above all the West. 'The initial demands of the democracy movement mark an attempt to establish within the existing political framework a mechanism by which to begin the important cultural process of wrenching from the state its monopoly on truth and the moral way and opening up a space for the individual subject.'[48]

In 1989 the generally orthodox philosophy journal *Philosophy Research* carried an article by Huang Kejian, who argued that free individuality constitutes the essence of modernity.[49] Drawing on Weber, Huang concluded that the transition to modern 'independent man' was a transformation of the value system resulting from the appearance of new values. The major difference between the old and the new was that the former was based on the group, the latter on the individual.

This presents China with an agonising dilemma. As long as China has no such value system, Huang maintains, modernisation will remain a delusion. Yet the West itself came to find, just as China was first encountering it, that the liberated individual was becoming prisoner of his own economic magic. China could only 'delude itself' in the utopian hope that the benefits of a modern economy could be achieved while preserving man's individual integrity. This delusion, as Huang sees it, has held sway over Chinese minds, including communist ones, for seventy years. The priority for China is first to establish what value orientations, in the context of world history, represent the best of our times. Huang insists that these are what Marx called 'independence' and 'free individuality'. In the yet-to-be-modernised China, priority should be given to promoting the ideal of individual freedom, since without this value modern civilisation and cultural transformation cannot succeed. Without this value, 'hard work' or 'patriotism' remain functions of the old authoritarian patterns. 'A hardworking slave remains a slave.'[50]

Neo-conservative developmentalism

One of the most influential alternatives to official ideology appearing in the Deng period was known as 'new authoritarianism'. Suppressed in the wake of 4 June 1989 because of links to former CCP General Secretary Zhao Ziyang, it resurfaced as 'new conservatism'. Outwardly in agreement with the Party's anti-liberalism, some of its representatives propose a quasi-liberalism, promising freedom and democracy after economic modernisation has had a chance to work.[51] More straightforwardly liberal intellectuals argue that this is simply the system which the current round of reforms is seeking to legitimate. It involves relatively large amounts of freedom in the economic sphere, and much of the freedom to indulge in a consumer culture which tends to satisfy the populations of modernised countries. However cynically intended, the theory departs decisively from Marxism-Leninism in that democratic freedoms are accorded a universal value. They will, however, be the gift of a benign authority when it sees fit. The developmentalist focus of new conservatism places it firmly in the category of discourse on civilisation and modernity which we have noted as dominant in this century.

Theorists of civil society

The theory of civil society represents yet another Western-derived ideology seeking to naturalise itself in Chinese soil. Its proponents seek to expand from a basis of modest zones of freedom for limited sectors in the present. The statist bias of Chinese intellectuals tended to limit their interest in society as a field of self-organisation. Following the spontaneous emergence of semi-autonomous social groupings during and after the Cultural Revolution, a body of theorising began to emerge. Another body of literature emerged in Taiwan accompanying the accelerated democratisation taking place there; this was filtered back to the mainland through intellectual circles. It is interesting to note that one expatriate mainland social theorist warns of a dangerous tendency of these formulations of civil society to be conflated with the rebellious knight errantry described above as the *hao han* folk ideology.[52]

The return to rapid reform in 1992 was marked by the appearance of a well-produced academic journal, *Chinese Social Science Quarterly*, whose editorials and major articles have been devoted to expounding and applying the civil society literature. In an article by the editor, civil society is proposed as alternative to the two extremes of radical democratisation and authoritarianism:

> Civil society has the capability to constrain the state, which is to say that civil society fights for and defends freedom to maintain its independence and autonomy, to exempt itself from abnormal intervention and infringement by the state. It is in just this sense that we say that civil society is the last bastion to protect freedom and prevent the reversion of authority to totalitarianism.[53]

Rather than waiting for a far-off transition to freedom, civil society is to be constructed in two stages, with increased personal freedom the lead indicator of the first of these. However,

> the main problems to be resolved in this stage are to secure the free space and prerequisite independence and autonomy of civil society *vis à vis* the state control. While these two problems remain unresolved, the dualistic structure of Chinese civil society and the state will have difficulty in forming. Attempts to regulate relations between the two by statute will be unable to be realized . . .
>
> It should be pointed out that the issue of gaining autonomy and freedom is unusually important for the construction of Chinese civil society, because there is a fundamental difference between the latter and the early period of the rise of civil society in the West, namely that in China the main motive force in its development originates in the state and not in the individual, shown for example by the dependence on state policies of the emergence and development for a period of independent enterprises, hence their quite evident dependency and subservience; while in the West the motive force came from the beginning from private capital and not the state, so that its independence and autonomy was stronger.

Dissidents and their detractors

In late 1996 two famous dissidents, Liu Xiaobo (1955–) and Wang Xizhe (a member of the three-man writing group 'Li Yizhe' who had been gaoled under the Gang of Four), wrote an open letter to the CCP leadership. Describing themselves as 'free persons of no party' (*wu dangpai ziyou renwu*) they castigated the leadership's failure to honour agreements signed with the Nationalists and other parties in the 1940s. These agreements had included clauses such as the following:

> In regard to the problem of the freedom of the people, we unanimously hold that government should guarantee the people enjoy all freedoms of the person, of belief, of speech, the press and of assembly enjoyed by all peoples of democratic countries in time of peace.[54]

As a result, in mid-October 1996 Liu was detained and summarily packed off for three years of 're-education through labour'. No discussion of intellectual involvement in the 1989 democracy movement and after would be complete without paying attention to Liu. He intervened dramatically in the events in Tiananmen Square on the evening of 3–4 June, having flown back from the comparative safety of New York to support and advise the students. He was imprisoned for over a year.[55] In many ways an atypical member of the Beijing intellectual world, Liu represents no sociological configuration directly; yet his writings sum up many of the attitudes of the rebellious youth who had seen the collapse of the Maoist order and were willing to call a spade a spade. Like Li Zehou, Liu's intellectual home ground is the field of aesthetics. In a series of works he threw down a polemical gauntlet to Li's blend of Hegelian-Marxist liberalism, denouncing it as 'despotic'. Official Marxism was subject to Liu Xiaobo's open criticism and rejection as well, so the attack on Li was not another case of dissent by proxy.

While Liu's philosophical output incorporates Nietzschean and Sartrean ideas of freedom as implicit in or 'essential' to human nature, he also attempts to incorporate the liberal tradition of Locke and Montesquieu. This is a consequence of his strong polemical interest in refuting accepted notions, typified by Li Zehou, of society as a moral order. In a move characteristic of his generation, Liu wants to replace the perfectibilist ideas common to both Confucianism and Marxism-Leninism with a notion of fallible human nature, and society as contract- or covenant-based.

According to Woei Lien Chong, Liu seemed unaware of the differences between the liberal and the Sartrean view on freedom.[56] Gu Xin, in a book examining Liu Xiaobo's main works to date, takes this criticism considerably further than Chong. For Gu, Liu Xiaobo remains, with Li Zehou himself, within a polemical tradition scarred by the ideological oversimplifications against which it tries to rebel.[57] Gu's main concern is that Liu Xiaobo counters both Marxism and the Hegelian-humanist halfway house with a caricatured existentialist freedom according to which one is still essentially free even if subject to slavery or repression by the regime. Invocations of Locke and Montesquieu are by the same token empty since there is no insight into the institutional disciplines which underlay their liberalism.

Li Zehou, Liu Xiaobo and Gu Xin are in no doubt that 'freedom' is a cultural litmus test for China, and the latter two exemplify successive attempts to apply it to self-critique of Chinese intellectuals. Even the proponents of new conservatism, or civil society, with their varying factional orientations and practical political focus, would seem to agree with Huang Kejian that modernisation will remain a delusion without an eventual change towards the recognition of more personal and civic freedoms.

Culturalist anti-liberalism

Regardless of political leaning, few doubt that 'freedom' is indeed a cultural watershed for China. Li Zehou's more radically 'liberal' critic Liu Xiaobo, and Gu Xin, a trenchant critic of both Li and Liu, fault him for not accepting personal and civic criteria of freedom. Still more radical, in a certain sense, are the writings of the theologically trained Liu Xiaofeng, who demands for China a standard of spiritual freedom which would sweep away most of the instrumental and historical rationalism which was swallowed whole – if not digested – in the May Fourth period, and by which, it is claimed, Li Zehou remains bound.[58]

China's history, it should be clear, does not by itself explain current intellectual opposition to freedom. What then are its roots? Some interesting case materials are provided by *Liangzhong Zhongguo Xin* ('Two kinds of Chinese patriotism'). This 1994 Hong Kong volume collects the polemics set off by an article by Yan Yuanshu, a professor of English in Taiwan.[59] Yan's article, 'Salute to one billion compatriot builders of China', appeared in a Beijing journal, *Zhongliu* ('Midstream'), controlled by leftist conservative Deng Liqun. In a way that not so many years ago would have spelt time in a Nationalist gaol, Yan defends the mainland communist regime for its committed nationalism. He reviles liberal intellectuals whose criticisms provide comfort to the enemy, above all to the Americans. Yan's deepest revulsion is for Su Xiaokang, principal writer of the TV series *He Shang* ('The River Dies Young'). Of interest to our present discussion is Yan's outburst:

> This is why on behalf of China at this point in history, I dare to proclaim, Down with democracy! Down with freedom! Down with Western democracy! Down with Western freedom! In abstract terms, freedom and democracy are not at all absolute goods; instead, placing ourselves firmly in the

flow of history, for China here and now, they are relative 'evils'! For freedom can only cause China to fragment, and democracy can only cause it to collapse. Some people may object, why should the Chinese be so pitiful that they cannot receive the 'blessings' of freedom and democracy! Of such people, who regard Western values as human values in general, I would ask in reply: What is so wonderful about freedom? And where is the virtue of democracy? Japan and Germany are again considered powers – is this because their democracy and freedom so exceeded those of England and America? Is England's present decline due to the decline of its freedom, of its democracy? Is America's supremacy due to the supremacy of its freedom, of its democracy? While the propagation of America's freedom and democracy became precisely the motive force of American imperialism! If tobacco tycoons did not have the freedom to exploit, how would Taiwan have become a dump for American tobacco? . . . but the real key is, what do these [values] offer China? Can they help China reach its historical goals? Students once asked me, 'Sir, which is more important for China, to have democracy or to be powerful?' I said, 'Silly, to be powerful, of course. Otherwise, even with freedom and democracy, wouldn't a China lacking any means of self defence be the same as late Qing-early Republican China, a minor colony, one in which "Chinese and dogs are not permitted [in the park]"?' Thus only if China places a belt around their myriad waists can its people be liberated, be liberated from modern Chinese history! From all its gaols and fetters.[60]

Yan Yuanshu's enthusiasm gained a mixed response. Predictably a series of more liberal writers lambasted his praise for China's military and technical exploits, generally with reference to the huge costs they had imposed. Yan had no right to castigate liberal critics, who sought to try Chinese achievements before the court of freedom and other 'Western' values, as traitors. They were on the contrary true heirs of Lu Xun, the early twentieth-century writer who manifested a higher kind of Chinese patriotism by holding a truthful, unflattering mirror up to China's deficiencies.

Yan stood pat and defended the 'blue ants' of the Maoist period again and again. Not for him Huang Kejian's admonition that 'a hardworking slave remains a slave'. Lu Xun, he held, had been contending with the debased semi-colonial China of the warlord era; the time had come to support the new China and give it face wherever possible. Even Yan's conservative mainland supporters, however, shrank from joining his diatribe against 'freedom and democracy'.[61] Was this because the 1982 Constitution upholds these principles, or does it flow from the fact that it is deeply uncomfortable for modern Chinese intellectuals to follow patriotism to the extreme exemplified by Yan, given their agonised sense of freedom as a civilisational watershed?

We may hint at an answer. Edward Said's celebrated critique of 'Orientalism' has met with a generally cool reception in China. Why?

From the civilisational perspective sketched here, Said is all too clearly motivated by *ressentiment*.[62] Bitterly rejecting the moral criteria of the West, as do Said and Yan Yuanshu, is unsatisfactory to those, whether liberal or neo-authoritarian, who hope ultimately to adopt these very criteria and prove superior to the West in realising them.

One of Orlando Patterson's central arguments is that all the components of the modern idea of freedom,

> derived as they are from the ancient relation of slavery, have the potential of being either refined upward into a civilized ideal or backward to the primal domination of slavery at its most elementary state: the savage right that inheres in one man's power of life and death over another.[63]

As we have seen, Chinese thinkers also tend to think that disputes over freedom must be brought before the bar of civilisation. Yan Yuanshu's position represents an extreme discounting of all standards external to China itself. He believes in subjugating everyone to the national cause: a nation of self-sacrificing blue ants capable of developing nuclear missiles and winning Olympic gold medals. It is a populism in which all are treated the same, in the name of national survival and supremacy over the West. While there are no survey data to test the popularity of such views, it should be pointed out that this is simply one current among many. Contrary to the populist rhetoric of Yan, many of today's educated audience are genuinely worried about the destruction of the élite culture which once sustained Chinese civilisation. Calls for a renewal of such a culture are common across the ideological spectrum. On the liberal side, a positive appraisal of freedom and democracy is often encapsulated in the notion of 'humanistic values'.[64] On the 'new conservative' side, populism is attacked from another angle, as an obstacle to development.

It would be an interesting exercise to score each of the three freedoms, personal, civic and sovereignal, in terms of their direction upwards or downwards in 'civilisational' terms in China today. Sovereignal freedom would likely be a civilisational minus. The power to act as one pleases regardless of the wishes of others is a reality in the hands of powerful officials at many levels. On the national, 'organic' level, the Han population exercises an unhealthy degree of this freedom over its national minorities – Tibetans, Mongols, Uighurs, Muslims. This kind of overdeveloped freedom is repeated all the way down from provinces and counties to criminal gangs and illegal enterprises which run rackets based on slavery pure and simple. Personal freedom which does not adversely affect others is, somewhat paradoxically, not entirely lacking; in fact, under the current conditions of economic growth, many people have enjoyed some sense of personal liberation, fleeting and limited to the sphere of consumption though this may be. There is still not enough of it to threaten becoming a new form of slavery. Finally, civic freedom is in a state of very slow growth indeed. Developments in the sphere of private law could be pointed to as offering legitimate channels for community members to voice contrary opinions. The reigning political culture is devoted to the proposition that too little is better than too much in this field, and that civic and personal freedom are, in Yan Yuanshu's terms, 'relative evils'. But he may not have had the last word.

That last word, from the point of view of this essay, lies rather with Bao Zunxin, one of the most outspoken dissidents to take part in the 1989 democracy movement. Bao and Yan Jiaqi, who together established the Beijing Association of Intellectuals in the course of the movement, were co-signatories of one of the most explicit denunciations of Deng's regime.[65] Bao was arrested and served five years in prison. He published the poignant article 'Hopes after "freedom"' in a Hong Kong monthly after his release in 1994; hence the title.[66] The subject, naturally enough, was the nature of freedom in China: why was it something always so remote for the Chinese people? True, Bao himself was no longer behind bars, but had no guarantee of staying that way, given the arbitrary legal limits set by the state. Yet Chen Duxiu, already a communist leader in 1923, had called Chinese to 'Fight for freedom!' and (as already noted above) sincerely believed Marxism to represent a higher goal of freedom.[67] When it suited him – notably in the 'New Democracy' period before the rise of the People's Republic – Mao too had been a champion of 'true freedom and democracy', notably only to damn them as bourgeois reaction.

Like Liu Xiaobo and Wang Xizhe, Bao seeks to grasp, from Mao's eventual insincerity, something which even his faithless disciples of today must respect. He concludes, first, that freedom has a 'stage-nature' rather than a 'class-nature'. In so far as the CCP had from the Anti-right movement of 1957 to the Tiananmen movement of 1989 suppressed calls for freedom and democracy as 'bourgeois liberalism',

> freedom and democracy are in fact products of the development of human civilization. While among different (i.e. democratic) nations and different (i.e. free) peoples they have specific forms, their basic characteristics are the same, namely, a respect for and protection of human rights. Therefore freedom and democracy have no distinction of East and West, still less of bourgeois and proletarian class character.

Second, hopes for freedom and democracy cannot rest with a saviour. The people's trust in such saviours (for which read Mao and the Party) has been betrayed. What is now needed is political reform to restrict their power; only accelerated democracy can provide genuine salvation. Third, Bao argues, only when the market economy is institutionalised can freedom and democracy survive. Both the traditional small peasant economy and the Soviet-style centrally planned system had led to despotism.

Bao rather depressingly concludes that the dream of seeing 'the flag of freedom and democracy fluttering over China' is simply his hope. It is up to the Party to see that its own survival can only be secured by undertaking political, democratic reforms. Bao argues simply and powerfully for a universal standard of civilisation from which a universal standard of freedom flows. He explicitly denies a uniquely Chinese 'national condition'. What is the appropriate form of political participation that Chinese liberalism should allow thus replaces the problem of whether it should allow any at all.

We have now registered the consistency of this outlook over a wide part of China's intellectual spectrum. Slavery, which was highly developed over long periods, never provided a definitive breakthrough to freedom as a vision of life or a political value. Nevertheless it has figured in China's acceptance of freedom as an attribute of modern civilisation. It remains to look back to Patterson's references to the Bangkok Declaration, to the view of Lee Kuan Yew that freedom can only exist in an 'ordered state' (see Chapter 1). The Asian response, one might suggest, would be to welcome the clarity offered by Patterson's analysis. However, even if fifty-seven varieties of freedom could be found in various historical formations, there is an eventual value-judgement about their relative claims on the present which cannot be endlessly delayed. Most of the Western development of freedom took place before the Enlightenment, but it is precisely the post-Enlightenment cluster of concepts central to liberalism that matter now.

The Bangkok Declaration is seriously at fault, however, in excluding the kind of voices listed above, from Liang Qichao to Bao Zunxin, in its account of freedom in Asia. This is in itself the most minimal of lists, and says nothing about countries apart from China. Hence one must underline Patterson's brief references to the moral indefensibility of the Declaration. If China is anything to go by, it is possible to identify all three freedoms in Asian history. What was stillborn was their 'chordal fusion'. Hence if Asia is the Antarctica of freedom it is thought to be, like the real Antarctica it turns out to be teeming with life under the forbidding coat of ice.

Notes

1 Lu Xun, 'Random Thoughts Under the Lamp', 29 April 1925. Cited by Orville Schell, *Mandate of Heaven* (New York: Simon & Schuster, 1994), p. 9.
2 Preamble to the *Constitution of the People's Republic of China* (adopted on 4 December 1982).
3 Mark Elvin, Mountains of Felicity, unpublished MS, Australian National University, 1994.
4 See, e.g., Xia Jiabao and Liu Yingqi, *Zhongguo bainian renquan shi* [A century of human rights in China] (Shenyang: Liaoning Renmin Chubanshe, 1994).
5 Mark Elvin, *The Pattern of the Chinese Past* (London: Eyre Methuen, 1973), p. 248. See Ch. 15, 'The Disappearance of Serfdom', *passim*.
6 James L. Watson, 'The Chinese Market in Slaves, Servants and Heirs', *Asian and African Systems of Slavery* (Oxford: Basil Blackwell, 1980), pp. 223–50.
7 William Theodore De Bary, *The Trouble with Confucianism* (Cambridge, Mass.: Harvard University Press, 1991); Roger V. Des Forges, 'Democracy in Chinese History', in R. V. Des Forges, Luo Ning and Wu Yen-bo (eds), *Chinese Democracy and the Crisis of 1989: Chinese and American Reflections* (Albany: State University of New York Press, 1993), pp. 21–52.
8 Shih Chih-yu, *State and Society in Chinese Economic Reforms: The Cultural Dynamics of Socialist Reform* (Boulder: Lynne Rienner, 1995), p. 126.
9 Chen Guying, 'Zhuang Zi and Nietzsche: Plays of Perspectives', in Graham Parkes (ed.), *Nietzsche and Asian Thought* (Chicago: Chicago University Press, 1991), pp. 115–29. Similarly, Burton Watson, in his translation of the book of *Zhuang Zi*, writes, 'The central theme of the *Zhuang Zi* may be summed up in a single word: freedom.' See Introduction to Burton Watson, *The Complete Works of Chuang Tzu* (New York: Columbia University Press, 1970), p. 3. 'Zhuang Zi used the flight of freedom (*xiaoyao you*) and the freedom of flight as a metaphor for the joy of the spirit and the liberation of the mind and soul.' Li Zehou, 'Zhuang Zi meixue zaji' [Notes on the aesthetics of Zhuang Zi], *Zhongguo wenhua yu Zhongguo zhexue*, December 1986, pp. 88–113; transl. in *Chinese Studies in Philosophy*, 20, 1 (1988), pp. 3–42.
10 Wolfgang Bauer, *China and the Search for Happiness* (New York: Seabury Press, 1976), s.v. 'Pao Ching-yen'; see part III section 1, 'Freedom and Anarchy', pp. 131–52, *passim*. Some of the Ge Hong quotes are reproduced in Chen Dinghong, 'Bao Jingyan shehui sixiang' [Social Thought of Bao Jingyan], *Zhongguo shehui sixiang shi* [History of Social Thought in China] (Beijing: Beijing daxue chubanshe, 1990), pp. 398–409.
11 Kung-chuan Hsiao, *A History of Chinese Political Thought* (Princeton: Princeton University Press, 1979), pp. 623–4.
12 Yü Ying-shih, 'The Radicalization of China in the Twentieth Century', in 'China in Transformation', *Daedalus*, 122, 2 (March 1993), p. 131.
13 Kung-chuan Hsiao, *History of Chinese Political Thought*, pp. 416–17.
14 Raymond Dawson, *Imperial China* (London: Hutchinson, 1972), pp. 111–14.
15 W. J. F. Jenner, 'A Knife in the Back for a Mate' (Morrison Lecture; Canberra: Contemporary China Centre, 1994), and *The Tyranny of History – The Roots of China's Crisis* (London: Penguin, 1992). He is not responsible for the way in which I have interpreted his ideas.

16 Comments on Ping-ti Ho, 'Salient Aspects of China's Heritage', in Ping-ti
    Ho and Tang Tsou (eds), *China in Crisis*, vol. 1, *China's Heritage and the
    Communist Political System* (Chicago: University of Chicago Press, 1968),
    Book I, p. 45. Franke linked this to his view of law as simply a governing
    tool in China, not an independent institutional order. He regarded this as
    an even more important difference between China and the West.

17 *Jiyū/ziyou* was coined by Japanese writers to translate expressions like
    freedom and liberty encountered in Western texts. They drew on classical
    Chinese poetry; Chinese students in Japan brought the new term into
    vogue in China.

18 Hu Weixi, Gao Ruiquan and Zhang Limin, *Shizi jietou yu ta: Zhongguo jindai
    ziyouzhuyi sichao yanjiu* [The Crossroads and the Tower: Studies in Modern
    Chinese Liberalism] (Shanghai: Shanghai Renmin Chubanshe, 1991).

19 Yang Dayong, 'Yan Fu's Philosophy of Evolution and the Thought of
    Lao Zi and Zhuang Zi', *Chinese Studies in Philosophy* (September 1992),
    pp. 55–84; Yü Ying-shih, 'The Radicalization of China in the Twentieth
    Century', p. 128. The classical treatment of Yan Fu is Benjamin Schwartz,
    In Search of Wealth and Power: Yen Fu and the West (Cambridge, Mass.:
    Harvard University Press, 1964).

20 'Lun ziyou' [On Freedom], in Li Huaxing and Wu Jiaxun (comps), *Liang
    Qichao xuanji* [Selections from Liang Qichao] (Shanghai: Renmin chuban-
    she, 1984), pp. 223–33. See also Ch. 10 of the present volume.

21 Wang Gungwu, 'Power, Rights and Duties in Chinese History', in *The
    Chineseness of China: Selected Essays* (Hong Kong: Oxford University Press,
    1991), pp. 165–86.

22 Xu Jilin, *Zhizhede zunyan – zhishifenzi yu jindai wenhua* [The dignity of the
    wise – the intellectuals and modern culture] (Shanghai: Xuelin chubanshe,
    1991), p. 206.

23 Wang Gungwu, 'The Chinese Urge to Civilize: Reflections on Change', in
    The Chineseness of China, pp. 145–64 (emphasis added).

24 Arif Dirlik, *Anarchism in the Chinese Revolution* (Berkeley: University of
    California Press, 1991), p. 28.

25 Xu Jilin, *Zhizhede zunyan*, p. 205.

26 Hu Weixi et al., *Shizi jietou yu ta*, p. 46.

27 Ip, Hung-yok, 'The Origins of Chinese Communism – A New Interpre-
    tation', *Modern China*, 20, 1 (January 1994), pp. 34–63. Cf. p. 42.

28 Ibid., p. 46.

29 Li Ming, 'Ziyou • minzhu • kexue – "Wusi" yundong yu Zhongguo xiandai-
    hua' [Freedom/democracy/science – 'May Fourth' and China's modernisa-
    tion], *Zhongguo Shehui Kexue Jikan*, no. 1 (November 1992), pp. 43–6.

30 The latter-day nostalgia of former Red Guards and educated youth for the
    'ten years of turmoil' often turns on the unforgettable, if strictly relative,
    liberation it brought them from humdrum existences and class roles.
    Cf. Lynn T. White III, *Policies of Chaos: the Organizational Causes of Violence
    in China's Cultural Revolution* (Princeton, NJ: Princeton University Press,
    1989), p. 15.

31 Maghiel van Crevel, *Language Shattered: Contemporary Chinese Poetry and
    Duoduo* (Leiden: CNWS Publications, 1995), p. 27.

32 Ann Kent, *Between Freedom and Subsistence: China and Human Rights* (Hong
    Kong: Oxford University Press, 1993). See also He Baogang, Liberal Ideas
    of Democracy in Contemporary China: A Constructive Critique of its

Moral and Intellectual Foundations, PhD, Australian National University, 1993.
33　Chen Yanqing (ed.), *Dangdai Zhongguo shehui zhexue* [Contemporary Chinese Social Philosophy] (Tianjin: Tianjin Renmin Chubanshe, 1990), pp. 555–81.
34　Ibid., pp. 556–7.
35　Ibid., pp. 563.
36　Marx and Engels, *The Manifesto of the Communist Party*, in Robert C. Tucker (ed.), *The Marx-Engels Reader* (New York: Norton, 1978), p. 491.
37　Chen Yanqing, *Dangdai Zhongguo shehui zhexue*, pp. 566–8.
38　'Dangdai Zhongguo shehui shixian rende ziyou de tiaojian', in ibid., pp. 574–81.
39　Ibid., pp. 579.
40　Bill Brugger and David Kelly, *Marxism in Post-Mao China, 1978–1985* (Stanford: Stanford University Press, 1990), Ch. 6. Also see David Kelly, 'The Emergence of Humanism: Wang Ruoshui and the Critique of Socialist Alienation', in Merle Goldman, Carol Hamrin and Tim Cheek (eds), *China's Intellectuals and the State: In Search of a New Relationship* (Cambridge, Mass.: Harvard University Press, 1987), pp. 159–82; and Merle Goldman, *Sowing the Seeds of Democracy in China: Political Reform in the Deng Xiaoping Era* (Cambridge, Mass.: Harvard University Press, 1994).
41　See also Gu Xin, 'Hegelianism and Chinese Intellectual Discourse: A Study of Li Zehou', *Journal of Contemporary China*, 8 (Winter–Spring 1995, pp. 1–27; Gao Ertai, 'Beauty as the Symbol of Freedom', transl. in *Chinese Issues in Philosophy*, 25, 1 (Fall 1993).
42　Li Zehou, 'Qimeng yu jiuwang de shuangchong bianzou' [Double variation on enlightenment and national salvation], *Zou xiang weilai*, 1988, pp. 18–36. Cf. p. 35.
43　Hua Shiping, 'All Roads Lead To Democracy: A Critical Analysis of the Writings of Three Chinese Reformist Intellectuals', *Bulletin of Concerned Asian Scholars* (January–March 1992), pp. 43–58.
44　Wang Ruoshui, 'Wenxue ziyou he ziyoude wenxue', *Xinhua wenzhai*, 6 (June 1986), pp. 161–3
45　Wu Jianguo, 'Guanyu ziyou wenti de "fansi"', *Hongqi*, 17 (September 1986), pp. 2–38; Yu Haocheng, 'Ziyou liangzhong gainian buneng hunyao' [The two concepts of freedom cannot be confused], *Wenhui bao*, 7 November 1986, p. 2. See David Kelly, 'The Student Movement of 1986 and its Intellectual Antecedents', *Australian Journal of Chinese Affairs*, 17 (January 1987), pp. 127–42; quote from p. 139.
46　Hua Shiping, 'All Roads Lead to Democracy: A Critical Analysis of the Writings of Three Chinese Reformist Intellectuals', *Bulletin of Concerned Asian Scholars* (January–March 1992), pp. 43–58. Discussion here closely follows David Kelly and Barrett McCormick, 'The Limits of Anti-liberalism', *Journal of Asian Studies*, 53, 3 (August 1994), pp. 804–31.
47　Li Zehou, 'Qimeng yu jiuwang de shuangchong bianzou'.
48　Kirk A. Denton, '1989 Democratic Movement and the May Fourth', *Journal of Chinese Philosophy*, 20 (1993), pp. 387–424.
49　Huang Kejian, 'Puzzles of Contemporary Chinese Culture', *Zhexue Yanjiu*, 2 (1992), pp. 10–19. My summary draws liberally on Michel Masson SJ, 'Chinese Culture and Christianity', supplement to *Correspondence* (HK) (January 1993), pp. 13–14.

50 Huang Kejian,'Puzzles of Contemporary Chinese Culture', p. 19.
51 Gu Xin and David Kelly, 'New Conservatism: Ideology of a "New Elite" ', in David S. G. Goodman and Beverley Hooper (eds), *China's Quiet Revolution* (Melbourne: Longman Cheshire, 1994), pp. 219–33. See also David Kelly (transl.), 'Realistic Responses and Strategic Options: An Alternative CCP Ideology and its Critics', special issue of *Chinese Law and Government*, 29, 2 (Spring–Summer 1996). On new authoritarianism see Stanley Rosen and Gary Zou, 'The Chinese Debate on New Authoritarianism', *Chinese Sociology and Anthropology*, 23, 2–5 (December 1990); and Barry Sautman, 'Sirens of the Strongman: Neo-Authoritarianism in Recent Chinese Political Theory', *China Quarterly*, 129 (March 1992), pp. 72–102.
52 Gan Yang, 'Minjian Shehui' [Civil society], *Zhongguo luntan* (Taibei), 1990.
53 Deng Zhenglai and Jing Yuejin, 'Jian'gou Zhongguode shimin shehui' [Constructing Chinese Civil Society], *Zhongguo shehui kexue jikan* (HK), 92, 1 (November 1992), pp. 58–68.
54 Wang Xizhe and Liu Xiaobo, 'Dui dangqian woguo ruogan zhongda guoshi de yijian' [Our views on some present major national issues], reprinted in *Zhongguo zhi chun* (November 1996), pp. 1–5.
55 See Geremie Barmé, 'Liu Xiaobo and the Protest Movement of 1989', in George Hicks (ed.), *The Broken Mirror: China After Tiananmen* (London: Longman, 1990), pp. 52–99.
56 Woei Lien Chong [Zhuang Ailian], 'The Tragic Duality of Man: Liu Xiaobo on Western Philosophy from Kant to Sartre', in Kurt Werner Radtke and Tony Saich (eds), *China's Modernization: Westernization and Acculturation* (Stuttgart: Franz Steiner Verlag, 1993), pp. 111–62. In the light of her work, I would now revise my own assessment (David Kelly, 'The Highest Chinadom: Nietzsche and the Chinese Mind, 1907–1989', in *Nietzsche and Asian Thought*, ed. Graham Parkes (University of Chicago Press, 1991), pp. 151–74).
57 Gu Xin, *Zhongguo fan chuantong zhuyide pinkun – Liu Xiaobo yu ouxiang pohuai de Wutuobang* [The poverty of Chinese anti-traditionalism: Liu Xiaobo and the Utopia of iconoclasm] (Taipei: Fengyun Shidai Chuban Gongsi, 1993).
58 Lin Min, 'Individual and Ultimate Concerns – Liu Xiaofeng's Formulation of Transcendent Human Universality in Contemporary Chinese Intellectual Discourse', *Issues and Studies*, 30, 2 (February 1994), pp. 91–106.
59 Zhongguo feng Chubanshe (ed.), *Liangzhong Zhongguo xin* [Two kinds of Chinese patriotism] (Hong Kong: Zhongguo feng Chubanshe, 1994).
60 Yan Yuanshu, 'Xiang jianshe Zhongguode yiwan tongbao zhijing' [Salute to one billion compatriot builders of China], in ibid., pp. 8–17. Quote from p. 15.
61 See ibid., p. 25.
62 Dong Yueshan, 'Dongfangzhuyi da hechang?' [Grand chorus of Orientalism?], *Dushu*, 1994, 5 (May 1994), pp. 99–103. Wang Hui and Zhang Tianwei, 'Wenhua pipan lilun yu dangdai Zhongguo minzuzhuyi wenti' [Theories of cultural criticism and issues about modern Chinese nationalism], *Zhanlüe yu guanli*, 4 (1994), pp. 17–20.
63 Orlando Patterson, *Freedom in the Making of Western Culture*, vol. 1 (New York: Basic Books, 1991), p. 365.
64 Wu Xuan; Wang Gan; Fei Zhenzhong; Wang Binbin, 'Women xuyao zenyangde renwen jingshen?' [What kind of humanistic spirit do we want?],

Dushu, 94, 6 (June 1994), pp. 66–75; Li Zonggui, 'Lun Dangdai Zhong-guode zhuliu wenhua', [The mainstream culture of contemporary China], *Taihai liang'an* (March 1993), pp. 46–51.

65 David Kelly, 'Chinese Intellectuals in the 1989 Democracy Movement', in George Hicks (ed.), *The Broken Mirror: China After Tiananmen* (Hong Kong: Oxford University Press, 1990), pp. 24–51.

66 Bao Zunxin, '"Ziyou" yihoude qiwang' [Hopes after 'freedom'], *Zheng ming* (HK), 2 (February 1995), pp. 66–8.

67 'Wei ziyou er zhan!' [Fight for freedom!], *Xiangdao*, February 1923.

CHAPTER 6

Freedom and the Family: Gendering Meiji Political Thought

Vera Mackie

Political debates of the late nineteenth century in Japan can be characterised as a contest between competing conceptions of society: a society based on hierarchy, obedience and order (often justified with reference to Confucian principles) versus a society based on principles of equality and freedom (justified with reference to the writings of European liberals). One important focus for discussion of these alternative visions of society was the family system. Competing models of the family and gender relations were fundamental to political discussions in the early Meiji period, as will become apparent in my analysis of the representation of freedom and its opposites in selected writings from the liberal movement. Some feminist and socialist writings which provided a critique of the limitations of liberalism will also be considered where relevant.

Roots of the Concept of Freedom in Japan

Although the word *jiyu* ('freedom') had been used as early as 1595 to translate the Latin word *libertas* in Christian literature,[1] it was not used consistently in Japan in its modern sense until the 1860s, when Fukuzawa Yukichi used it in his translation of the Declaration of Independence.[2] The concept gained wider currency in 1871 with Nakamura Masanao's translation of Mill's *On Liberty*.[3] In June 1874 Mitsukuri Rinshō in the intellectual journal *Meiroku Zasshi* explained that *jiyū* was the translation of 'liberty', derived from the Latin *libertas*, 'the social situation that was not slavery'.[4] Mitsukuri linked liberty with constitutional government: 'When men acquire liberty by changing their status from slavery in republics, they can become men who possess in their persons the rights of liberty from a political point of view, but this is impossible under monarchical despotisms.'

121

The different nuances of 'liberty' and 'freedom' were elaborated on by Nishimura Shigeki in May 1875, as part of a series of articles on foreign words.[5] The very translation of this word at this time suggests that there was a societal need for such a concept. Rather than assuming that such a concept was necessarily 'foreign' or derivative, I want to concentrate on the social context which made such a coinage necessary.

In Europe the development of liberalism and individualism has been identified with the rise of Protestantism, capitalism, and free-market ideologies. From these roots came the first bourgeois revolutions, the rise of democratic ideas, and, eventually, feminism. Liberal ideas were said to be particularly congruent with the transition from the subsistence values of feudalism (custom, status, authoritarianism) to the free-market ideology of capitalism (mobility, freedom, market values). Ideas of natural rights were employed to justify democratic ideas. Natural rights entailed the notion of equal rights and universal values, and it became logically difficult not to extend these to women. The first major tracts of European feminism were almost contemporaneous with the French Revolution,[6] and some of these writers attempted to use the supposed universalism of liberal theory in order to argue that women were entitled to the same rights and freedoms as men.[7] Recent feminist writing, however, has argued that the exclusion of women from early liberal discourse was more than an oversight. Rather, patriarchal values form the very basis of liberal discourse.[8]

In the nineteenth century Japan was also undergoing the transition from feudal to capitalist economy, and market relations were already prevalent in particular sections of the economy.[9] Roger Bowen, drawing on the work of T. C. Smith, links these economic changes with the development of liberal ideologies in rural Japan:

> The free rural market of late Tokugawa, Smith shows, likewise demonstrated such aspects of capitalistic society as occupational migration and mobility; employment contracts; competitive hiring practices; competition to secure adequate supplies of raw materials; a small-producer hatred of government-supported monopolies; the concentration of wealth and political power in the hands of large landholders; and wide-scale commercial farming . . . 'Such men were far from being peasants with an abacus,' Smith writes. Instead, 'we find them in conflict with government over its intervention in local affairs, in matters concerning village common land, irrigation rights and the selection of headmen . . .' Local political autonomy, 'a more open system above,' and unrestricted rights of commerce were the 'liberties' demanded by the rural beneficiaries of the expansion of the market economy.[10]

Peasants under the feudal relationships of the Tokugawa period had been conscious of the 'right to subsistence', and had been positioned as 'supplicants' who could petition a benevolent government when subsistence was threatened. When their petitions were unsuccessful, their dissatisfaction was at times expressed in riots and uprisings.[11] In other words, peasants in the nineteenth century were now participants in a market economy who wanted to see the freedoms and rights of the market economy extended to the political sphere. E. H. Norman has contrasted the urban roots of British liberalism with the rural origins of liberalism in Japan: 'The point to note is that Japanese liberalism had its roots in the countryside, unlike English liberalism which was a movement of the cities.'[12]

The tensions between the feudal hierarchy and liberal aspirations came to a head through the catalyst of external pressure on Japan. In the years between Commodore Perry's first visit in 1853 and the Meiji Restoration of 1868, there was a reconfiguration of power relations at the élite level, resulting in the end of the military rule of the Shōguns and a reaffirmation of the authority of the Emperor. The creation of a new regime was symbolised by the move of the Imperial court from Kyōto to Edo (renamed Tōkyō), and the designation of a new era name: *Meiji*, or 'enlightened rule'. In the first few years after the Restoration, the feudal domain system was abolished and the feudal class system dismantled, although former *samurai* retained some privileges. The Meiji Constitution was not completed until 1889 (to become effective in 1890), so that the 1870s and 1880s saw intense debates on alternative models of society.

These debates were carried out under the shadow of threats to national sovereignty. Although Japan was not subject to direct colonial intervention like so many of its Asian neighbours, a major goal of nineteenth-century governments was revision of the unequal treaties which denied tariff autonomy and protected foreign residents through extraterritoriality.

Despite the resonance of liberal ideas for many individuals experiencing the economic and social transformations of Meiji Japan, the legitimacy of liberal ideas could be challenged by the dominance of Confucianist ideas, which emphasised hierarchy and obedience rather than equality and freedom. But it was also possible to find justification in the Confucian tradition for rebellion against a ruler who did not show the necessary benevolence. In the feudal period we can also find such iconoclasts as the eighteenth-century thinker Andō Shōeki, a man who had endeavoured to construct 'a philosophy vindicating resistance to unbridled authority and oppression',[13] and who stated that 'in nature there is no distinction between high and low, rich and poor, first and last'.[14]

Irokawa Daikichi argues that many of the participants in the Freedom and People's Rights Movement of the 1870s and 1880s understood their participation in terms drawn variously from Confucianism, from the *Kokugaku* (National Learning) School, or from the millenarian *Yonaoshi* movements of the late Tokugawa period.[15]

The *gōnō* [wealthy farmer] advocates of Freedom and People's Rights took the ideal of primitive Confucianism to consist in the ideology of the love of Emperors Yao and Shun for the people – the ideology of 'dynastic change' which stated that incompetent emperors should abdicate or be replaced, and that the absolutism of the sovereign was not the natural 'will of heaven', and also the utopian vision of the simple society in which people live in happy contentment, as the 'will of Heaven.' The *gōnō* then, by joining this ideology with the revolutionary ideology of Europe and America (the modern doctrine of natural rights) and the doctrine of joint rule by sovereign and people, formed the ideology of Freedom and People's Rights.[16]

The language of Confucianism was therefore not simply a remnant of premodern times, which somehow retarded the development of liberal or democratic ideas. Rather, Confucianism was constantly being reinvented and reconstituted, and Confucianist language could be used to justify the most modern practices and institutions. But there were limits to the usefulness of a philosophy based on principles of hierarchy and obedience, no matter how much this was tempered by benevolence, and many liberal thinkers of the nineteenth century in Japan found European liberal ideas more congenial in expressing their aspirations. The contradictions between Confucianism and liberalism became most apparent in discussions of the family system, as we shall see below.

    That notions of natural rights and freedom resonated for many Meiji intellectuals is perhaps demonstrated most effectively in Ueki Emori's song of popular rights. His 'Country Song of Civil Rights' (*Minken Inaka Uta*) used the imagery of nature to give metaphorical force to the notion that the rights being demanded were the natural inheritance of men and women:

> . . . Though the birds have wings they cannot fly;
> The caged bird can see the outside.
> Though the fish have fins they cannot swim;
> The netted fish sees the sea beyond.
> Though the horses have hooves they cannot run;
> The tethered horse sees the grass out of reach.
> [We] are endowed with arms and legs;
> We have hearts and minds.
> But today we have no liberty or rights.
> If we call ourselves [human]
> Then each person must . . . stand up and say
> '[Humans] have rights.'[17]

The songs of Ueki and others were popular during some of the uprisings of the 1880s, suggesting that they had a broad resonance. Ueki also wrote his own draft constitution based on popular sovereignty, democratic principles, and equality between men and women, and said to be the most liberal of the thirty-odd drafts around at the time. This constitution enumerated the necessity for freedom of 'thought, speech, publication, communication, travel, petition, assembly, public association, religion, commerce, arts, education, residence, and protection of self and property'.[18]

A Liberal Party (*Jiyûtō*) was formed by Itagaki Taisuke and other prominent liberals, including Ueki. The Liberal Party, active from 1881 to 1884, produced a newspaper, *Jiyū Shinbun* (*Liberty*), edited for a time by Nakae Chōmin, translator and interpreter of Rousseau into Japanese. Other publications of the liberal movement carried similar titles. In 1887 Nakae published 'A Discourse of Three Drunkards on Government', where one of his characters promotes ideas of democracy and freedom, and argues that equality is necessary for the exercise of freedom. One of Nakae's characters advocates equal political rights for all, but does not elaborate on concepts of gender.

Gender and Liberalism

In this period it was thought vital for the prosperity and stability of the state that the most suitable form of the family be instituted. This reflects the Confucian utilitarian belief that family, school and other institutions are inseparable from the functioning of the state.[19] The family also played a crucial role in imagining the new Japanese nation-state. The Meiji Restoration had threatened traditional power relations by the abolition of the feudal domains and the modification of the feudal class system. By identifying the state with the family, it was possible to use emotional attachment to the family in the service of the state.

In 1873, the sixth year of the Meiji era, Mori Arinori[20] and others established the *Meirokusha* (Meiji Six Society), a society devoted to the dissemination of 'modern' ideas. The activities of this society contributed to the development of civil society in Meiji Japan, providing a physical space for lecture meetings, and promoting further discussion through the journal *Meiroku Zasshi* ('Meiji Sixth Journal'). These practices were built on in the creation of other intellectual journals and mass newspapers, and in the liberal movement which deployed 'lectures, debates, demonstrations . . . speaking tours aimed at various villages and their agricultural associations; political party and society newspapers and bulletins; handbills, and even songs and poems'.[21]

In addition to discussion of the concepts of liberty and rights, alternative systems of government, the role of the intellectual, and issues related to education and language planning, *Meirokusha* members used their journal to discuss notions of women's role, challenging the double standard that allowed such practices as prostitution and concubinage.

In 1872 the new government had given legal recognition to concubines, and in the following year had allowed that the children of concubines need not be treated as illegitimate, although these provisions were later modified. The *Meirokusha* writers saw this as tantamount to official recognition of polygamy.[22] Thus as early as the 1870s liberal thinkers were interested in the situation of unfree women: wives and concubines under the patriarchal family system.[23] Tsuda Mamichi, in particular, continued to criticise the institution of prostitution. In the *Meiroku Zasshi* of October 1875, Tsuda lamented the growth of prostitution in Japan, despite the recent outlawing of indentured labour.

Slavery and Prostitution

Even before the creation of the Liberal Party, and before the first petitions for representative government, concepts of individual freedom were highlighted in an international incident involving the transportation of Chinese 'coolie' labourers. The existence of another group of un-free labourers, prostitutes indentured into sexual labour in Japanese brothels, also attracted public attention as a result of this incident. In 1872, two Chinese labourers escaped from the Peruvian ship the *Maria Luz*, which was transporting them from Macao to Peru.[24] After investigation, the Kanagawa Prefectural Court found the Captain of the *Maria Luz* guilty of abusing and forcibly detaining the Chinese passengers. The sentence, however, was commuted. The Captain initiated a civil suit for the return of the labourers, which was not upheld by the court.[25] The governments of Japan and Peru entered into discussions, which were eventually resolved by the mediation in May 1875 of the Czar of Russia, who upheld the decision of the Japanese courts. As early as 1873, however, relations between Japan and Peru were normalised through a treaty of trade and amity.

This incident was the occasion for embarrassment on the part of the Japanese government, when the Peruvian advocate pointed to the existence of indenture in Japan. The government hurriedly responded by making contracts of prostitution unenforceable.[26]

The language of a subsequent statement by the Ministry of Legal Affairs, however, was a long way from recognition of the freedom and autonomy of the women. It was argued that the prostitutes were in the same situation as cattle which had been bought and sold, and therefore could not be expected to meet the obligations of the contract.[27] The effect of these regulations was short-lived, and reformers continued to lament the situation of prostituted women, as prostitution continued under revised regulations in 1873, which recognised individual contracts between brothel owners and their workers.

The *Maria Luz* affair, as other commentators have noted, revolved around issues of national sovereignty rather than the individual freedom of the Chinese labourers or the Japanese prostitutes. The Japanese officials were keen to demonstrate their facility in the conventions of international legal protocols, as part of a process of working towards revision of the unequal treaties which denied Japan sovereignty in tariff matters and which granted extraterritoriality to citizens of the United States, the United Kingdom, and other treaty partners. As in so many other historical situations, the bodies of the Chinese labourers and Japanese prostitutes were tokens to be wielded in a larger fight for national sovereignty.

In other discussions of slavery, the issue was located in Ancient Greece, in China, or referred to the transportation and use of negro slave labour by Europeans.[28] Indeed, it seems that African or African Americans were associated with images of slavery in the Meiji mind, images safely externalised, with no apparent connection with Japanese conditions. By contrast, the figure of the prostituted woman would return in the discussions of liberals throughout the 1870s.

Although all the contributors to the journal agreed that the form of the family was crucial to the prosperity of the state, there was no one way of theorising the relationship between family and state. Some argued for a direct congruence between family structure and political system: a liberal polity required a family system based on equality and freedom, while the order of a society organised on Confucian principles would be threatened by a family that did not uphold the proper hierarchies of age and gender. Others argued for a separation of family and state. In most cases, however, they were more interested in the relationship between family and state than the welfare of the individual women, whose interests were often equated with those of the family.[29]

Even those writers who were promoting radically new ideas of gender relations in the context of Meiji Japan couched their arguments in Confucian terms, complete with quotations from Confucius and Mencius. Mori Arinori, for example, who advocated (and attempted to practise) a form of contractual marriage based on mutual consent, used the Confucian language of 'righteousness' to denounce the practice of concubinage:

> When righteousness does not prevail, the strong oppress the weak and the smart deceive the stupid. In extreme cases, immorality becomes an amusement providing a source of livelihood as well as pleasure. Among the customs common among barbarians, mistreatment of wives by their husbands is especially intolerable to witness.[30]

Sakatani Shiroshi quoted Mencius in order to argue for 'separate spheres' for men and women, but questioned the concept of equal rights:

> In sum, the word rights includes evil. There is a tendency for the advocacy of rights to generate opposing power. This was never the intention of the wise men of Europe and America and the translation [of the word 'right' as *ken*] is not appropriate. Instead it would be well to speak of preserving the spheres of men and women (*danjo shubun*) or of the harmonious bodies of husband and wife (*fūfu dōtai*). Further, from the point of view of rights, the man should stand slightly above the woman, just as elder brother takes precedence over younger brother.[31]

Nakamura Masanao, credited with coining the phrase *ryōsai kenbo* ('good wives and wise mothers'), argued for purity on the part of both husbands and wives.[32] Most of these writers argued that education was necessary in order to instil notions of purity in both sexes, and they advocated monogamy and a single sexual standard for both sexes. Similar demands would be made by the *Nihon Kirisuto Kyō Kyōfūkai* (the Japanese chapter of the Women's Christian Temperance Union). At the first session of the Diet in 1890, Yajima Kajiko, the leader of the *Kyōfūkai*, appealed for an end to prostitution and concubinage. The *Meirokusha* members limited their discussion of women's role to marriage, however, and even those who referred to 'equal rights' within marriage were reluctant to grant women equal rights in society at large. Katō Hiroyuki was actively hostile to the notion of equal rights for women in any sphere.[33] Fukuzawa Yukichi realised that Meiji men were not ready to relinquish their privileges, and allowed that they could 'tacitly' keep concubines, as long as they did not flaunt the fact.[34] In other writings Fukuzawa challenged the Confucianist identification of family and state, pointing out that the expectation of obedience to Emperor and father rested on the unrealistic assumption that the people needed constant help and guidance from a wise and enlightened Emperor. Fukuzawa later wrote 'enlightenment' versions of didactic texts for women.[35]

We should note the gap between theory and practice in these writings: the most liberal of writers were often far from exemplary in their private conduct. We should also note that this first debate on gender roles and the connections between family and state was carried out by male writers only.

By the 1880s, however, women were participating in the liberal movement, claiming by their actions a place in the emergent civil society. Sharon Sievers reports that the first woman's speech given to a political gathering (of which there is a record) 'came in late 1881, when a sixteen-year-old woman spoke to a Kyūshū group. That speech was followed in late March 1882 by a talk on behalf of equal rights for women given by a policeman's wife at a political rally in Nakatsu.'[36] One of the most prominent female participants was Kishida Toshiko, who toured the country making speeches demanding political rights for women and contributed articles to liberal newspapers such as *Jiyū no Tomoshibi* ('The Light of Freedom') and the women's magazines which developed during this period. Kishida's contribution to the first issue of *Jiyū no Tomoshibi* underlined the lack of freedom for women in Japan at the time. Kishida at first appears to take the meaning of *tomoshibi* quite literally, enumerating the dangers which await a woman who walks alone at night without a light. But then she turns to a more metaphorical understanding and describes the lack of rights of women, who cannot escape a situation of enslavement. She hopes that the light of freedom will light the way for women for ages to come.[37]

In other writings and speeches Kishida focused on the family as the site of women's oppression. In one essay she used the conventional phrase that described the upbringing of young ladies, *hakoiri musume* ('daughters raised in boxes') but turned it into an image of deprivation.[38] Daughters raised in this fashion were like plants whose growth had been stunted, in comparison with flowers growing wild in the mountains and valleys. Like Ueki Emori in his song, Kishida identified freedom with nature and unfreedom with an unnatural state.[39] Kishida also discussed the Confucian view of women's place in the family, and criticised education which taught women the 'three obediences': to their father in the natal home, to their husband on marriage, and to their son in old age.[40] She further argued that women's present education (in singing, dancing, and needlework) was training them to be the playthings of men. Such was the subversiveness of her message that Kishida was arrested in 1883 after a public speech. Subsequent regulation of political activities by women showed that the Meiji government was developing a clearly gendered vision of the rights and duties of citizens and subjects.

These competing visions of society were highlighted again in discussions and commentaries on the Meiji Constitution of 1890, the Imperial Rescript on Education of 1890, and the Meiji Civil Code, which could not be completed until 1898 because of controversy over family law. The final form of the Meiji Constitution reflected the desire to pay lip-service to democratic ideals while at the same time ensuring the power of the élite in the name of the Emperor. Although an elected assembly was allowed for, its powers were limited, and the franchise was limited by a qualification depending on the amount of tax paid.[41]

Where other constitutions carried a Bill of Rights, the corresponding section of the Meiji Constitution (Chapter 2) outlined the Rights and Duties of Subjects. There was no mention of inalienable human rights; rights were granted to the people as subjects of the Emperor, who was 'sacred and inviolable' (Article 3).[42] Freedom of religious belief and freedom of speech and association were only granted 'within the limits of law' and 'within limits not prejudicial to peace and order' (Articles 28 and 29). Any of these provisions were subject to the exercise of the powers of the Emperor 'in times of war or national emergency' (Article 31). Thus the Meiji state failed to support democratic or liberal ideas in any real sense. The preamble to the Constitution referred to Shintō mythology in its affirmation of the divinity of the Emperor. The 'monarchic principle' of the German Constitutions of the 1850s was adopted to justify the notion that sovereignty resided in the Emperor.[43]

For Meiji women, the constitutional system meant that they were to live in a state which did not recognise the notion of 'natural rights', let alone extend them to women. Although the language of the Constitution was gender-neutral, women were implicitly excluded in various ways. The duty to perform military service, for example, could be said to imply a male subject. Although some liberals championed the cause of political freedom for both men and women, the Meiji government reacted by prohibiting public, political activities by women. The first regulations on public meetings and associations were passed in the 1880s.[44] The new regulations, from 1890 on, added clauses specifically directed at women. The Japanese Law on Political Associations and Meetings of 1890 (*Shūkai oyobi Kessha Hō*) prevented women from engaging in any political activity, whether it be attending a political meeting, holding one, or joining a political party. These bans were reiterated in Article 5 of the Public Peace Police Law of 1900 (*Chian Keisatsu Hō*). State regulation of public political activities circumscribed the possibilities for further development of civil society independent of the state, and prevented women from further participation in this arena.

Women and the family were not explicitly mentioned in the Constitution itself, except for the statement that Imperial Succession was based on the male line (Article 2), but the Imperial Rescript on Education of 1890 upheld a Confucian view of a state based on hierarchy and obedience, with the family seen as the basic unit of society.

Freedom and the Family

The link between patriarchal authority in the family and imperial power in the state was the focus of discussions leading up to the promulgation of the Meiji Civil Code, eventually completed in 1898. The liberal Ueki Emori lamented that those who grew up under authoritarian states failed to develop independence and autonomy. He used natural rights theory to argue for equal rights for men and women, and identified the patriarchal power of the family head (*koshu*) with the absolute power of the monarch (*kunshu*). He argued that the country should be made up of individuals, not a collection of families. Those who grew up under an autocratic power structure, he argued, failed to develop independence and autonomy. He called for a Civil Code based on the 'new ideas' of the nineteenth century.[45] On the other side of the debate, conservative legal scholar Hozumi Yatsuka criticised a draft of the Civil Code which failed to affirm the principle of primogeniture.[46] He stated that the form of the Japanese state depended on the Japanese family system, and described an idealised, trans-historical form of this system.[47] The promulgation of a Civil Code based on liberal principles, he implied, would result in the destruction of society as we know it. Hozumi's appeal to antiquity is a common feature of modern nationalist thought.[48]

What was at stake in both Ueki's and Hozumi's laments was the construction of the modern Japanese nation-state. The identification of family with state was a socially constructed ideal. Perhaps we can reconsider this identification with reference to Benedict Anderson's discussion of nationalism as the construction of an 'imagined community'. In Japan, it seems, the identification of family and state was to facilitate the imagining of a new community: the nation-state as family, referred to in the Japanese literature as *kazoku-kokka* (family-state). Gluck has described this process succinctly: 'confronted with increasing individuation and even anomie, ideologues enshrined the family – the hyphenated metaphor of the family-state in effect sanctifying the family at least as much as it domesticated the state.'[49]

We should distinguish the Japanese discussion of family and state from European bourgeois ideology. In Europe, bourgeois marriage developed as the site of production moved out of the home, and middle-class men engaged in paid labour outside the home while their wives looked after the management of the home.[50] The ideological construction of the private sphere rendered aspects of gender relations 'invisible', and naturalised the gendered hierarchy in the home. In Japan, however, there were different configurations of 'public' and 'private'. According to Confucian ideology, power relations in the family were articulated directly into the power relations of the state. In Europe the concept of 'separate spheres' was used by some feminists to argue for equal political rights for women, on the grounds that women made an equally significant contribution to society. In Japan, under the constitutional system, notions of a gendered hierarchy within the family were made explicit, and the family itself was politicised rather than being seen as a private haven. Under the Meiji Civil Code and related legislation, women were prevented from public political activity; inheritance was based on the principle of primogeniture; married women lost the right to control any property brought into a marriage, and were prevented from entering into independent contracts; and all family members were subject to the control of the patriarch, who mediated between family members and the state. But the extended discussion of alternative family forms had the contradictory effect of bringing the family and gender relations into public discourse and creating a discursive space for feminist ideas.

Despite the victory of conservative views of family and state, progressive thinkers continued to try to imagine a society based on freedom and equality, and the family continued to be a focus for these imaginings. Such was the power of linking family and state that this rhetoric also appeared in oppositional texts.

Family, Community and Freedom

One line of thought that developed from the early liberal movement was socialism. An early socialist organisation was the *Heiminsha* (Commoners' Society); the name referred to the thought of the Meiji journalist Tokutomi Sohō, who had espoused the ideal of *heiminshugi* ('commonerism'). Socialists in the early 1900s saw the family as the repository of communal values and continued to debate ideal family forms and the relationship between family and society. A constant topic of discussion in the socialist press was marriage and the family. Issues related to marriage and 'free love' (*jiyū ren'ai*) were aired repeatedly. Many of the speakers and writers on socialism assumed a natural connection between socialism and 'free love' and seemed to assume that their female listeners and readers were primarily interested in romantic matters. While Nishikawa Fumiko linked socialism with the 'feminine' values of nurture and compassion, Murai Tomoyoshi invited women to 'fall in love' with socialism.[51]

Views on love and marriage ranged from descriptions of the European bourgeois ideal of companionate marriage, to an espousal of 'democratic' family arrangements reminiscent of the early Meiji debate on women, to an affirmation of 'free love' which accompanied a complete rejection of marriage and the family system. Women's role within marriage was occasionally likened to slavery,[52] and the condition of wives could be linked with the situation of other women, such as prostitutes, who laboured under unfree conditions.[53]

In 1905 Matsuoka (Nishikawa) Fumiko, a member of the *Heiminsha*, reported on a walk through the Yoshiwara licensed district with two other socialist women. Matsuoka's account focuses on the conditions of the prostitutes, comparing their confinement behind wooden gratings to that of caged animals in the zoo. She laments that the women are treated like 'non-human commodities' (*ningen igai no butsuhin*), and that they have 'lost the freedom [to express] human emotions'. She understands that they are probably doing this work for the sake of aged parents or invalid relatives, and 'in thinking about their fate', she hated 'the society which placed our comrades (*dōhō*) in such pitiful circumstances'. For some later socialist writers, prostitution would be used as a symbol of the exploitation of women in capitalist society.[54]

An editorial in the socialist women's paper *Sekai Fujin* ('Women of the World') in December 1908, 'The Family in Communal Society', considered the view that socialism necessarily meant a rejection of the family in favour of communal solutions to problems of childcare and care for the aged,[55] and concluded that people might be reluctant to resort to solutions which could conflict with the ideal of *ninjō* (human feeling and compassion). The writer referred to the transformations which the family has undergone through history and suggested that while the family would continue to exist in a communal society, it would undergo further transformation. Once the wealth of society was communalised, the family would no longer be held together simply by economic necessity. This would allow the emergence of relationships within the family where the motive power was that of the pure human feelings of love between husband and wife and between parents and children. In response to the view that love within the family is based on selfish individualism (*shiyoku*), and should thus be abolished, the writer argued that it was the present social system which set up this conflict between the needs of the family and society, and that under a communal society love would be able to emerge in a purer form.

The search for a socialist view of marriage and the family involved, first of all, a questioning of the relationship between husband and wife, which could be extended to an interest in relationships in society at large. As in the early Meiji period, the family could be seen as paradigmatic of social relations in general. The deficiencies of the present family system were seen as symptomatic of problems with the existing economic system, and the family was a site for imagining the forms and practices of an ideal communal society.

The family could be used as a metaphor for any organisation run on communal principles.[56] Sakai Toshihiko, for example, described the *Heiminsha* as a family, a refuge from the restrictions of society.[57] In the Society, even women who were not actually married to one of the male socialists were metaphorically constructed as 'wives'. The senior woman of the group, Fukuda Hideko, was referred to as *shūtome*, 'mother-in-law'. The use of such fictive kinship terms implicitly constructed the *Heiminsha* as an extended family, a metaphor which was made explicit by Matsuoka Fumiko in an account published in the *Heimin Shinbun*. Matsuoka identifies herself as being responsible for the *Heiminsha* kitchen, and describes the *Heiminsha* as an extended family (*daikazoku*), complete with a pet dog, which performs the function of bringing out the human side of the *Heiminsha* members.[58] Within the metaphorical *Heiminsha* family, however, women performed the very real labour of providing meals and supporting the activities of their male comrades.[59] In socialist rhetoric on the ideal society, however, the whole of society was sometimes described as a family where all would be looked after.

The *Heiminsha* 'family' was seen as a space where communal values could be put into practice, in keeping with the relatively gentle brand of socialism espoused by this group. Values of co-operation and community were more apparent here than the class struggle. For women in the *Heiminsha*, however, the use of familial metaphors also had hierarchical connotations, and women in the socialist movement were primarily constructed as wives and lovers, daughters and sisters. This was reflected in a sexual division of labour in the day-to-day running of the Society and in the different ways in which women and men contributed to the early socialist publications. Articles addressed to women in the socialist movement tended to address the 'feminine' concerns of marriage and family, romance and reproduction.

There had been limits to the usefulness of the family as microcosm in liberal discourse, and socialist invocation of the family as a microcosm of a communalist society also showed the limited usefulness of this metaphor. The family demonstrates the tensions between the twin ideals of community and freedom which must be dealt with in any vision of an ideal society. While liberals and socialists invoked the values of caring and community represented by the family, feminist critics showed that the family was the site for the construction of gendered hierarchies, and the place where women's freedom was most severely restricted.

Feminism, the Family and Freedom

The search for a more democratic family form was linked to a questioning of the subordination of women as 'helpmate' within marriage. This led to questioning the role of woman as 'helpmate' to the state, and a re-evaluation of the possibilities for women's political activities. Thus the issue of women's lack of personal freedom under existing family relationships was linked with their lack of civic freedom under the Imperial system. While the Meiji nation-state was constructed as a family, there was only a limited role for women, in public or in the domestic sphere. As 'helpmate' to the state women provided support for militarism through the Patriotic Women's Association (*Aikoku Fujin Kai*), formed in 1901, which gained in popularity after the Russo-Japanese War.[60]

In the 1900s socialist women campaigned for the most basic of civic freedoms, the right to attend and participate in public political meetings, a campaign led by Fukuda Hideko, a veteran of the nineteenth-century liberal movement, and editor of the socialist women's paper *Sekai Fujin* ('Women of the World').[61] The progress of the petitions and proposals to reform Article 5 of the Public Peace Police Law was followed in the socialist press. When the reform proposal was rejected by the House of Peers, the *Commoners' News* reported to its women readers (in an unsigned article called 'The Women and the Peers') that they had been dealt a grave public insult. It said that the members of the ruling class 'do not see women as human individuals (*ikko no jinrui*) or as citizens of the nation (*ikko no kokumin*). They treat their wives and [other] women as slaves and concubines, and turn them into ornaments and playthings'.[62]

Several features of the participation of women in the early socialist movement can be understood from an analysis of this campaign for the reform of Article 5. We can perhaps detect a middle-class bias in this campaign, and a blindness to the class differences between women. With a few exceptions, women within the socialist movement at this stage tended to see the 'woman question' in terms of rights and freedoms which should be extended equally to males and females. In criticising the activities of the Patriotic Women's Association, and campaigning for the reform of Article 5, these women were attempting to reconstruct women as citizens.

The conduct of the campaign followed liberal political practice. The women wrote articles, collected signatures, lobbied, and (with the help of sympathetic parliamentarians) presented their demands to the Diet. The activities and demands of these socialist women may seem moderate when compared with the militant activities of the British suffragettes (they were certainly aware of the suffragettes, whose activities were reported regularly in *Sekai Fujin*).[63] The proposal was defeated, however, by the unelected Upper House, proof that Japan was a long way from the liberal democratic society whose ideals these women espoused.[64]

Thus in Meiji political discourse the family became a crucial focus for discussion of competing visions of society: a Confucian-style family-state where hierarchy and obedience were emphasised, or a liberal polity which emphasised freedom and democracy. The limits of liberal ideology were addressed by early socialist and feminist critiques, but even these oppositional discourses still referred to the family as microcosm and as metaphor. The Meiji debates on the family highlighted the tensions between the ideals of community and freedom, and demonstrated that an institution like the family, where the freedom of its members was systematically restricted, could not form the foundation of a society that valued freedom and autonomy.

Notes

1 Ishida Takeshi, 'The Assimilation of Western Political Ideas and the Modernization of Japan', *Fukuoka Unesco Bulletin*, 4 (1968), p. 63.

2 Fukuzawa Yukichi, *Seiyō Jijō* (Tokyo, 1866), cited in Ishida, 'The Assimilation of Western Political Ideas', p. 64; Sōgō Masaaki (ed.), *Meiji no Kotoba Jiten* (Tokyo: Tōkyōdō, 1986), pp. 215–18.

3 *On Liberty* was translated by Nakamura Masanao under the title *Jiyū no Ri* ('The Principle of Liberty').

4 Mitsukuri Rinshō, 'Jiyū', *Meiroku Zasshi*, 9 (June 1874), translated by William Braisted, *Meiroku Zasshi: Journal of the Japanese Enlightenment* (Cambridge, Mass.: Harvard University Press, 1976), pp. 117–19. See also Nakamura Masanao's comments in issue 12, in a postscript to an instalment of his translation 'An Outline of Western Culture'. He comments that early attempts to translate the word into Japanese included 'jishu no ri' (the principle of self-rule) and 'nin'ikō no ken' (the power of voluntary action), ibid., p. 162.

5 Nishimura Shigeki, 'An Explanation of "Liberty" and "Freedom" (Second of a Series of Expositions on Foreign Words)', *Meiroku Zasshi*, 37 (May 1875), in ibid., pp. 451–4.

6 Karen Offen, 'Liberty, Equality and Justice for Women: The Theory and Practice of Feminism in Nineteenth Century Europe', in Renate Bridenthal, et al. (eds), 2nd edn, *Becoming Visible: Women in European History* (Boston: Houghton Mifflin, 1987), p. 336.

7 Roger W. Bowen, *Rebellion and Democracy in Meiji Japan* (Berkeley: University of California, 1980), pp. 180–5; Richard Evans, *The Feminists* (Croom Helm: London, 1977), pp. 13–39; Barbara Taylor, *Eve and the New Jerusalem* (London: Virago, 1983), pp. 1–18.

8 Carole Pateman, *The Sexual Contract* (London: Polity Press, 1988), *passim*.

9 T. C. Smith, *The Agrarian Origins of Modern Japan* (Stanford: Stanford University Press, 1959), *passim*.

10 Bowen, *Rebellion and Democracy in Meiji Japan*, pp. 120–1.

11 For discussion of peasant rebellions during the Tokugawa period, see Stephen Vlastos, *Peasant Protests and Uprisings in Tokugawa Japan* (Berkeley: University of California, 1986); Herbert Bix, *Peasant Protest in Japan: 1590–1884* (New Haven: Yale University Press, 1986); Anne Walthall, *Peasant Uprisings in Japan: A Critical Anthology of Peasant Histories* (Chicago: University of Chicago, 1991). Bowen, in *Rebellion and Democracy*, discusses the participation of commoners in some early Meiji rebellions which drew on the notions of 'freedom and popular rights'.

12 E. H. Norman, *Origins of the Modern Japanese State*, ed. John Dower (New York: Pantheon Asia Library, 1975), p. 279.

13 John Dower, 'E. H. Norman, Japan, and the Uses of History', in ibid., p. 4.

14 Ibid., p. 10. For a detailed study of Andō Shōeki, see E. H. Norman, 'Andō Shōeki and the Anatomy of Japanese Feudalism', *Transactions of the Asiatic Society of Japan*, 3rd series, vol. 2 (December 1949).

15 Andrew Gordon discusses the use of such concepts as *giri* (obligation) by participants in twentieth-century labour disputes, and concludes that 'Japanese cultural values' could 'work to sanction resistance to authority'. Andrew Gordon, *Labour and Imperial Democracy in Prewar Japan* (Berkeley: University of California, 1991), p. 73.

16 Irokawa Daikichi, 'Freedom and the Concept of People's Rights', *Japan Quarterly*, 14, 2 (April–June 1967), p. 181.

17 Ueki Emori, 'Minken Inaka Uta', in Ienaga Saburō (ed.), *Meiji Bungaku Zenshū*, 12 (Tokyo: Chikuma Shobō), pp. 128–9; translated in Bowen, *Rebellion and Democracy*, pp. 206–8; see also: G. T. Shea, *Leftwing Literature in Japan: A Brief History of the Proletarian Literary Movement* (Tokyo: Hōsei University Press, 1964), p. 6. I have modified Bowen's translation slightly as he uses 'man/men' for the gender-neutral *hito* and *ningen*. In Shea's translation he has used feminine pronouns for the caged bird.

18 Ibid., p. 208. The full text of Ueki's constitution appears in Ienaga Saburō (ed.), *Ueki Emori Senshū* (Tokyo: Iwanami Shoten, 1974), pp. 89–111. For a discussion of alternative draft constitutions, see Joseph Pittau, *Political Thought in Early Meiji Japan: 1868–1889* (Cambridge, Mass.: Harvard University Press, 1967), pp. 99–130; Irokawa Daikichi et al., *Minshū Kenpō no Sōzō: Uzumoreta Kusa no Ne no Ninmyaku* (Tokyo: Hyōronsha, 1970).

19 Nagai Michio, 'Westernisation and Japanisation: The Early Meiji Transformation of Education', in Donald Shively (ed.), *Tradition and Modernisation in Japanese Culture* (Princeton, NJ: Princeton University Press, 1971), p. 76.

20 For details of Mori's life and thought, see Ivan Hall, *Mori Arinori* (Cambridge: Cambridge University Press, 1971), *passim*. For an account of the founding of the *Meirokusha*, see David Huish, 'Meiroku Zasshi: Some Grounds for Reassessment', *Harvard Journal of Asiatic Studies*, 32 (1972), pp. 208–29. The full text of the journal is translated by William Braisted, *Meiroku Zasshi: Journal of the Japanese Enlightenment* (Cambridge, Mass.: Harvard University Press, 1976). The *Meiroku Zasshi* writings on women have also been surveyed by Sharon L. Sievers in *Flowers in Salt: The Beginnings of Feminist Consciousness in Meiji Japan* (Stanford: Stanford University Press, 1983), pp. 16–25.

21 Bowen, *Rebellion and Democracy*, p. 5.

22 Mitsuda Kyōko, 'Kindaiteki Boseikan no Juyō to Henkei: Kyōiku suru Haha kara Ryōsai Kenbo e', in Wakita Haruko (ed.), *Bosei o Tou: Rekishiteki Henkō* (Tokyo: Jinbun Shoin, 1985), vol. 2, pp. 107–8.

23 Debates on prostitution and concubinage are surveyed in Noriyo Hayakawa, 'Sexuality and the State: The Early Meiji Debate on Concubinage and Prostitution', in Vera Mackie (ed.), *Feminism and the State in Modern Japan* (Melbourne: Japanese Studies Centre, 1995).

24 Suzanne Joncs Crawford surveys the *Maria Luz* affair from the point of view of international diplomacy, arguing that the resolution of the situation owed more to Japan's concerns about national sovereignty than to concern for indentured labourers. See 'The Maria Luz Affair', *The Historian*, 1984, pp. 583–96. For the significance of the incident with respect to campaigns for the abolition of prostitution, see Takemura Tamio, *Haishō Undō: Kuruwa no Josei wa dō Kaihō sareta ka* (Tokyo: Chuko Shinsho, 1982), pp. 2–12.

25 Crawford, 'The Maria Luz Affair', pp. 586–7.

26 Dajōkan Order no. 295. 2/10.1872; *Jinshin Baibai Kinshi Rei*. Takemura, *Haishō Undō*, pp. 3–4.

27 Takemura, *Haishō Undō*, p. 4.

28 See Fukuzawa Yukichi's notes on slavery in *Fukuzawa Yukichi Zenshū*, vol. 18. On images of black people from early modern Japan to the recent present, see: Gary P. Leupp, 'Images of Black People in Late Mediaeval and Early Modern Japan, 1543–1900', *Japan Forum*, 7, 1 (April 1995), pp. 1–13; John

G. Russell, 'Race and Reflexivity: The Black Other in Contemporary Japanese Mass Culture', in John Whittier Treat (ed.), *Contemporary Japan and Popular Culture* (Richmond: Curzon Press, 1996), pp. 17–40.

29 Cf. the comments on the 'elision between women and the family and women and mothers' in Lesley Caldwell, 'Women as the Family: The Foundation of a New Italy?', in Floya Anthias and Nira Yuval-Davis (eds), *Woman – Nation – State* (London: Macmillan, 1989), p. 173.

30 Mori Arinori, 'Saishōron', *Meiroku Zasshi*, 15 (November 1874), in Maruoka Hideko (ed.), *Nihon Fujin Mondai Shiryō Shūsei* (Tokyo: Domesu Shuppan, 1977), vol. 8, pp. 73–7; translated in Braisted, *Meiroku Zasshi*, pp. 189–91.

31 Sakatani Shiroshi, 'Shōsetsu no utagai', *Meiroku Zasshi*, 32 (March 1875); translated in ibid., pp. 392–9.

32 Nakamura Masanao, 'Zenryō naru haha o tsukuru setsu', *Meiroku Zasshi*, 33 (March 1875), in *Nihon Fujin Mondai Shiryō Shūsei*, vol. 15, pp. 348–50; translated in Braisted, *Meiroku Zasshi*, pp. 401–4.

33 Katō Hiroyuki, 'Fūfu Dōken no Ryūhei ron', *Meiroku Zasshi*, 31 (March 1875); in *Nihon Fujin Mondai Shiryō Shūsei*, vol. 8, pp. 77–9; and translated in Braisted, *Meiroku Zasshi*, pp. 376–7.

34 Fukuzawa Yukichi, 'Danjo Dōsū Ron', *Meiroku Zasshi*, 31 (March 1875), in *Nihon Fujin Mondai Shiryō Shūsei*, vol. 8, p. 79; quoted in Sievers, *Flowers in Salt*, p. 21.

35 As a challenge to the dominance of such writings as Confucian Scholar Kaibara Ekken's *Onna Daigaku* [Greater Learning for Women], Fukuzawa penned *Nihon Fujin Ron* [On Japanese Women] and *Hinkōron* in 1885; *Danjo Kōsai Ron* [On Relations Between Men and Women] in 1886; *Onna Daigaku Hyōron* [A Critique of Greater Learning for Women] and *Shin Onna Daigaku* [The New Greater Learning for Women] in 1899. For discussion of these writings, see Carmen Blacker, *The Japanese Enlightenment: A Study of the Writings of Fukuzawa Yukichi* (Cambridge: Cambridge University Press, 1964) pp. 67–89; Sievers, *Flowers in Salt*, pp. 18–25; Kiyooka Eiichi, *Fukuzawa Yukichi on Japanese Women: Selected Writings* (Tokyo: University of Tokyo Press, 1988); Hane Mikiso, 'Fukuzawa Yukichi and Women's Rights', in Hilary Conroy et al. (eds), *Japan in Transition: Thought and Action in the Meiji Era, 1868–1912* (Cranbury, NJ: Associated University Presses, 1984), pp. 96–112.

36 Sharon L. Sievers, 'Feminist Criticism in Japanese Politics in the 1880s: The Experience of Kishida Toshiko', *Signs*, 6, 4 (1981), p. 609. On women in the liberal movement, see Maruoka Hideko, *Fujin Shisō Keisei Shi Nōto* (Tokyo: Domesu Shuppan), vol. 1, pp. 35–41; Itoya Toshio, *Josei Kaihō no Senkushatachi: Nakajima Toshiko to Fukuda Hideko* (Tokyo: Shimizu Shoin, 1975); Sievers, *Flowers in Salt*, pp. 26–53.

37 Kishida Toshiko, 'Jiyū no Tomoshibi no Hikari o Koite Kokoro o Nobu', *Jiyū no Tomoshibi*, 1 (11/5/1884), reprinted in Suzuki Yūko, ed., *Kishida Toshiko Hyōronshū* (Tokyo: Fuji Shuppan, 1985), pp. 53–4.

38 Kishida Toshiko, *Hakoiri Musume, Kon'In no Fukanzen* (Tokyo, 1883), reprinted in Suzuki, *Kishida Toshiko Hyōronshū*, p. 34; discussed in Sievers, *Flowers in Salt*, p. 34.

39 Images of oppression and liberation are analysed in detail in Vera Mackie, *Imagining Liberation: Feminism and Socialism in Early Twentieth Century Japan*, Working Papers in Feminist Cultural Studies, No. 1 (Sydney: Women's Research Centre, University of Western Sydney, 1995).

40 Kishida, *Hakoiri Musume*, pp. 37–9.
41 In 1890 the electorate numbered 450,000, or 1.1 per cent of the population. Those who paid 15 yen per annum in direct taxes were enfranchised. Carol Gluck, *Japan's Modern Myths: The Ideology of the Late Meiji Period* (Princeton, NJ: Princeton University Press, 1985), p. 67.
42 Hideo Tanaka and Malcolm Smith, *The Japanese Legal System* (Tokyo: University of Tokyo, 1976), p. 637.
43 Ibid., p. 631.
44 Regulations for Political Meetings and Associations, 1880; Revised Regulations for Political Meetings and Associations, 1882; *Hōan Jōrei* (Peace Preservation Ordinance), 1887; Revision of Public Meeting Regulations, 1889; W. W. McLaren (ed.), 'Japanese Government Documents', *Transactions of the Asiatic Society of Japan*, vol. 62, part 2 (1914), pp. 495–505.
45 Ueki Emori, 'Ikanaru minpō o seitei subeki ka', *Kokumin no Tomo* (22/8/1889, 2/9/1889), reprinted in Yuzawa Kazuhiko, *Nihon Fujin Mondai Shiryō Shūsei*, vol. 5, pp. 383–7.
46 Hozumi's view emphasised 'a community based on private property rather than individual interests'. Cf. Rosalind Coward, *Patriarchal Precedents: Sexuality and Social Relations* (London: Routledge & Kegan Paul, 1983), p. 137.
47 Hozumi Yatsuka [1891], 'Minpō idete, chūkō horobu', *Hōgaku Shinpō*, 5, reprinted in Yuzawa, *Nihon Fujin Mondai Shiryō Shūsei*, pp. 237–9.
48 Benedict Anderson, *Imagined Communities: Reflections on the Origins and Spread of Nationalism* (London: Verso, 1983), p. 19: 'If nation-states are widely conceded to be "new" and "historical", the nations to which they give political expression always loom out of an immemorial past.'
49 Gluck, *Japan's Modern Myths*, p. 265.
50 On the development of concepts of public and private in European bourgeois culture, see Leonore Davidoff and Catherine Hall, *Family Fortunes: Men and Women of the English Middle Class* (London: Hutchinson, 1987); Jean Bethke Elshtain, *Public Man: Private Woman* (Oxford: Robertson, 1981); Eva Gamarnikow et al. (eds), *The Public and the Private* (London: Heinemann, 1983); Philippe Ariès et al., *A History of Private Life*, 5 vols (Cambridge, Mass.: Belknap Press 1987–91).
51 Murai Tomoyoshi, 'Nihon Fujin ni Taisuru Nidaimeisō' (part 1), speech presented to the Socialist Women's Seminar 13/2/1904, reported in 'Shakai Shugi Fujin Kōen no Ki', *Shūkan Heimin Shinbun*, 15 (21/2/1904); reproduced in Suzuki Yūko (ed.), *Shiryō: Heiminsha no Onnatachi* (Tokyo: Fuji Shuppan, 1986), pp. 277–80.
52 For some examples of the use of this analogy, see Sakai Toshihiko, 'Ryōsai Kenbo Shugi'; Imai Utako, 'Fujin no Chii', *Nijūseiki no Fujin*, 1, 7 (1/8/1904); H. A. Sei, 'Tate yo Shimai', *Sekai Fujin*, 1, 1, p. 7; Kamikawa Matsuko, 'Ori ni Furete', *Sekai Fujin*, 1, 3 (1/2/1907), p. 5.
53 Cf. Nishikawa [Matsuoka] Fumiko, 'Yoshiwara Kenbutsu no Ki', *Chokugen* (11/6/1905), also reprinted in Nishikawa Fumiko, *Heiminsha no Onna: Nishikawa Fumiko Jiden*, ed. Amano Shigeru (Tokyo: Aoyamakan, 1984), pp. 210–11.
54 See also Yamaguchi Gizō, 'Shakaishugi to Inbaifu', *Shūkan Heimin Shinbun*, 21 (3/4/1904), p. 7. For the views of later socialist writers on prostitution, see Vera Mackie, *Creating Socialist Women in Japan: Gender, Labour and Activism, 1900–1937* (Cambridge: Cambridge University Press, 1997), Ch. 5.

55 Such negative views had been a feature of Marxist writings on the family. See Denise Riley, 'Left Critiques of the Family', in Cambridge Women's Studies Group (eds), *Women in Society: Interdisciplinary Essays* (London: Virago, 1981), pp. 75–91; Michèle Barrett and Mary McIntosh, *The Anti-Social Family* (London: Verso, 1982), p. 18; Coward, *Patriarchal Precedents*, Chs 5 and 6.

56 Cf. Barrett and McIntosh, *The Anti-Social Family*, p. 40.

57 Sakai Toshihiko, 'Heiminsha yori', *Chokugen*, 2, 12 (23/4/1905), quoted in Suzuki Yūko (ed.), *Shiryō: Heiminsha no Onnatachi*, p. 28.

58 Matsuoka Fumiko, 'Heiminsha no Katei', *Shūkan Heimin Shinbun*, 60 (1/1/1905), reproduced in Suzuki, *Shiryō: Heiminsha no Onnatachi*, pp. 53–5. The dog's name is 'Maru', short for Marx; ibid., p. 54.

59 Sakai Toshihiko, however, seems to have taken an interest in improving the practical conditions of the work of the women, in purchasing, for example, a device to simplify the process of washing rice. Cf. Nishikawa Fumiko, 'Kometogi Kikai no Ohanashi', *Heimin Shinbun*, 63 (22/5/1905), reproduced in Suzuki, *Shiryō: Heiminsha no Onnatachi*, p. 56. Sakai, indeed, was distinguished as one of the male socialists in the early twentieth century who showed a prolonged commitment to pursuing answers to 'the woman question'. Cf. Suzuki Yūko, 'Sakai Toshihiko no Josei Ron Nōto', *Undō Shi Kenkyū*, 12 (August 1983); Suzuki Yūko (ed.), *Sakai Toshihiko Josei Ron Shū* (Tokyo: San-Ichi Shobō, 1983).

60 On the Patriotic Women's Association see Wakita Haruko et al. (eds), *Nihon Josei Shi* (Tokyo: Yoshikawa Kōbunkan, 1986), p. 223; Jane Mitchell, Women's National Mobilization in Japan: 1901–1942, unpublished thesis, University of Adelaide, 1986; Sharon H. Nolte and Sally Ann Hastings, 'The Meiji State's Policy Toward Women', in Bernstein, *Recreating Japanese Women*, pp. 151–74.

61 For accounts of this campaign, see Kodama Katsuko, 'Heiminsha no Fujintachi ni yoru Chian Keisatsu Hō Kaisei Seigan Undō ni Tsuite', *Rekishi Hyōron*, 323 (1977); Kodama Katsuko, *Fujin Sanseiken Undō Shōshi* (Tokyo, Domesu Shuppan, 1981), pp. 29–34; Suzuki, *Shiryō: Heiminsha no Onnatachi*, pp. 14–16; Miki Sukako, 'Meiji no Fujin Zasshi o Tadoru', pp. 86–90; Sievers, *Flowers in Salt*, pp. 122–34; Mackie, *Creating Socialist Women*, Ch. 3.

62 'Fujin to Kizoku', *Nikkan Heimin Shinbun*, 62 (30/3/1907), reprinted in Suzuki, *Shiryō: Heiminsha no Onnatachi*, pp. 301–2.

63 See the *Kaigai Jiji* (Overseas Topics) column of *Sekai Fujin*: 1 (1/1/1907), p. 3; 3 (1/2/1907), p. 3; 7 (1/4/1907), p. 3; 21 (1/1/1908), p. 3; 22 (5/2/1908), p. 2; 24 (5/4/1908), p. 2; 25 (5/6/1908), p. 10; 26 (5/7/1908), p. 2; 28 (5/9/1908), p. 3.

64 The critique of the family system would eventually be developed by the 'new women' of the Bluestocking Society in the Taishō period; the next campaign for the modification of Article 5 was carried out by the *Shin Fujin Kyōkai* (New Women's Association) in the 1920s. (The provisions of Article 5 relating to women were eventually modified in 1922, making possible the creation of the first organisations devoted to the attainment of women's suffrage, although this goal was not achieved until after World War II.)

CHAPTER 7

Merdeka:
The Concept of Freedom in Indonesia

Anthony Reid

> Merdeka – melody to me that word . . . On its account the red
> blood of courage was spilt brave and bold . . . But in the end
> it evoked greater joy and pride and honour than was ever
> known before in South East Asia.
>   Merdeka, in the language of Indonesia, means freedom.
> Nothing more. Historians may come in time to chronicle its
> evolution and interpret its development in textbook terms
> of political autonomy and nationhood. To me Merdeka is a
> native battle-cry beautifully sad, echoing far into the night
> across the island kampongs and fires.[1]

Today's Indonesia is low on the league tables for the practice of political
and civic freedoms. Its government does not put the expansion of
personal liberty high on its own list of national priorities. In the contemporary debate about the universality of human rights, the Soeharto
government tends to line up with the 'Singapore School' argument
that individual freedom is a peculiarly Western cultural preoccupation, while Indonesian human rights activists see it as an inherent
aspect of that modernity towards which the country aspires in other
domains. Freedom as a key concept is either Western or it is modern. It
would appear not to be inherently Indonesian.

In other circles, however, the equation of liberty with progress has
been challenged. Slavery was once seen as the antithesis of both freedom and progress, its gradual elimination from the world as 'proof of
a transcendent purpose in history'.[2] We now have to confront the paradox that freedom is most valued where it is most denied, so that we
should look towards cultures in which slavery played a major part for
potential seedbeds of the idea of liberty. Perry Anderson and Moses
Finley each perceived that the conjunction in ancient Greece of an
urban social system based on slavery and the birth of concepts of democracy and personal liberty was not coincidental.[3] These two phenomena
rose together, and they declined together. The similar symbiosis

between slavery and liberty in the birth of American democracy was explored by E. S. Morgan.[4]

Orlando Patterson's *Freedom in the Making of Western Culture* has finally made explicit and universal the connection between slavery and the idea of freedom. It was slaves, and those owning them, who conceived 'the unusual idea that being free was not only a value to be cherished but the most important thing that someone could possess'. Though one of his main objectives is 'to show that freedom was a peculiarly Western value and ideal', Patterson devotes only one chapter to the question 'Why freedom failed in the non-Western world'. He concedes that 'some notion of freedom existed wherever slavery was found', and specifically that among the (Bare'e-speaking) Toraja of central Sulawesi, his only Asian example, 'freedom did become something of an ideal ... it would certainly have been listed among the important things in life'.[5] He categorises this freedom, however, as only the most basic of his three elements – the one he calls sovereignal freedom, the ability to do as one likes with others. The Toraja scarcely ever freed their slaves. They needed neither to motivate their slaves with the hope of eventual freedom nor to placate non-slave-owning freedmen by giving them some rights in society. There was no progress, he argues, towards either of the other central elements in the Western triad: personal freedom and civic freedom.

In arguing that the centrality which freedom came to occupy in the value-systems of several European cultures grew out of particular social conjunctions rather than disembodied intellectual debates, Patterson has taken an important step forward. Nevertheless this path invites a response from those in a position to study particular Asian social forms more carefully. In an earlier study of slavery I had already called for comparative work on how far slave institutions in non-European societies generated values analogous to that which freedom represents in European languages.[6] Here I wish to respond to the challenge in relation to the development of the concept of 'merdeka' within Indonesian cultures.[7] As one of the few Asian terms for political freedom which resonates positively with the ancient world's distinction from slavery, this is a particularly important case. The Torajas of central Sulawesi are only a small part of it, for other Indonesian societies proceeded much further, both in freeing slaves and in building civic traditions.

Origins of the Merdeka Idea

The word came to the Indonesian Archipelago from the Sanskrit *maharddika*, meaning eminent, wise, rich or illustrious. It appears in this form in a number of Javanese texts from the tenth to the eighteenth century.[8] In the seventh-century Telagu Batu inscription of southern Sumatra, on the other hand, it had already adopted a Malay form, *murdhaka*, with a meaning more like the leader of a group of subjects or bondsmen.[9] Since in some Borneo, Sulawesi and Philippine languages (e.g. Sa'dan Toraja *ma'dika*; Tagalog *maharlika*) it refers to the intermediate group above slaves but below the ruler, we might guess that the term was first dispersed by Indian-influenced kingdoms in the Archipelago to mean a rank of official or headman, and later a superior social category.

In the first clearly dated dictionary to mention the word, the Malay word-list collected by Frederick de Houtman in Aceh in 1600, it had already assumed its modern sense as the antonym of slavery: '*mardeka*: vryman/geen slaef zijn' ('freeman, not being a slave').[10] At some point in the sixteenth century or before, this meaning had spread to all the Indonesian languages which were in contact with Malay-speaking urban life – at least Acehnese, Minangkabau, southern Sumatran languages, Javanese, Bugis and Makasarese, as well as the Malay lingua franca itself. In the cosmopolitan Malayo-Muslim world of the sixteenth- and seventeenth-century cities, slaves and slave-owners came from different cultural backgrounds, and clear legal notions were required to govern their status. It is in this context that *merdehika* (the classical Malay form of the word) became a term with defined legal status, the equivalent of Arabic *hurr* in Islamic law, in which criminals, victims and citizens were given different values according to whether they were slave or free.

In the interior of Java this meaning appears to have arrived fairly late, presumably because slaves never became an important or clearly defined legal category (despite a lively export of slaves from pre-Muslim areas in the sixteenth century). In eighteenth-century texts the Sanskrit form *maharddhika*, or *amardika*, was still being used in the sense of an old or wise person, or perhaps someone freed from obligations by retirement.[11] Although by the late nineteenth century Javanese had imported from Malay the opposition between merdeka and slavery, the older and deeper Javanese uses of the word had more to do with being pensioned or liberated from government service. The *pardikan desa* ('freed villages') of Java were given a charter freeing them from any tax or service to the king.[12]

John Crawfurd developed a theory of slavery on the basis of his experience in Indonesia in the second decade of the nineteenth century: 'wherever the manners of the lower orders are most untractable, there slavery most prevails, and where they are most docile, it is rarest. For the extremes of both, Celebes and Java may be quoted as examples.'[13]

While the servility of nineteenth-century Javanese towards their superiors made slavery unnecessary, and therefore freedom ill defined,
Bugis and Makasarese slave-holders were the most passionate about
their freedom. Because the slave/free dichotomy had only a small part
in the way Javanese understood this concept, merdeka in modern
times came to have 'few resonances in Javanese' in contrast to its emotive power in Malay and Indonesian.[14] One of the pioneers of the
teaching of Javanese to Dutch officials in the 1840s had insisted that the
inherently hierarchic nature of Javanese speech made it indispensable
for retaining control of the colony. Malay, he complained, encouraged
a sense of equality and freedom, and if these ideas spread, 'Java is lost
to us'.[15]

Following a dichotomy developed by James Watson, I have argued
elsewhere that Southeast Asia had both 'open' and 'closed' slave systems.[16] In relatively self-contained 'closed' systems such as those of the
Batak, Niha, Ngaju Dayak and Toraja (including those discussed by
Patterson), slavery was a means of retaining the labour of a valuable
subordinate group, who were therefore ritually defined as distinct,
subordinate pariahs with very little prospect of obtaining their freedom. But during the rapid commercialisation of the Archipelago in
the fifteenth to seventeenth centuries there was an immense trade in
slaves and captives, and larger cities such as Banten, Aceh, Palembang
and Makasar grew by incorporating slaves into the dominant society.
In these 'open' systems freeing slaves was a well-established legal
procedure, expressed in Malay, Javanese and Bugis legal codes.

Freedmen and freemen were both merdeka (correctly *merdehika*) in
the Malay of the sixteenth and seventeenth centuries, and the verb for
manumission was *merdehikakan* (to free). In the most important Malay
legal text, the *Undang-undang Melaka*, often copied but thought to have
been initially drawn up about 1500, both freemen and slaves have
specified values and rights, including the right to defend their dignity
if abused.[17] This would hardly be imaginable in the 'closed' systems of
outcast slaves.

This code also gives sufficient attention to issues of contested manumission to make clear that this was a frequent occurrence.

> If someone lays claim to an adult person, saying that he is his slave, but that
> person says, 'I am a freeman (*merdehika*) from birth,' the claimant should be
> asked to produce his witnesses, or his documents to support the claim. If
> neither party can produce a witness or a document to that effect, the case
> will be cancelled.
>   If a man lays claim to another person, saying 'you are my slave,' but the
> one claimed replies, 'It is true I was your slave, but you freed me,' or 'the
> person who sold me to you had already set me free,' then he will be asked for
> witnesses that he was set free by his master.

In this latter case, the code specifies that if each side can produce contradictory witnesses, the person seeking his freedom will be given the benefit of the doubt, and will be free.[18]

Ethnographic evidence of the nineteenth and twentieth centuries indicates that laws relating to freeing of slaves were present in many other societies. In the Makasar area there were complex rules to govern the case of slaves whose testimony that they were promised manumission at the death of their owner was contested by the heirs.[19] There were various Makasarese methods of manumission (*pamaradeka*), including the making of a written declaration by the master, but most commonly the slave passed coins obtained from the master to thirty different people, who then became the witnesses of his status.[20] Derek Freeman describes the ritual of 'enfranchisement' (a term he prefers to manumission because he is arguing that slavery is anomalous among Ibans) by which Ibans freed enslaved captives and rendered them members of the dominant society.[21] Among the most successful trading states which incorporated large numbers of servile outsiders through capture or purchase, there is no doubt that similar patterns of incorporation obtained. Slavery was the major source of labour mobility, and each city or commercial frontier had its subclass of unfree labourers, who could hope that they or their locally born descendants would be able to rise to free status.[22]

The growing role of Europeans as slave-owners, and the increasing trend for Islamic societies to restrict enslavement to non-Muslims by preference, gave the boundary between slave and non-slave a sharper racial or cultural character in the seventeenth and eighteenth centuries. Slavery also declined as the wealth of the Indonesian indigenous cities decreased, and as long-established rural patterns of exploiting labour through corvée became more dominant (especially in Java). Nevertheless the importance of non-slave status as an aspect of the good life was established by the seventeenth century, and gave the subsequent career of the concept of merdeka a positive start.

James Scott in Chapter 3 of this volume observes perceptively that the freedom of Southeast Asians at a practical level has generally depended, and still depends, on 'the relative autonomy of the social units within which they live'. It is therefore important that some of these social units described their autonomy in terms of merdeka. The tax-free *pardikan desa* of Java, already referred to, are one such case. Another developed in the upper reaches of the Musi River in southern Sumatra, where a number of highland peoples considered themselves *orang mardeka* (free people) because they had no king themselves and explicitly declined to submit in even the most nominal way to the downstream ruler of Palembang. A Dutch official in 1870 recorded the origin story of the six self-governing clans of the Besemah (Pasumah) plateau, and the council known as 'Four mats and two frees' (*Lampik empat merdike due*), which regulated their affairs in times of crisis. Local legend had it that when their founding ancestor had failed to make peace among the six Besemah clans, four of the clan leaders had journeyed to Palembang where they received each a mat from the Sultan as a token of pre-eminence, while the other two refused to go for fear of losing some of their treasured freedom, and hence became known as the 'two frees'.[23] The Besemah were reported by Dutch officials in the nineteenth century to constitute 'a Republic in the most democratic sense. The people rules itself; for that purpose great public meetings would be convened in which all important matters would be discussed'.[24] Another source noted, 'The untamed, freedom-loving masses in Besemah are the tyrant of their own leaders; democracy prevails there to the point of anarchy'.[25]

Freedom in State Institutions – the Bugis Case

The existence of a concept of free status as the antithesis of slavery is a necessary step, but only a first step, towards modern understandings of rights to personal freedom. In all parts of the world where slavery was important and recognised as a legal category there was such a concept, but most state ideologies developed without regard to it. The precolonial Indonesian states for which both slavery and freedom were most important were the pluralistic port-states of the period roughly 1450–1630, in which law codes such as the *Undang-undang Melaka* originated. The merchant-aristocrats who dominated these states found ingenious ways of evading the absolutist ideology of kings, such as female and child rulers and dual monarchies, but for the most part they failed to generate an alternative ideology which protected the rights of others against the king.[26] Precolonial states remained unstable, caught in the tensions among weak state institutions, strong local traditions, and royal claims to untrammelled authority.

This background makes the particular case of the Bugis, the dominant people of southern Sulawesi, important as the most advanced precolonial attempt to institutionalise freedom in the way states were run. The Bugis and Makasar peoples of the southwestern peninsula of Sulawesi developed their states relatively late and with little of the Indian-derived rhetoric of universal kingship which influenced Java and Sumatra. Each local community which acknowledged a political and military leader identified the legitimacy of that leader with the sacred regalia of the place, believed to be found by the heaven-descended founder of the local lineage. When these communities federated into larger states in the fifteenth and sixteenth centuries they retained most of their autonomy, still magically sanctioned by the intrinsic power of the regalia (*arajang*).[27] Federations remained therefore contractual, and the terms on which they formed broader units were sanctioned by powerful supernatural forces.

Makasar, the most powerful state in the period 1550–1660 by dint of its dominant port and brilliant leadership, might have been expected to absorb the whole of southern Sulawesi into a new state in this period, as happened with sultanates in Java and Sumatra. But this contractual pattern stood in its way. Makasar's own strength was built on a central dualism between the two states of Gowa and Tallo', which in turn were federations of seven or nine lineages each with rights within the united kingdom. The Dutch admiral who conquered Makasar with Bugis help in 1667, astonished at the series of extremely complex rights, contracts and obligations to which he became heir, noted that 'the kings of Gowa and Tallo' cannot make one false step once outside their own gates'.[28]

Southern Sulawesi also had a distinctive form of slavery, where slaves were regarded with the sort of contempt which obtained in the closed systems like those of the Toraja, but where commercialisation and warfare produced all the movement of the 'open' system, with thousands of Bugis slaves being exported every year in the eighteenth century. Although freemen used the term *ata* to refer not only to slaves but to themselves as loyal subjects of a ruler, they knew very well what slavery and non-slavery meant. As indicated above, they had elaborate procedures to publicise the emancipation of individual slaves, indicating that this was also common.

The autonomy of several of the Bugis kingdoms was severely threatened in the seventeenth century when Indonesian kings, like European ones, profited from new wealth, weapons and ideas to extend their power. Makasar twice conquered Bone, the largest Bugis state, and reduced it to the invidious status of slave (*ata*), without a ruler of its own. When Bone freed itself from this humiliating yoke by its alliance with the Dutch, it in turn subjected other states including Wajo' to the same unacceptable 'slavery'. When full independence and equality were again achieved, as in 1737 when Wajo' threw off Bone rule, liberation was naturally described with the term merdeka.[29]

The Bugis state of Wajo', based around Lake Tempe and the Cenrana River to the north of Bone, was particularly attached to the contractual autonomies of its freemen, repeatedly expressed in the ideal of merdeka. Wajo' was also, from the late seventeenth century to the late nineteenth, the source of most of Sulawesi's seafaring entrepreneurs, the renowned Bugis mariners who traded throughout the Indonesian Archipelago and as far as Cambodia. There was clearly a connection between this individual entrepreneurship and the attachment to an ideology of freedom, both of which were well established in the eighteenth century. The Wajo' chronicles were rewritten after the 'liberation' of 1737, and the resounding declarations then placed in the mouths of the state founders of two or three centuries earlier may reflect eighteenth-century values better than fifteenth-century ones.

These texts were clearly written with the intention of codifying what they call 'the freedoms of Wajo'' (*am-maradeka-ngenna to Wajo'*). Though chronicles and local traditions differ, the declaration that 'the people of Wajo' are free' (*maradeka to Wajo'*) is common to all of them. In a more elaborate version put into the mouth of one of the founding fathers, 'the people of Wajo' are free; free from birth. Only their land is subject, the owners of the land are all free. Their only master is the customary law which is agreed consensually'.[30]

The major chronicle tradition of Wajo', the *Lontara Sukku'na Wajo'*, is largely an exemplary account of how the state was formed by agreement, how two of the earliest rulers transgressed the 'freedoms' of the people and were duly killed, and how the people ensured through agreements solemnly witnessed by the (pre-Muslim) gods that their freedoms would thereafter be safeguarded. These freedoms are repeatedly enlarged on. At one point the Wajo' people declare:

> To secure freedom, only three things are decisive: firstly not to interfere with people's wishes; secondly not to forbid the expression of opinions; thirdly not to prevent [people going] to the south, the north, the west, the east, upstream or downstream. These are the freedoms of the people of Wajo'.[31]

Elsewhere more extensive lists of concerns are spelled out. The people of Wajo' must not be unjustly punished. Even if they are guilty the punishment must be mild, no others should suffer for the crime of one, and death sentences should be commuted to fines or exile. Their family, their property and their slaves must not be taken from them. They must be free to come and go, with the doors of Wajo' always open to them.[32]

The rituals by which new Arung Matoa of Wajo', as well as heads of local communities, were installed, repeated for each generation the consensual ideals of the eighteenth-century chronicle writers. The new ruler protested his inadequacy: 'I am not worthy to be appointed ruler of Wajo', for I am stupid, fearful, poor and weak', to which the people's representative replies, 'Simply accept the decision of Wajo', for Wajo' is clever, Wajo' is brave, Wajo' is rich and Wajo' is strong'.[33] The head of each constituting lineage would then express his loyalty at the same time as his autonomy: 'I will conduct my own affairs, I will preserve my manners, I will maintain my custom, only if I need it will I appeal to your advice.' In return the ruler declared to the assembly, 'I will not oppose myself to your will; I will not contradict your words; I will not prevent you from leaving Wajo' or returning to it'.[34]

At least one Indonesian people appear to have arrived quite independently at a well-defined idea of freedom by the eighteenth century. English liberals such as Thomas Forrest and James Brooke, children of a British Enlightenment not a great deal older than that of the Bugis, could discern in these attitudes and institutions a parallel to their own ideas. After visiting Wajo' in 1840, the future 'white raja' of Sarawak declared that, 'amid all the nations of the East, amid all the people professing the Mahometan religion from Turkey to China, the Bugis alone have arrived at the threshold of recognised rights, and have alone emancipated themselves from the fetters of despotism'.[35]

Slavery and Freedom in the European Settlements

Of declining commercial importance in the late nineteenth century, the Bugis were not central to the development of modern Indonesian political culture, except in so far as they carried their intellectual traditions to the cities. It was in the European-ruled but multicultural cities of the Archipelago, including Singapore, that the Malay language (the basis for both Indonesian and Malaysian national languages) was adapted to cope with modern political ideas such as freedom and democracy. Since it was also in these cities that slavery was most sharply defined, it was not surprising that merdeka (non-slave) became the term to translate that freedom.

Europeans in the Archipelago themselves adopted the word merdeka (usually in the Dutch form *Mardijker*) to refer to the earliest Asian slaves who were freed after becoming Christian. The Portuguese were more inclined than the Dutch to Christianise their slaves, but it appears to have been the Dutch who perceived the resulting Portuguese-speaking, Christian Asians as a distinct ethnic or social group whom they called Mardijkers – 'freed people'. The Dutch Company captured many on Portuguese ships or in Portuguese settlements such as Melaka and Pulicat and found them useful as a military force. They were gradually converted to Dutch Calvinism and became a vital source of relatively loyal support for the Dutch in Batavia. A 1673 enumeration of the Batavia population showed 5362 Mardijkers, twice as numerous as Dutch and Eurasian groups combined. They formed the backbone of the local militia, and were responsible for Portuguese becoming the predominant language of Dutch Batavia.[36]

Far more numerous in the 1673 register were the slaves, at 13,278 about half the Batavian population within the walls. Indonesian slaves continued to be imported to Batavia at a rate of about 1000 a year in the seventeenth century and 3000 a year for much of the eighteenth. After 1760 larger numbers were needed as replacements for the slaves, who were then dying at a rate in excess of 1300 a year in Batavia's unhealthy conditions. The total slave population of Batavia from 1680 to 1770 remained at between 20,000 and 30,000, but the numbers of freed slaves and their descendants gradually rose to become the dominant factor in Batavia's population by the time of the English interregnum in 1812–16.[37] The slave trade was made illegal by Britain in 1807 and the Netherlands in 1818, but there were still about 3350 slaves in the Batavia area when slave-holding was finally abolished in Dutch colonial territory in 1860.

The British settlements of Singapore and Pinang, which were among the most important points of interaction between Malay-speakers and the outside world in the nineteenth century, did not legally countenance slavery. Nevertheless several hundred slaves each year from Bali, Sumbawa, Flores, southern Sulawesi, the Batak area and Nias were being shipped to these settlements in the first half of the century, where they were valued by some as 'of immense advantage in procuring a female population'.[38] Munshi Abdullah bin Abdul Kadir, Malay writer for the British founders of Singapore, gives a poignant description of one such cargo of about 300 slaves being sold at the Singapore dockside around 1820. When he reported it to Stamford Raffles, he received a predictable lecture on the evils of slavery, but the hope that 'if we live a long time we may see all these slaves become free (*mardehika*) as we all are free'.[39] Later he describes how John Crawfurd, British Resident of Singapore, freed twenty-seven girls, 'young and beautiful to look at', who were slaves of the British protégé Sultan Husain Shah. Crawfurd explained to the fearful girls that they might go 'wherever you wish, and nobody can order you about or do anything to you'. Abdullah then described Crawfurd's meeting with the indignant Sultan, when he firmly insisted that 'instructions have come from the Governor-General in Bengal that in any English state no one whatsoever may keep slaves, but on the contrary everybody is free (*mardehika*)'.[40] These events clearly made a great impression on Abdullah, and his subsequent influential writings dwelt on the contrast between the oppression exercised by the Malay sultans of the Peninsula and the freedom conveyed by the British rule of law. Anthony Milner has recently hailed Abdullah as the unrivalled 'founder of Malay modernism' in the nineteenth century, not least in his insistence on the importance of personal freedom for the individual to develop his own intellect.[41]

It may have been the influence of Abdullah and Raffles, for both of whom freedom from slavery and civic freedom were undoubtedly linked, which led English dictionaries of Malay in the nineteenth century to see merdeka as the natural equivalent of the liberty of which

Locke and Mill wrote. Although the more pedestrian word *bebas* was always available to indicate freedom of movement, the English dictionaries gave primacy to merdeka. The first post-Enlightenment effort to render liberty into Malay went as follows:

> Free (manumitted) *mardika*; (on an equality) *sama rata*; (unrestrained) *bibas* . . .
> Freedom *hal mardika* . . .
> Liberty (enfranchisement) *ka-mardika-an*; (permission) *mohon, bibas*[42]

As the century progressed, English writers tended to broaden the reference of merdeka to cover all the political meanings of English 'free'. Crawfurd's 1852 dictionary translated it as 'free, not enslaved; manumitted, emancipated',[43] while Wilkinson in 1903 broadened it right out, perhaps under the influence of Munshi Abdullah, whose use of the term he quotes: 'Freedom, in contrast to servitude; free.'[44]

The Dutch scholarly tradition differed significantly, accepting merdeka as the equivalent of the abstract 'freedom' (*vrijheid*), but finding numerous other words for 'free'.[45] Ignorant or resentful of what the nationalist movement had done to build revolutionary implications into merdeka, the editors of the 1947 edition of Klinkert's much-used dictionary (significantly still called Malay, despite long-held nationalist insistence on 'Indonesian') continued to define it with breathtaking Orientalist irrelevance.[46]

It would be wrong to suggest that in the rural heartlands of nineteenth-century Indonesia merdeka was prominent as an ideal. The numerous rebellions and wars fought against the Dutch in the Archipelago in that period do not appear to have expressed themselves in terms of freedom so much as through holy wars, obligations on the Islamic faithful to fight against the unbeliever, or simply defence of territory or prerogatives.[47] It may have been only in southern Sulawesi and parts of southern Sumatra, where the slave/free dichotomy of the early modern period had been developed in inter-state or inter-group relations, that nineteenth-century battles were fought in the name of freedom. Elsewhere the older concept of freeman had faded before new concepts of a free man had begun to penetrate.

Freedom as a Modern Political Goal

Nevertheless merdeka remained a positive and expansive term with 'not a slave' connotations which could not be unhitched from personal freedom. As Dutch rule became vastly more pervasive around the turn of the twentieth century, merdeka became again a central concept for those who resented taxes, corvée, registrations, vaccination campaigns and a host of other intrusions by the colonial state. One such manifestation, remarkable because it occurred far from the influence of Western ideas, was the Samin movement in rural areas around Blora, central Java, at the beginning of this century. Its members rejected paying taxes or having anything else to do with the government, considering themselves free (merdeka) and self-sufficient.[48]

But it was in the second decade of the century that the idea of freedom as both a personal and political goal moved to the centre of the agenda of young Indonesians. The first generation to benefit from the expansion of Dutch schooling opportunities under the so-called 'Ethical Policy' (developmentalism in today's terminology) then began to absorb ideas of progress, education, science, freedom and democracy, and to form organisations to promote them. The large Dutch and Chinese communities also began to generate modern organisations to promote such ideas. Between 1908 and about 1922 there was an extraordinary hothouse of diverse ideas before the colonial authorities began to take fright and impose ever tighter controls.

In this atmosphere the concept of 'free' appears to have commended itself first as a description of the new kind of person being brought into being by these new conditions – free from traditional loyalties and able to make their own decisions about what to believe and what organisation to join. The first association set up by the pioneer Javanese journalist and activist Tirtoadisurjo, a commercial association to rival the Chinese Chamber of Commerce, proclaimed itself 'an association of free people' in 1909, using the Malay *kaum mardika* to translate the Dutch *vrije burgers*.[49] The first women's organisation for Indonesians was called *Puteri Mardika* (free daughters), and aimed at encouraging not only female education but also a 'merdeka attitude' among women.[50]

The newspapers which began to service the mushrooming organisations also sought to call themselves free. First into the field may have been the Dutch-language publication *Het Vrije Woord*, put out by the Dutch-led Indies Socialist Party from 1917. When the party produced a Malay-language newspaper two years later it was called the same thing – *Soeara Merdika* ('Free Voice', or equally 'the Voice of Freedom'). In 1920, as the Indonesian wing of the Indies Social Democratic Association transformed itself into the Indonesian Communist Party this became the People's Voice – *Soeara Ra'jat*. But meanwhile a number of other newspapers had begun to trumpet the importance of freedom. *Benih Mardika* ('Seeds of Freedom'), a Medan (Sumatra) daily of the years 1916–22, was the most important, but Tasikmalaya had its *Sora Merdika* (1920), Purwokerto its *Doenia Merdeka* ('Free World', 1924), Padang Panjang its *Djago Djago* (*Soeara Mardeka*) ('Champion – Free Voice', 1923–24), while the Surakarta leftist publishing firm was simply called Mardika.

In the period before communism, radical Islam, democracy and nationalism had taken fixed positions against each other, this concern for freedom was especially found in the inchoate Islamic-communist radicalism associated with Sarekat Islam and Sarekat Rakyat. At the grassroots level the Russian revolution itself was interpreted as having blazed the trail to merdeka: 'The communists have seized freedom in Russia . . . Now Russia is free. Everybody is equal there, free from all oppression.'[51] One of the powerful expressions for this group was *rasa merdeka*, which could be translated as 'the taste, sense or experience of freedom', but also 'a free spirit'. It resonated with the cultivation of the inner being (*batin*) for which Javanese are especially renowned. The early Javanese Communist Semaun defined it in terms of two other words often applied to the *batin*: *selamat* and *ayem* (literally 'secure' and 'contented', but with mystical overtones).[52] Even the Dutch-educated Communist Tan Malaka had *rasa merdeka* inscribed on the red scarves worn by the students at his revolutionary school, while the same phrase was used as the title of his propagandist novel by another leader of the then left wing of the Sarekat Islam.[53] This did not (yet) refer to national independence in the first instance; rather it was a way of standing up against all kinds of authorities. Shiraishi has well described the magical effect of Haji Misbach's oratory in the rural areas of Java as he told ragged groups of oppressed and hungry farmers that they should stand up as free men. 'The peasants experienced their taste of "freedom" in the suppression of their shared fear of the state'.[54]

One writer in central Java made the connection with Javanese tradition by explaining that there were two forms of freedom: *kemerdekaan lahir* ('outer', or 'ordinary' freedom) and *kemerdekaan batin*, which he explained in religious terms as 'the freedom of a person who has liberated himself from every worldly temptation'. The ordinary or outer freedom was also distinguished in ways which seem to prefigure Patterson's 'sovereignal freedom'. There was the kind of freedom from restraints which stemmed from conquest and imperialism, but the freedom this writer sought to focus on was 'a *kemerdekaan* based on humanity . . . which seeks and values common goals'. This freedom was a universal right, universally desired, but he was sure his readers would feel that they did not enjoy it.

Merdeka is a right given by God to each one of us, that is a right which cannot be taken away or reduced by anyone at all . . . The flood of desire to demand freedom cannot be dammed; it arises spontaneously in the thinking of each person, who until now still feels in a situation which is far from the name of merdeka. Every person feels it is essential to possess and use that right . . . only with that freedom will people be able to overcome whatever is not pure.[55]

This enthusiasm for freedom brought about a reaction, and not only from the side of an increasingly reactionary colonial government. In October 1925, as pressure was building for an ultimately disastrous revolutionary outburst, an article appeared in the leading Surakarta left-Muslim newspaper:

> The word 'free' [Merdeka] can be heard from every direction. Wherever people gather, there we hear people talking about freedom. We want to sit free, sleep free, eat free, work free, talk free, play free, have a good time . . . is there anything that people do not want [to do] freely? In short, to be free is generally understood to mean 'not to be interfered with,' 'not to be prohibited from,' etc. Thus people who pursue freedom can fall into violent, brutish, and ill-considered ways, and sometimes thus become people who are indifferent, or senseless.
>
> If one seeks freedom, [one should] not simply dare to speak low Javanese [i.e. not using the polite high form to superiors], dare to quarrel, dare to go on strike, and dare to make a big hoo-hah in brothels and hotels, but first of all one must have seriousness to study the science of true freedom and to perform all the obligations thereby involved.[56]

The author, and both the communist and Islamic wings into which the Sarekat Islam had now split, were sure that the intoxication with freedom had gone too far. Discipline was called for to reach specific goals, and the Party would define what they were.

Nevertheless the roots of this *rasa merdeka* ran deep. The most creative attempts to build a non-colonial, autonomous education system between the wars, those of Ki Hadjar Dewantoro and Tan Malaka, both put at the top of their agenda the development of a sense of personal freedom in their students. Tan Malaka's attempt was relatively short-lived, consumed in the communist rebellions of 1926–27 and the subsequent government crackdown on radicalism of all sorts. But Ki Hadjar Dewantoro founded a national education system which still endures and was an important intellectual influence on the whole nationalist movement. The aim of his schools, as he explained in opening the first one in 1922, was 'to develop our culture by planting the seeds of freedom in the hearts of the people, by using a system of education with a national character'.[57] Building on the educational ideas of Montessori and Tagore, he sought schools that were totally independent of government control. *Kemerdekaan* ('freedom' or 'independence') was the second of the five principles on which Taman Siswa based itself.[58] But like others on the more conservative side of the national movement, he increasingly stressed self-control and self-reliance as the true essence of liberty. In 1940 he defined merdeka a little differently: 'It is not the absence of authority, it is knowing how to control oneself.'[59]

If freedom began to be defined more cautiously after the upheavals of the mid-1920s, it was also increasingly harnessed to the purposes of nationalism. As controls tightened in the colony, it was to Indonesian students in Holland that radical nationalist leadership fell. In 1925 their organisation, the Perhimpunan Indonesia, launched a new journal, *Indonesia Merdeka*, and a new radical policy which declared the national liberation of Indonesia as the prime objective. Increasingly in the years that followed, nationalists linked the new word Indonesia to the old word merdeka, defining the latter above all as independence. The politically repressive policies pursued by colonial governments after 1926 tended to confirm the idea that this was the one freedom which had to be won before anything else could change.

This shift was encouraged during the Japanese Occupation of 1942–45. Nationalists such as Soekarno co-operated with the Japanese in the hope of achieving Indonesia Merdeka, and were finally rewarded in the last year of the Occupation. Facing one defeat after another in the Pacific, the Japanese promised independence in September 1944. The nationalists finally had something to show for the miseries of wartime life and seized the opportunity to build up expectations of independence. Other aspects of merdeka such as individual rights, however, were anathema to the Japanese military. Messianic expectations centred around the fact of independence itself, not its content. Ancient prophecies of King Joyoboyo were adapted to suggest that after ruling for three and a half years the Japanese would go and Indonesia would be free.

It was during the Indonesian revolution of 1945–49 that merdeka became a talisman, the key word of an aroused people. It happened quickly and spontaneously during the almost delirious days of September and October 1945, when the youth of Java and Sumatra realised that Japanese power had collapsed without any other regime taking its place. Merdeka suddenly became not just a political program but a felt reality. Crowds of people swarmed into the streets 'in response to the magic summons of Merdeka',[60] and nobody stopped them. The youth who mobilised first to confront the Japanese and then to fight the Dutch found themselves virtual masters of the cities in which they had lived. The *rasa merdeka* was theirs.

During this period merdeka became the battlecry with which the citizenry was summoned to support the cause, the salute with which revolutionaries would greet each other, the cry of solidarity at every mass rally, and the signature at the end of every Republican document. Newspapers, hotels, offices and city squares were renamed Merdeka.

In the fighting against the Dutch, radical youth groups were animated by the slogan 'freedom or death' (*merdeka atau mati*). One Australian correspondent who travelled with Soekarno through East Java in December 1945 noted that his train pulled up 'amidst a vast roar of "Merdekas" . . . [People thought it] a fine thing to have the privilege of shouting "Merdeka" . . . [and] speeches always ended with a triple "Merdeka" salute, thunderously returned by the crowd'.[61] Later in the difficult struggle for independence it may have become as routine as 'citoyen' did in the French Revolution, but during the first emotive year 1945–46 when the world was overturned, it was almost supernaturally powerful.

What did it mean to the revolutionaries? Certainly different things to different people. It began by meaning national independence, and the defence of the declaration of independence of 17 August 1945. For the leaders of the Republic this had to remain its primary reference, and all other freedoms should if necessary be sacrificed to that end. Yet there is no doubt that the people, and especially the young people who spontaneously supported the revolution and gave it momentum, experienced it as a freedom far more immediate and personal. For some urban youth the exhilaration of merdeka was felt when they discovered they could ride free on the trams and trains. For others it meant the escape from family and institutional authority to the new-found solidarity of revolutionary youth (*pemuda*). In some areas of Java's north coast where the 'social revolution' against local power-holders was particularly intense, the cry of 'Merdeka' by one revolutionary would be answered by another shouting its twin: *bebas* ('free' in the sense of 'unfettered'). As Anton Lucas described the memories of the hundreds of revolutionaries he interviewed, 'nothing should be too organized; each person was seeking his own freedom in the exhilaration of looking for new personal liberty, which in turn formed a new consciousness'.[62]

This freedom quickly got out of hand, and the more disciplined elements of what was slowly becoming a national army went to considerable lengths to suppress its more radical manifestations. The military ideologues of Soeharto's New Order government after 1966 sought to redefine the revolution as a struggle for independence, and the spontaneous social revolutions within it as outbreaks of counter-productive terror. Merdeka itself was increasingly defined in official texts and state rituals as simply independence – that which was proclaimed in August 1945 and ritually celebrated on every 17 August since. Yet its other connotations will not go away. The positive resonance of a merdeka that is opposed to slavery, oppression and control is rooted too deep in Indonesian history ever to be forgotten.

Notes

I acknowledge with gratitude the contribution of the late Abdurrahman Surjomihardjo to the conception of this chapter, and to M. C. Ricklefs, Helen Creese, Amrih Widodo and A. C. Milner for their contributions.

1 From a manuscript in K'tut Tantri's private papers, as cited in Timothy Lindsey, *The Romance of K'tut Tantri and Indonesia* (Kuala Lumpur: Oxford University Press, 1977), pp. 232–3.

2 David Brion Davis, *Slavery and Human Progress* (New York: Oxford University Press, 1984), p. 111.

3 Perry Anderson, *Passages from Antiquity to Feudalism* (London: Verso, 1978), pp. 1–23; M. I. Finley, 'Slavery', in *International Encyclopedia of the Social Sciences* (Crowell, Collier and Macmillan, 1968), p. 308.

4 E. S. Morgan, *American Slavery – American Freedom: The Ordeal of Colonial Virginia* (New York: Norton, 1975).

5 Orlando Patterson, *Freedom in the Making of Western Culture* (New York: Basic Books, 1991), pp. 9, 20, 41, 32.

6 Anthony Reid (ed.), *Slavery, Bondage and Dependency in Southeast Asia* (Brisbane: University of Queensland Press, 1983), p. 21.

7 I use the modern Indonesian and Malaysian word merdeka without italics as the general term, leaving variants in various languages of the Archipelago in italics.

8 P. J. Zoetmulder, *Old Javanese-English Dictionary* (The Hague: Nijhoff, 1982), p. 1086. Th. G. Th. Pigeaud, *Java in the Fourteenth Century. A Study in Cultural History* (The Hague: Nijhoff, 1960–63), vol. 3, p. 110; 4, p. 331.

9 K. R. Hall, 'State and Statecraft in Early Sri Vijaya', in *Explorations in Early Southeast Asian History: The Origins of Southeast Asian Statecraft* (Ann Arbor: University of Michigan Center for South and Southeast Asian Studies, 1976), pp. 71, 99.

10 Denys Lombard, *Le 'Spraeck ende Woord-boek' de Frederick de Houtman: Première méthode de malais parlé (fin du XVIe s.)* (Paris: EFEO, 1970), p. 215.

11 M. C. Ricklefs, *The Seen and Unseen Worlds in Java* (forthcoming). The 1847 *Javaansch-Nederduitsch Woordenboek* of Gericke and Roorda did not even derive *pardikan* from *Maharddhika*, but from *wartika* = proclamation. Later dictionaries always associated *pardikan* with *mardika*, and derived both from *Maharddhika*. I owe this information to Merle Ricklefs and Helen Creese.

12 The most famous *pardikan desa*, Tegalsari, was given this privileged status in 1742 in return for the spiritual assistance to the king of the holy mystic who lived there. Claude Guillot, 'Le rôle historique des *perdikan* ou villages francs: le cas de Tegalsari', *Archipel* 30 (1985), pp. 137–62.

13 John Crawfurd, *History of the Indian Archipelago*, (Edinburgh: Archibald Constable, 1820), vol. 3, p. 43.

14 Benedict Anderson, 'A Time of Darkness and a Time of Light: Transposition in early Indonesian Nationalist Thought', in *Perceptions of the Past in Southeast Asia*, ed. Anthony Reid and David Marr (Singapore: Heinemann, 1979), p. 245.

15 Cited by C. Fasseur, 'The French Scare: Taco Roorda and the Origins of Javanese Studies in the Netherlands', in *Looking in Odd Mirrors: The Java Sea*, V. J. H. Houben, H. M. J. Maier and W. van der Molen (eds) (Leiden: Vakgroep Talen en Culturen van Zuidoost Azië en Oceanië, 1992), pp. 249–50.

16 James L. Watson (ed.), *Asian and African Systems of Slavery* (Berkeley: University of California Press, 1980), pp. 9–13; Reid, *Slavery*, pp. 156–81.

17 Liaw Yock Fang, *Undang-undang Melaka. The laws of Melaka* (The Hague: Nijhoff for KITLV, 1976), pp. 74–76.

18 Ibid., p. 154.

19 *Adatrechtbundels*, vol. 17 (The Hague: Nijhoff, 1910–55), pp. 169–70.

20 *Adatrechtbundels*, vol. 9, p. 277; B. F. Matthes, *Boegineesch-Hollandsch Woordenboek* (1874), p. 260.

21 Derek Freeman, *Some Reflections on the Nature of Iban Society* (Canberra: Department of Anthropology, Australian National University, 1981), pp. 43–9.

22 Reid, *Slavery*, pp. 166–9; Reid, *Southeast Asia in the Age of Commerce*, vol. 1 (New Haven: Yale University Press, 1988–93), pp. 132–6.

23 William Collins, Besemah Concepts: A Study of the Culture of a People of South Sumatra, PhD, University of California, Berkeley, 1979, pp. 90–3.

24 Rombouts (1870), cited in ibid., pp. 93–4.

25 Gromberg (1865), cited in ibid., p. 94.

26 Reid, *Age of Commerce*, vol. 2, pp. 251–66.

27 Leonard Andaya, *The Heritage of Arung Palakka: A History of South Sulawesi (Celebes) in the Seventeenth Century* (The Hague: Nijhoff for KITLV, 1981), pp. 11–15.

28 Speelman, Notitie II, p. 117, cited in Reid, 'Kings, Kadis and Charisma in the Seventeenth Century Archipelago', in Anthony Reid (ed.), *The Making of an Islamic Political Discourse in Southeast Asia* (Melbourne: Monash University Centre for SE Asian Studies, 1993).

29 J. Noorduyn, 'Arung Singkang (1700–1765): How the Victory of Wadjo' Began', *Indonesia*, 13 (1972), p. 62; cf. Andaya, *Arung Palakka*, p. 111.

30 Andi Zainal Abidin, *Wajo' pada Abad XV–XVI. Suatu Penggalian Sejarah Terpendam Sulawesi Selatan dari Lontara* (Bandung: Penerbit Alumni, 1985), p.v. cf. ibid, p. 115; Christian Pelras, 'Hiérarchie et pouvoir traditionnel en pays Wajo', *Archipel*, 1 (1971), p. 174.

31 Zainal Abidin, *Wajo'*, p. 148.

32 Zainal Abidin, *Wajo'*, pp. 93–4, 122–4; J. Noorduyn, *Een achttiende-eeuwse kroniek van Wadjo': Buginese historiografie* (The Hague: Smits, 1955), p. 54; Pelras, 'Hiérarchie', pp. 170–4.

33 Zainal Abidin, *Wajo'*, pp. 135–6; cf. Pelras, 'Hiérarchie', p. 174.

34 Pelras, 'Hiérarchie', pp. 174–5.

35 R. Mundy, *Narrative of Events in Borneo and Celebes Down to the Occupation of Labuan. From the Journals of James Brooke, Esq. Rajah of Sarawak* (London, 1848), pp. 65–6.

36 Susan Abeyasekere, *Jakarta: A History* (Singapore: Oxford University Press, 1987), pp. 19–31; Leonard Blussé, *Strange Company: Chinese Settlers, Mestizo Women and the Dutch in VOC Batavia* (Dordrecht: Foris for KITLV, 1986), p. 165; Paramita Abdurrachman, Portuguese Presence in Jakarta, paper presented to the Sixth IAHA Conference, Yogyakarta, August 1974.

37 Reid, *Slavery*, pp. 29–30; Abeyasekere, *Jakarta*, pp. 19–65.

38 Reid, *Slavery*, pp. 30–1. The quotation is from John Anderson (1826).

39 My translation from the romanised text in *Hikajat Abdullah*, R. A. Datoek Besar and R. Roolvink (eds) (Jakarta: Djambatan, 1953), pp. 234–5. A full English translation is 'The Hikayat Abdullah', transl. A. H. Hill, *JMBRAS*, 28, 3 (1955), pp. 161–3.

40 *Hikajat Abdullah*, pp. 294–5; cf. Hill translation, p. 195.
41 Anthony Milner, *The Invention of Politics in Colonial Malaya: Contesting Nationalism and the Expansion of the Public Sphere* (Cambridge: Cambridge University Press, 1994), pp. 31, 82.
42 William Marsden, *A Dictionary and Grammar of the Malayan Language* (1812, reprinted Singapore: Oxford University Press, 1984), pp. 451, 482.
43 John Crawfurd, *Grammar and Dictionary of the Malay Language* (London, 1852), vol. 2, p. 113.
44 R. J. Wilkinson, *A Malay-English Dictionary (Romanised)* ([1903] reprinted London: Macmillan, 1959), p. 768.
45 Roorda van Eysinga, *Algemeen Nederduitsch-Maleisch Woordenboek* (Leiden: Gualph Kolff, 1853), pp. 1000–1. This pioneering dictionary was revised by Grashuis in 1878 without significant change to these terms, while Klinkert's more popular twentieth-century dictionaries also borrowed heavily from their predecessors.
46 '*Merdaheka* Skr., also pronounced as *merdika*, a spiritual leader or priest, who is freed from corvée obligations; free from slavery or service obligations' [my translation of the entry in its entirety], H. C. Klinkert, *Nieuw Maleisch-Nederlandsch Woordenboek*, 5th edn (Leiden: Brill, 1947), p. 975. The more subversive connotations of merdeka in the Straits Settlements than in Netherlands India in the nineteenth century, at least as suggested by these dictionaries, provides an interesting contrast to post-1957 Malaya/Malaysia, which was more successful than Indonesia in limiting the term to national independence.
47 Examples of the ideologies of these nineteenth-century struggles are Sartono Kartodirdjo, *The Peasants' Revolt of Banten in 1888. Its Conditions, Course and Sequel* (The Hague: Nijhoff for KITLV, 1966), esp. pp. 341–3; Ibrahim Alfian, *Perang di Jalan Allah: Perang Aceh 1873–1912* (Jakarta: Pustaka Sinar Harapan, 1987), pp. 105–50; Peter Carey, *Babad Dipanegara: An Account of the Outbreak of the Java War* (1825–30) (Kuala Lumpur: MBRAS, 1981), esp. pp. xxxix–xlvii.
48 Ruth T. McVey, *The Rise of Indonesian Communism* (Ithaca, NY: Cornell University Press, 1965), p. 176.
49 Takashi Shiraishi, *An Age in Motion: Popular Radicalism in Java, 1912–1926* (Ithaca, NY: Cornell University Press, 1990), p. 34
50 A. K. Pringgodigdo, *Sedjarah Pergerakan Rakjat Indonesia*, 1949, 5th edn (Jakarta: Pustaka Rakjat, 1964), p. 30.
51 Communist speaker in Sawah Lunto, West Sumatra, 1926, as translated by Ruth McVey, 'The Enchantment of the Revolution: History and Action in an Indonesian Communist Text', in Reid and Marr, *Perceptions*, p. 340.
52 'merasa merdika artinya merasa "selamat" dan' "ayem"': *Hikayat Kadirun*, p. 92. I owe this reference to Semaun's novel to Amrih Widodo, to whom I am grateful for other insights into Javanese rural ideas.
53 Shiraishi, *Age in Motion*, p. 246; Benedict Anderson, *Language and Power: Exploring Political Cultures in Indonesia* (Ithaca: Cornell University Press, 1990), pp. 235–7. These two authors attribute the 1924 novel *Rasa Merdika* to Soemantri, whereas earlier writers usually ascribed it to Mas Marco Kartodikromo, another SI/PKI journalist and politician; see A. Teeuw, *Modern Indonesian Literature* (The Hague: KITLV, 1967), p. 16.
54 Shiraishi, *Age in Motion*, p. 165.
55 Gati Semarang [pseud.], 'Kemerdeka'an' in *Rasa-Doenia* (Jogjakarta, 1923).

56 Cited Shiraishi, *Age in Motion*, pp. 324–5.
57 Quoted in *Pedoman Rakyat* (2 May 1981).
58 Kenji Tsuchiya, *Democracy and Leadership: The Rise of the Taman Siswa Movement in Indonesia* (Honolulu: University of Hawaii Press, 1987), esp. pp. 55–63.
59 Quoted in Denys Lombard, *Le carrefour javanais: Essai d'histoire globale*, 3 vols (Paris: EHESS, 1990), vol. 3, pp. 125, 185.
60 Benedict Anderson, *Java in a time of Revolution, Occupation and Resistance, 1944–1946* (Ithaca: Cornell University Press, 1972), p. 126.
61 Anton Lucas, *One Soul One Struggle: Region and Revolution in Indonesia* (Sydney: Allen & Unwin, 1991), p. 157.
62 Ibid., p. 158.

CHAPTER 8

Slavery and Modernity:
Freedom in the Making of Modern Siam

Thanet Aphornsuvan

Central to the modern idea of freedom in Siam was the discovery of slavery as an oppressive and un-Thai institution. Until the mid-nineteenth century, slavery was not viewed by the élite as opposite to freedom or even as an exploitative institution and practice. It was in the first two decades of the twentieth century, after the abolition of slavery and unequal treaties with foreign countries, and with the rise of official nationalism, that the modern idea of slavery (*thaat*) as the opposite to freedom (*thai*) was internalised.

During this social transformation, Western missionaries and other agents of influence disseminated the familiar narratives of progress and modernity, which the Thai élite accepted virtually without question. At all events, it was only with the inception of Thai ethnic nationalism (*chat thai*), around the time of the First World War, that words for freedom as a modern concept (*thai/seriphap*), were able to take root. These in turn could allow for the gradual accommodation of the ideas of slavery and freedom, influenced by modern (Western) sensibilities, referred to in Chapter 1 of this book. Hence it was only after the abolition of slavery (1905) and the rise of state nationalism that the concept of freedom as a social and political value for the common people emerged. The irony of this development is significant for the comparative enterprise of the present volume and deserves closer examination.

From Kingly Prerogatives to Citizen Rights

Freedom in the West has been posited as the antithesis of slavery. The origin and development of freedom were rooted deeply in the complexities of Western culture and political economy.[1] In Thailand, by contrast, the concept of freedom is not defined in opposition to other concepts but is subsumed under the idea of duty and rights as sanctioned by the power of the king. Freedom as sovereignty or autonomy carried the further implication of hierarchical privilege, exercised according to one's rank or status in a family, community or in the service of the king. The Thai word for liberty, *itsaraphap*, traditionally meant 'being great'.[2]

Thai social critics and academics have recently engaged in public criticisms of Western concepts of rights and freedom and argued for 'Thai' rights and dignity. These critics claim that liberal concepts of freedom and rights based on individual claims and interests are deficient and even detrimental to the common good and society itself. Such attacks are of course not new. Throughout the modern history of Southeast Asian countries, resistance to, and suppression of, individual freedom was the rule rather than the exception. In the origin and development in Southeast Asia of the modern idea of freedom, individual rights and political liberty came largely as a result of Western colonial expansion and influence.

Against a background of the rising hegemony of capitalism in the nineteenth century, slavery was perceived by westerners as a general and universal system throughout the world, while in fact it was not.[3] Recent studies of slavery and freedom in non-Western societies have shown that modern Western slavery, its origins, development and abolition, was exceptional, or particular. In non-Western societies, slavery was only one of many forms of servitude and in many cases had little of the far-reaching impact on the society's economy and politics that it had in the West. Furthermore, the idea of freedom as the antithesis of slavery and as universal human value has undergone changes in the Western and non-Western worlds. Interestingly, freedom, as a social value and an expression of the citizen's individual rights and personal liberty, was in non-Western countries not generated from the experience of slavery but ironically from the élite's political entanglements with colonialism.

In the case of Siam, there emerged a different kind of 'freedom' in the process of Thai social formation as a response and reaction to the impact of westernisation in the late nineteenth century. Rather than why and how 'freedom' in Siam failed to live up to the Western idea, my question is how did it originate? How was it reconstructed by the Thai élite in the process of modernising the traditional social system? For, in striving to define itself in relation to 'modernity', the élite placed in question the old social relations and hierarchical structure. In this context, and contrary to what happened in the West, freedom did not emerge as a byproduct of Thai slavery. Rather, as the Western perception of slavery as an uncivilised practice became known, it was reinterpreted as un-Thai or as against the Thai tradition. As a corollary, freedom was conceptualised as the essence of the Thai nation and race as an independent and sovereign state. Ultimately, Thai freedom was conceived to mean Thai-ness.

Traditionally, the practice of freedom in the Thai kingdom, from the Sukhothai (*c.*1325–50) to Ayudhya periods (1351–1767), was basically determined by the concept of power and authority of the king. *Sitthi* ('authority, right'), an old word in wide use since the dawn of Thai written history in the fourteenth century, was associated with the privilege and power of the king to rule over his subjects, deriving from his claim to protect and preserve order for the common good. In Sukhothai inscriptions *sitthi* means 'authority and success'.[4]

As the right to rule over subjects, and the successful execution of affairs of state, *sitthi* is thus an attribute of rulers rather than of commoners. Against the background of a political society aspiring to a harmonious, implicitly hierarchical social order, *sitthi* was incorporated in a broader language of rights. Rights, whether as idea or practice, are bound up with contestation between ruler and ruled to define the structure of power. In this process the changing concept of *sitthi* played an important mediating role: it allowed a transfer of some of the attributes of the sovereign to his subjects. Thus in the early Bangkok period (1782 to *c.*1868), the meaning of *sitthi* was gradually extended to include more of the rights of commoners. The *pra racha kamnod mai* (new royal decree) of King Rama I stipulated that *phrai* (common people) who had suffered hardships and were obliged to labour for the king could now be given one-third of the time to labour for their own sake, one-third to the master, and the last third to the king.[5] One of the important *sitthi* that *phrai* secured even in the Ayudhya period was the right to choose and change one's master. Other *sitthi* permitted them to have choices whether to pay a certain amount of money in lieu of going to labour for the king.[6]

Following the abolition of slavery and the end of corvée labour in the early twentieth century, this traditional notion of rights restricted to the king and the upper class was challenged by the growing labouring and bourgeois classes. The concept of *sitthi* was now appropriated by these emerging classes, who claimed them as their legitimate rights as citizens; such rights were as inherent to workers and common people as to the upper class. The 1932 coup, which ended the absolute monarchical regime and replaced it with constitutional monarchy, made this clearer. From now on, the new, popular political democracy would dominate Thai political discourse. However, the débâcles of democratic governments in Thai politics and the persistence of the élite cultural domination can be seen in the official meaning of the word. From the 1940s to the 1970s *sitthi* had been defined by the Royal Institute in the Thai official dictionary as, '*kwam sumret* (success), and *amnaj an chob tham* (legitimate power)'.[7] In the 1980s, with the coming of political liberalism and economic prosperity, the definition of *sitthi* was finally liberalised to include 'power to perform legally accepted things freely'.[8] *Sitthi* thus emerges as an important analogue of modern 'freedom' not by the transposition upwards of a slave value but by the extension downwards of sovereign privilege.

This traditional view of freedom and right as privileges of the ruler had persisted well into the Bangkok period (1782 to the present) and underwent major transformations starting in the middle of the nineteenth century when the kingdom confronted Western colonial penetration. The élite's discourse of freedom was, in effect, an appropriation of a modern value and practice that were lodged in the narrative of modernity and progress now so important to the élite's conception of itself in relation to the rest of the world. The new and foreign ideas thus became *old* and very *Thai* and, of course, contained within themselves many tensions and conflicting meanings.

Slaves and Free People

Traditional Thai social organisation was strictly based on hierarchical relations, with the king at the top of the social pyramid, followed by the royal family and the nobility forming the upper class or élite. The lower classes consisted of *phrai* (common people) and *thaat* or *dasa* (slaves; *thaat* is vernacular Thai and *dasa* the Pali equivalent). In Old Siam, slavery, within the *sakdina*[9] or corvée system, functioned as a social alternative for *phrai* who wanted to escape state obligations or dire personal straits.

The premodern Thai view of society as an organic whole imposed strictly prescribed roles of reciprocal obligation on both masters and servants. One derived one's social identity from these prescribed sets of relationships: first there were primordial relations with one's parents, spouse, friends, and kin, relations deemed 'natural' (or 'karmic' in reference to the Buddhistic notion of causation). But potentially the most meaningful social relation for a commoner was living under and maintaining 'good' relations with a master.[10] Thus in Thai society the individual person or the self is subordinated to society taken as a greater whole; a person is defined in terms of his or her vertical relations, that is, obligations and duties to others. The Thai concept of the 'social' does not begin with individuals, abstracting them into a totality (i.e. 'society'), but rather with the concrete *relations* operating between the members of the social order.

Furthermore Buddhism, the source of many of the categories which underlie this set of relations, alludes on the one hand to egalitarian notions, while it teaches, on the other, the impermanence of all things both natural and social. Under the law of karma individual existences are conditioned by their karma and merit accumulated in previous lives. To be free and attain happiness is not a social matter, but essentially an individual or existential one. The basic injunction is to eliminate one's own ego and greed, hatred and delusion so as to live harmoniously with nature and the world, and ultimately live happily and contented with oneself regardless of external conditions. Personal freedom on this interpretation is something inward, and as such antithetical to gaining control over and altering the world. Practically, for the common people, freedom from this world of suffering lies in performing one's duties as best as one can in one's given status, no matter how high or low.[11]

Under élite rule, such a social ethic tended to obscure and at times obstruct the introduction of legal status and social recognition for 'free' or 'independent' people, that is, people defined as independent of duties and obligations to others, and who thereby led an autonomous existence. In the premodern ethical view, people as individuals have duties and not rights. This is because the source of power and moral worth lies outside the individual. Theoretically all men are in essence heteronomous: obligated to external sources of power and value. Such a world-view does not give rise to or support the idea that man himself is the source of moral worth.[12] Humankind is understood from the angle of people in their relations with each other, not as individual persons.[13] In the sense of being entitled to live one's life and to deal with others without the need to answer to a superior, in the whole Thai kingdom only the king could be said to be 'free'.[14]

On the other hand, a religious creed like Buddhism was also a source of legitimation for rulers but provided a channel for spiritual freedom in the ruled. Unlike Christianity, which facilitates and encourages the development of freedom of the self, Buddhism teaches the opposite: freedom is realised through the negation of the self. The more one subdues one's own ego and the three poisons of lust, hatred, and delusion, the closer to freedom one will come. In this, Buddhist monks and religious leaders could be said to have 'power' and to enjoy quite a degree of 'freedom'. In Thai society, therefore, the source of rights and legitimacy comes from both external and internal forces. Crucial to the understanding of Thai freedom is the role of Buddhist thought, which creates grades of inequalities based on individuals' karma.

The dominant form of premodern Siam government and rule was codified into a system of social relations known as *sakdina*.[15] *Sakdina* comprehensively divided society into various categories and social

statuses. The majority of the population was the peasantry or *phrai*.
The *phrai* could be called on to perform involuntary labour for fixed
amounts of time. Initially, in the the Ayudhya period, they were subjected to such corvée labour for six months of the year; later, in the
Bangkok period, this was reduced to four months. At the bottom of the
sakdina system was *thaat* (here meaning 'slavery' as well as 'slave'), a
defined period of servitude which could in principle extend to one's
entire lifetime.

Bearing in mind the inefficiency and limited capacity of states like
that found in traditional Siam,[16] within the *sakdina* system both *phrai*
and *thaat* were categories considered to be within the state's control
(they stood in contrast to certain other peasant groups who were
outside the state's purview). The duties and rights of *phrai* and slaves,
comprising the commoners, were stipulated by laws and customs.
Unlike Western slave codes which dealt exclusively with slaves, the Thai
slave codes were part of the *thammasat*,[17] a form of legal code derived
from the Hindu *dharma-sastras* as restated by Mon legal specialists,
which governs *all* subjects of the land. According to the *Thai thammasat*
or the Three Seals Law, slaves were not outsiders, nor were they
an alienated or 'peculiar' element of the community as was the case
in American Negro slavery. There were no sharp colour or ethnic
distinctions between slaves and free persons.

Many other general formal elements characteristic of slavery in
general were, however, true of Thai slaves. They were, importantly, a
form of property,[18] and could be bought and sold at the whim of the
master. But there were a number of notable aspects that distinguish the
Thai from the Western case. Many Thais were enslaved 'temporarily'
according to the debt-bondage system, that is, until they repaid their
debt. Additionally, at least in the Bangkok period, slaves were not
outsiders, but came from within Thai society. Consequently there
also were many practices, customs and laws under which slaves were
recognised as humans rather than as chattels.

These facts, while in striking contrast to Western slavery, do little to
justify these practices. Slavery was an unenviable stigma placing the
bearer in the lowest level of society.[19] By implication, slave status
deserved scant respect or trust from other people. Since all relations
with others, including one's rights and duties, were strongly influenced by one's status, slavery was a dishonour to its bearer. But there
are some complications in the relative social rank and prestige of slave
and free commoners. The two groups were closely related: people
could change from one to the other quite readily. As well, the status
and prestige of *phrai* and *thaat* derived from their master's social rank.
In this case, a slave of a *somdet chaophraya* or a *chaofa* (prince) would no

doubt rank higher than the *phrai* of a minor official.[20] Status, in other words, did not in and of itself always define one's social relations. Likewise, slavery did not in and of itself always degrade or deprive one of one's rights in the community. It was simply that being at the bottom of a strictly hierarchical structure made one's life unworthy in the eyes of others. This negative evaluation attached to servitude would later provide a pivotal base in the rationalisation of the monarch's abolition laws.

The Monetary Value of Slaves

Another important variable, apart from status, was the slave's monetary value. Legal measures of the value of a person provided the main means of establishing this. In the *sakdina* system, the entire population was given a personal monetary value according to social rank, together with consideration of age and sex. While this practice may sound very capitalistic, its actual source was the old Thai Buddhist cosmography in which merit as well as status positions were quantified.[21] Ironically, it was only when Siam was about to embrace the free labour system – in which human labour is commodified – that the personal exchange-value would be abrogated. In the Ayudhya period the personal value of an adult male was given at 218 *baht* and 3 *salyng*.[22] Up till the reign of King Rama V in the late nineteenth century, the legal price of slaves was determined by different formulae in three categories of age:

1 male slaves from the first month to 3 months. The price began at 6 *baht* or *ticals*, then increased with age, from 4 months up to 25 years old;
2 slaves between 26 and 40 years. Their value was set at the highest or full price (56 *ticals*);
3 Between the ages of 41 and 90 the value gradually decreased till it reached the lowest level. This was set at 4 *ticals* for slaves aged between 91 and 100 years. There was a similar, slightly lower, scale of personal values for female slaves.[23]

Personal value was important in the commodity trade in humans, as the exchange-value of slaves and free men largely derived from it. But more critically, the personal value was taken as a basic measure by the state in accepting and deciding legal cases brought up by slaves and freemen. Though there were several types of slaves, in practice the slave codes dealt mainly with *redeemable* and *non-redeemable* slaves. Redeemable slaves were those who had been sold for less than their full personal value.[24] They were in general commoners who borrowed money from money masters, offering themselves or their family as collateral. Others in this category had been condemned to slavery by the state because of their crimes. There were also those who had lost cases in court and could not pay the fines. This group of slaves still possessed limited civil rights. But they could lose their rights absolutely if, as bonded people, they were sold again at a higher price to another master. This, according to the slave codes, was because the slave had become the absolute property of the master. The latter could exercise almost absolute rights over these slaves, including that of punishing (short of killing) them.[25]

Non-redeemable or absolute slaves, on the other hand, consisted of war captives, monastery slaves (*lek wad* or *kha phra*), and commoners who had sold themselves for their full personal value or more. This group had no civil rights. They could neither purchase their freedom nor change masters by letting another person purchase them. Finally, the offspring of absolute slaves were by law the property of their parents' masters. Slaves of this category more closely approximate Western chattel slaves. Even so, there were still further subdivisions regarding the rights of slaves over their children and other matters, by means of which the law determined (given the amount of money involved) the extent of the rights to which slaves would be entitled. As Terwiel puts it, 'in general the larger the sum borrowed the fewer rights an individual retained'.[26]

According to the Three Seals Law, slaves were deprived of many rights pertaining to themselves and their interests. Rights over their children provide a case in point. The offspring of slaves were the property of the parents' master. The bilateral principle of Thai kinship still determined rights over slave children, but a tendency towards a matrilocal system could be seen.[27] For example, if children were born to slave parents or to a slave mother but free father, the mother's master retained full right. If both were slaves, the children were divided between the masters of each parent, but the mother's master would get more share from this. Slaves were entitled to marry. However, the female slave needed the master's consent, while the male slave did not. Slaves could possess individual property and transmit it by inheritance. The special provisions in the laws and customs protecting both free and slave women no doubt reflect the importance attached to the reproductive role of women and the scarcity of male labour power.

As to access to law, slaves could not act as witnesses. Yet this stipulation also applied to persons in debt, because these people had already used up their personal value. In terms of legal procedure, slaves had similar access to courts and magistrates as free men. The difference was that most of these rights were conditional. For example, in order to take the master to court, the slave had first to pay the amount of his personal value unless the master had committed serious crimes such as robbing the state treasury, rebellion, or banditry. But if the court found that the master was not guilty, then the slave would be punished severely by being put on a three-legged wooden frame, with a sign on his forehead. Next he would be carried around the town while being compelled to shout out, 'Don't follow my example – I'm a villain caught trying to slander my master'. After caning with rattan and having his tongue cut out, the slave was finally sold off. If the master was found guilty, on the other hand, the slave would be rewarded with freedom.[28] It is easy to imagine the hesitation slaves would feel about taking their master to court.

Slavery had an important contractual aspect. Unlike the modern contract of sale, the old Thai contract, rather than a solely commercial relationship, represented a power relation between the master/giver and the slave/borrower. The contract included money *and* the physical person of the borrower, which was placed under the master's power. The master not only demanded the borrowed money but also the return at any time of his favour as 'gratitude'. While monetary debts were of fixed duration, 'gratitude' had no temporal limitation, but was a lifetime relation: a debt-slave may have paid off the debt-money, but the gratitude was never paid off. The Thai word for borrowing is *khu*, which means to save or redeem one's life. In borrowing money in traditional times, *khu* acquired the meaning of saving the life of another. The borrower, either free or slave, theoretically sacrificed his or her *itsaraphap* (liberty) over his or her body and came under the power of the master. Practically, the distinction between a free and slave Thai commoner in relation to those with power or money was not too significant. It was in virtue of these patriarchal social contracts that R. Lingat denied that Thai slaves were property of others or were people without freedom. He reasoned that most Thais lived under some kind of seigneurial power and lacked freedom anyway.[29] Physically, some fortunate slaves who lived in the big houses of wealthy and powerful nobility could enjoy more good food and clothing and security than *phrai* commoners. But this was a double-edged sword, because such slaves were also more vulnerable to abuse and, in time of political crisis, faced grave punishment from enemies of their master.

The sale of slaves did not depend solely on the free will of the parties. Independently of the wishes of each side, for example, a well-to-do man was obligated to save the life of a poor one even though he did not want to buy him as a slave. At the same time, many commoners, out of necessity rather than willingly, put themselves into slavery. From this it can be seen that the slave contract was not based solely on individual rights and interests but depended very much on the nature of the community and its social order. The slave contract of sale reflected social relations or obligations. It not only stipulated property relations but more importantly also the 'duty within a social order' which binds both parties to the best interest of the community.

For example, the dissolution of sale contract should not interfere with or disrupt the farming of either party. If a debt-slave wanted to pay back money owed to a master during the harvest season, the master was entitled to reject the payment; the slave could not bring the case to court. The justification in the slave law was that both sides had to observe the natural order of things first, that is, during the harvesting the priority was the rice. So other practices that might disrupt this order were deemed unjust.[30] Interestingly, this provision was repealed by King Mongkut in the mid-nineteenth century, allowing the slave to repay the borrowed money to the master at any time.

In general, life in Old Siam was insecure and harsh. Little legal and financial security was available from the state to commoners or even nobles. Freedom from other people, especially potential supporters and patrons, was not desirable or even imaginable. It was tantamount to suicide; one was looked upon as a *thuan* (raw, wild, untamed) person. A life without patrons or clients was thus scarcely a desirable one. Both patrons and clients needed each other's protection and support. That is why many *phrai* who had to labour six months for the state tried to get out of this hard work by becoming *thaat* or slaves or *phrai som*[31] under a local or provincial master. In time of war, many *phrai* escaped the hardships of conscription, seeking security for their families by turning themselves into slaves of wealthy patrons and lords. Historically, then, slavery was less desirable to the state than *phrai*. At times slavery put pressure on, and even disrupted, the *phrai* system which was the backbone of the kingdom's military strength and order and the basis of taxation.[32]

Legally, under the systems of corvée labour and slavery, there were only duties and no freedom for the people. But in practice *phrai* and slaves manipulated these systems to the benefit and survival of their families and village security and well-being. In so doing, both poor and slave managed to avoid, as much as possible, adhering to the works or duties assigned by the master which might be disadvantageous to them. Aspects of these systems which obstructed their freedom would be resisted and protested by making them unworkable and finally forcing a change or revision by the state. To achieve these goals, the people managed to exploit state power and its systems in various ways, for example by exchanging masters, resisting the labour duties, sheltering runaway slaves, and ultimately by becoming outlaws or rebels. Freedom was thus a result of both conflict and compromise between the ruling class and the people. So restricted and exploitative was the state system that the peasants learned about freedom from their efforts to strike back at it. Choosing one's master thus became one way of expressing one's freedom.[33] Paradoxically, though the system was based on vertical, hierarchical relations, people gained some freedom by using such personal relations as that between patron and client to protect their rights against the power of other masters and even the central state.

This is probably closer to an act of freedom of the individual, though it can certainly be interpreted as an act of passive resistance. Such freedom carried with it a totally opposite notion from the modern Western notion of individual freedom, which emphasises individual responsibility and burdens of self-perfection and self-determination. For the powerful and upper classes, freedom meant privilege, the right to do or not to do what they deemed beneficial and good for them and their world. For poor and lower classes, freedom meant opportunity to escape and deliver oneself, as far as possible, from the burden of the state's and master's services. Given these unequal social relations, freedom was hardly a social value to be cherished. On the contrary, it simply spelt a means for both the élite class and the people to gain (unequal) access to wealth and resources.

Freedom in premodern Thai social organisation thus involved relations set up between people seeking to fulfil their obligations to the state. Structures within a strictly hierarchical social order made the notion and practice of inequality much more significant and meaningful than freedom. In fact freedom in Siam was conditioned and shaped largely by the idea of inequality. While freedom tended to give rights and liberty to individuals, inequality would bring individuals back into the group and community. For commoners, freedom could well be expressed in their resistance to the state's duties and obligations. Freedom meant deliverance from all kinds of political and economic oppression under state power, from natural adversity and disasters, and from private worldly sufferings. Above all, the point and meaning of such freedom to the commoners lay in the realisation of collective goods – food, shelter, and security for their families and communities.

Slavery and Progress

The first moves towards the eventual abolition of slavery were made during the reign of King Mongkut (r. 1851–68), whose reign officially opened Siam to free trade with Western powers. By the mid-nineteenth century, as the kingdom came more and more under the world capitalist

system, slave relations were affected by urban commerce and manu-
facturing. The seven traditional classes of slaves – redeemable, born
slaves, slaves acquired by inheritance, by gift, by legal penalties, by
famine, and war captives – had become reduced into one major group
of debt or bond slaves.[34] Realising the threats and dominant positions
of the West, Siamese élites for the first time took foreigners' views and
reactions seriously. The missionaries' outlook on slavery as a sign of
backwardness and barbarism was a case in point. Mongkut displayed a
sensitivity to such attitudes when he publicly commanded his noble-
men and officials, together with rich merchants and other persons of
influence, not to beat up their servants and slaves in front of foreigners,
for this would have been regarded by Westerners as barbaric and uncivilised. Note that the king was not forbidding his nobility to beat
up their servants and slaves but only not to beat them up *in front of
foreigners*! Western colonisation thus affected Siam in a particular way
by imbuing the Siamese élite with a sense of shame about the visibility,
to Western eyes, of slavery in the kingdom.

An 'enlightened despot', Mongkut revoked and revised many old
laws to give more justice to his subjects. He revised the old law that
regarded women as buffaloes and men as human beings (*phuying pen
khwai, phuchai pen khon*), and made them both human (though not
equal). It is interesting to note that the social and moral worth that
Mongkut referred to was 'human beings', a new expression in the Thai
political lexicon. Himself a rigorous scholar of Buddhist thought,
Mongkut developed some nascent ideas of free will and autonomous
self. The emphasis was on the individual self instead of relying on
meta-human power or karma as traditionally conceived. Such an idea
represented a break with the old concept of power and authority in the
traditional Thai world, which emphasised the power of one over the
other. Emphasis on the individual self and free will implies one's power
or authority over oneself. The former signifies unlimited power of the
authority, the latter the subversion of that power. This contradiction
would become clearer and more political in the 1920s and subsequent
political changes.

On the eve of the new and forceful Western penetration in the nineteenth century, Siamese political thought was undergoing changes,
with emphasis, significantly, now placed on the concept of 'humanity'.
The concept became part of modern Siamese political thought as it
changed from the late eighteenth century as a result of the defeat and
destruction of the Ayudhya kingdom. Buddhism, also greatly revised
in the early Bangkok period, was an important component of this
humanitarianism. This new version of Buddhism, together with the
new political entanglements of this period, combined to promote

rationality in the interpretation of traditional social ideas as well as Buddhism itself.[35] Theory now held that a king, no longer divine as in the past, was a 'Great Elect', who followed certain precepts of just rule and abided by the ten kingly virtues (*thosapitrajatham*).[36]

Another factor was the recognition of law as a guarantor of right and justice to the subjects. Before the full impact and penetration of Western concepts of government and society, Siamese political thought had evolved from the contradictory bases of Hinduism and Theravada Buddhism into a more rational and pragmatic political outlook, emphasising reciprocal relationships in a hierarchical social order. That is why the concept of 'humanity' was gaining ground by the time of King Mongkut when the kingdom was confronted and threatened by Western power and knowledge.

The idea of humanity, however, did not imply freedom and equality among all men (and women), or justice for all people solely before the law. It was in fact grounded on a hierarchical idea of man and society and was shaped by the Buddhist idea of social organicism. Modern Siamese political concepts, developing this theme, emphasised that man and his world are guided and ultimately determined by nature and karma. Human nature is oriented towards the interest and preservation of the self: everyone always desires and wants more for one's self. Accordingly, man is not born 'free' for he or she is subject to the egoism and delusion incorporated in mankind's karma. The life of nature, therefore, is suffering because it is hemmed in by all things that are transient. Man needs religion and a king to control and mould his inner desires in order to avoid committing sinful deeds, which, according to the élite's belief, are inherent in the nature of the common people. Thus government and rulers are necessary and good for the people. This political tradition sees no division between the state and society; nor does it accept the existence of individuals as rational agents *per se*. Politically, it does not recognise the people outside the realm of the state, and individuals of themselves have no rightful place in the political community.

Emancipation: the Modernisation of Slavery

The abolition of slavery was also part of the historical struggle and transformation of Siam in the late nineteenth century. Returning from a trip to Europe, King Chulalongkorn realised that one of the criteria for 'progress' (*kwam charoen*) was doing away with signs and symbols of oppression. So he set up the Council of State in 1874 to advise him in matters of government in order to improve and make progress in the country. The first issue that the king asked the Council to consider was the plight of slaves in Siam. Even though the upper classes remained relatively united in favour of having slaves, they could not oppose the king's wish to move towards progress and modernisation.

King Chulalongkorn wisely argued for and adopted measures for the abolition of slavery from within the Thai political tradition and world-view. His initial plan for the abolition of slavery was unwelcome to both masters and slaves, who were afraid of losing the means of patronage from the master. But with his absolute authority he managed to solicit full support from the ministers and the newly appointed councillors of the state. Only then did the king, avoiding the public resentment that would have been attendant on outright repeal of the old unjust slave laws, resort to closing off legal loopholes of these laws.

First he studied the Three Seals Law and found the loopholes in the *Prom Sakdi* law. This set the value of slaves in such a manner that few could ever be emancipated, because of the high personal values deemed applicable over much of their life. The king repealed this, issuing a new law stipulating that the full price of a slave apply at 21 years of age. On reaching 21, the price of a slave would fall, thus making it unprofitable to hold slaves indefinitely. These measures offer an example of his remarkable ability to balance and exploit both the modern Western discourse and the 'old' constructed past of Thai knowledge and practice to suit the country's need. The royal call for an end to bondage labour and the slave status would thus prepare the way for the emergence of free labour and capital, new sources of living for people besides labouring in agriculture.[37]

The abolition of slavery in Chulalongkorn's reign meant terminating the conditions under which slaves in Thai society were able to reproduce themselves. Rather than directly and immediately abolishing slavery, his measures simply stopped its circulation and renewal. Redeemable or debt-slavery in particular was ended by revising the scale of slave children's monetary value. This was set by the expenses that a master had in raising children of his or her slaves. The king focused especially on the injustice imposed on the children simply by their birth to slave parents. With the freeing of these children, no person or groups could claim to have suffered a particular grievance.

The next crucial step was to prevent slave and free children from entering slavery again. The measures adopted here successfully exploited the way Thai slavery had gradually developed from debt-bondage. As we have seen, this kind of slavery took the form of a private transaction between a buyer and seller over a human body. Traditionally, parents could sell their children to money masters for a specified sum; their children were, literally, collateral – if they could pay the interest, the children did not have to stay with the master but remained with their parents. Thus debt-slaves who performed labour for masters did that as a payment of their interests. In this case the slave lived with the master and worked according to what his or her master commanded.

There were several proclamations putting an end to the institution of slavery in Siam, covering a period of thirty years. The first proclamation leading to legal emancipation was the 'Proclamation on Born Slaves' issued on 8 October 1874. The law required that creditors and money masters who had from one to ten slaves or who owned slave families must note particularly those who had been born in their house as slaves and record the year of their birth, particularly those who had been born in the year of the Dragon. The local judges had to write down this information on the back of the sale papers for every slave. The idea was to prevent those slave children born in the year of the Dragon from any future sale by registering their names with the judges.

Chulalongkorn's next step was to issue 'Laws Concerning the Limits of the Age of Servitude and Freedom'[38] in 1874. As we have seen, the old slave law put money value on slaves at all stages of their lives, so there was no time when there was not a legal value upon their persons. This was cruel and unjust. The subtext of this law was that slaves remained in bondage for life if they could not pay back their money-value in full. Chulalongkorn saw this point clearly when he announced that this law was unjust to the children of slaves. 'As the children who are born in slavery know nothing and saw nothing of the evils which their parents had perpetuated, in enforcing upon them slavery, for life, and the endurance of penalties and misery belonging properly to the parents, it is not right that such children should be slaves for life.'[39]

The laws concerning the limits of slaves and their children pointed out clearly the goal of legal abolition of slavery in Siam. It was designed to 'abolish the legal personal value of the children of slaves'. This was to make certain that slave children had no money-value up to a certain age, namely 21 years old. The thrust of the decree therefore was, rather than awarding personal freedom, to render them valueless as human commodities, hence their parents and the money masters found no benefit in transactions concerning them. After enforcing this law for thirty years, the king finally decreed the 'Abolition of Slavery Law' in 1905, terminating for good the slave status in the kingdom, and the practice of selling and buying people into slavery. Later, in 1908, the sale and purchase of people into slavery was considered a criminal act and punishable by laws like those against theft and offences on property.

In order to abolish slavery, and to prepare for free labour, the state had to devalue and finally destroy the personal money-value of the new generation of children. This value was called in Thai *kasian aayu*, meaning the compensation to cover expenses that the master paid to raise slave children.[40] Ironically, this generation of Siamese were to be free throughout their lives because they could no longer enslave themselves to money masters. But at the moment of legal freedom, they also were facing more state regulations and control, as well as the intervention of a market economy in their everyday lives. They would never know what personal value might have been fixed on them. From now on the market would decide.

In reality, the freed slaves were free not only from masters and protection but also from the ability to own any property and to work for themselves: there was no private property for them to own since land was still largely Crown property and social life was still structured in a rigid hierarchy. Note that the first land-title code was established in 1905, the year of the legal abolition of slavery. The absence of absolute ownership on land prevented Thai peasants from becoming propertied individuals in the modern sense. The freed slaves thus went straight from one form of exchange-value in the *sakdina* system into another form of commodity in an increasingly market-dominated economy.

The paradox of the Thai abolition of slavery, therefore, was seen clearly in many of the complaints, not from the masters, but, emotionally, from commoners. For them, the end of 'freedom to sell' children or wives spelt poverty and starvation for the family as a whole. For those poor families, the end of slavery ended as well a flow of extra income from the master. In particular, the families whose children were born in the year of the Dragon, the year of the abolition, would be trapped in poverty until they died, because they could get financial help from no one. They lamented that children of the poor would always be poor all their lives because nobody would trust and lend money to them in lieu of personal mortgage.[41] In years to come, the road to freedom as against serfdom/slavery would scarcely be a bright and promising one to commoners. It should not therefore be less surprising to find that after years of Third World industrialisation, the use of oneself or children, in addition to their labour, as a basis for money income should not yet have been totally extinguished. Child slavery and involuntary labour have in modified forms survived from the abolition of slavery right up to the 1990s.

Freedom and Slavery

Intellectual reflection on slavery was initiated and elaborated by Prince Damrong, the 'Father of Thai History', at the request of King Chulalongkorn during the launching of the reforms in 1890. Only then did it become a major political issue for the government and élite in Old Siam, leading to new thinking.

Prince Damrong's writing on slavery is still unsurpassed in depth and breadth. One of the king's most able brothers, Damrong was one of several royal brothers to hold ministerial posts in the reformed absolutist government; the knowledge and administrative skills of these men were instrumental in the construction of the first modern Thai nation-state along Western lines. Damrong made particular contributions in the field of history. Disengaging from traditional Thai historiography, which took the form of chronicle and Buddhist tales, he prepared the way for a modern historical narrative of the nation, drawing on historicist and positivist influences.[42]

Damrong's writings were important in constructing a narrative of progress for the emerging Thai national community which attempted to explain the traditional Thai society in the light of modern ideas. Contradictory impulses can be observed in this process: on the one hand, by situating Thai slavery in a comparative, historical context, Damrong sought to rationalise it. On the other hand, he also argued that slavery was in its origin and in its essence very 'un-Thai'. The competing tendencies within Damrong's thought reflect the juncture at which he wrote in Thai history. Conscious of Westerners' scrutiny, Damrong sought to make Thai slavery comprehensible in their terms. At the same time he was articulating a proto-nationalist stance, a position which in its full flowering would maintain that Thai-ness was the opposite of slavery; and therefore slavery *could not be Thai*.

His arguments to this effect drew significantly on the *thammasat*, the ancient Thai law derived from the Mons and Indians, on Buddhist texts and on English sources. He pointed out that *thaat* (*dasa* in Pali) was equivalent to the word 'slave' in English and *servitus* or *servus* in Latin, which he glossed as *kheekha* (the servile), that is, persons who are property or belong to other people's will. The master has power over the slave, such that the latter may be treated as he (the master) wills. Significantly, Damrong stressed that because of changes in the practice of slavery these definitions were harsher than the reality undergone by latter-day slaves. It is worth noting that in this article he used the term *tai* for free.[43] By contrasting *thaat* and *tai*, he effectively made a temporal dimension in Thai history in which slavery belonged to the past and existed as a result of Khmer influence on the Ayudhya kingdom. In contrast, the modern Thai nation (still known at that time as Siam) was independent from others' domination, which essentially made Thai people free. The notion of *thaat* (slave) thus was imbued with colonial subordination.

Assertion of the un-Thai-ness of slavery is, as noted, the critical step here. The term *Thai* begins to be synonymous with 'free(dom)'. As an erudite man, Damrong applied the history of slavery elsewhere in the world to explain Thai slavery. Slavery served as a benchmark in his effort to identify what 'modernity' should mean for Thais. Thus the image and existence of slavery in Thai society was seen not simply as negating the freedom of people as individuals but more abstractly, as symbolic of backward and uncivilised institutions impeding the progress of the nation. For the first time, Damrong argued that slavery had originally been borrowed from the Khmer empire in the early Ayudhya period, along with other Indianised institutions. It did *not* originate in the Thai kingdom and society because, he explained, 'there was no such thing as slavery in the old Thai tradition'. Later Thais who moved to the south began to practise slavery according to the Khmer custom. Even then, King U-Thong, the founder of Ayudhya, did not send back runaway slaves from Sukhothai according to the request of the northern masters. Hence King U-Thong called freed slaves *tai*: 'originally in the Thai race (*chon chat thai*) there was no place for slavery'.[44] The basic form of servitude among Thai people after the Sukhothai kingdom was the status of 'servant' (*kha*). This was defined more by paternal relations than by labour exploitation or human property. Even when slavery later came into general practice in Siam, it was ameliorated by Thai paternalism and theravada Buddhism.

This attitude to slavery is still prevalent in Thai society and among Thai historians. The invention of a gentle Thai slavery, the Prince argued, was to prove one of the unique characteristics of the Thai race, which also included a love of national independence, toleration and the power to assimilate.[45] The most important contribution of Damrong's discourse on Thai history in general and on slavery in particular was in laying the groundwork for the coming of Thai nationalism. This would indeed draw powerful ideological sustenance from, among other sources, the abolition of slavery by the early twentieth century. Damrong's historiography would serve as a model for later élite discourse on Thai history and government. On the one hand, the élite would not object to the claims of Western systems of knowledge and practice to represent progress and modernity. On the other, they would also argue that Thai society had a long history of freedom and independence, that Thais were exceptional and must continue their special culture.

This 'Thai-ness' of the élite was criticised strongly by Jitr Phumisak, a radical intellectual, in the late 1950s. Jitr took an opposite stand on the issue of slavery and Thai-ness, arguing that the kingdom from the early period was a slave society, which then evolved the *sakdina* social formation. Jitr clearly borrowed Marxist historiography to attack Prince Damrong's discourse. Interestingly, though, he mimicked the élite's use of Western ideas to defend their privileged institutions. Like the élites before him, Jitr appropriated Western knowledge for political purposes. But this time he turned upside down the old methods and arguments of Thai particularity and Thai-ness. In effect, Thai élites took 'universal' principles (generally of Western origin) to argue for Thai particularity; they thereby underscored their roles as interpreters and mediators of what 'Thai' was and should be. They, the élite, reserved for themselves the right to 'know' which of the new ideas were appropriate for Thailand. Jitr, on the other hand, universalised Thai-ness, forcing comparative frameworks on hitherto sacrosanct particularities of Thai history and society, most particularly equating *sakdina* with feudalism. Positing that Thai slavery conformed to slavery in general, Jitr defined it as essentially a system of class exploitation and struggle.[46]

Not until the last decade of the nineteenth century did Siamese élites and the growing middle class begin to see slavery as an institution and practice which stood against freedom or liberty in some sense. There were good reasons for them to do so at the time. Siam was under pressure to transform its legal system into a modern one in order to renegotiate for an equal treaty with Western powers. In the first two decades of the twentieth century, Siamese élites, therefore, were busy translating and inventing Thai words from Western law and political concepts into Thai political discourse and practice. The struggle to gain more equal and just relations with the Western powers and Japan thus taught an understanding of freedom from foreign domination and coercion.

The transformation of the old into the modern lexicon was a complex process. For example, by the early twentieth century the term *itsaraphap*, originally meaning 'having power and authority', became, somewhat like the English 'sovereign', an attribute of the nation, the antithesis of colonised status. *Itsaraphap* was used extensively by the royal Thai governments after the signing of the unequal treaties with Western nations in the 1850s in which the issue of extra-territorial rights arose. During the struggle to be free from these unequal relations, Siamese ruling élites adopted the modern idea of rights and liberty of the nation as an independent state and incorporated it into the old word *itsaraphap*.

For the common people, the increasing free-trade and market system, particularly print-capitalism, expanded their world-view and, importantly, allowed them more opportunities to be able to assert themselves and indirectly involve themselves in *kan pokkhrong* (affairs of state), which had been the exclusive domain of the élite for so long. Note that at that time the term *kan muang* ('politics') had not yet been invented. The dominant aspect of the idea of freedom in Siam, when it was used in political discourse, was the persistence of the old and traditional ideas in favour of the state's rights and privilege.

In dealing with Western colonialism, the Jakkri (or Bangkok) kings, Rama IV (r.1851–68), Rama V (1868–1910), and Rama VI (1910–25), discovered, to their advantage, that the Thai language was an important means of withstanding the Western encroachment and a vital way to the formation of a new national community.[47] For the Jakkri élite the political potential of Thai language modernisation was on a par with the creation of the modern bureaucracy, government and legal system.[48] The national Thai language proved to be a sign and symbol of social and political distinction. It restored and assured the Thai ruling group's sense of integrity, power and authority, and even the formation of their class consciousness.

Furthermore printing, introduced and operated by Western missionaries, began to open wider circles of people to modernity's influence. For the first time, people other than the court could also 'own' and use the written language. The court therefore tried to control the new development of communication within its power and authority by creating the precise 'royal' standard of the language, thereby regulating and limiting its popular use.[49] All of these kings were very conscious in prescribing linguistic usage, including its orthography, semantic content, and its precise use in translating Western languages – especially English – into a canonical, central Thai language. In this realm of cultural modernisation, the Thai élite was borrowing, translating, and modifying words and their meanings as they saw fit. With the growth of print-capitalism in the country, especially in the late nineteenth and early twentieth centuries, the court could not, of course, remain the only institution to shape and build the nation's intellectual development. In fact its rivals – courtiers and other members of the urban literati – were also disseminating their own interpretations of what politics and a modern form of government ought to be.[50]

Until the First World War, there was no Thai word for 'freedom' in the modern (Western) sense except the word *tai*, which originally referred to Thai ethnicity. *Tai* has been used since the Sukhothai period in the twelfth century for a category of subjects who were not slaves; it was later promoted as the ethnic name of the Thai people and of the nation. Originally *tai* meant human being or humankind, so that many groups of people living in mainland Southeast Asia called themselves Tai-Dam, Tai-Dang, Tai-Yai, Tai-Noi, etc. In the Sukhothai inscriptions, the word *tai* referred to non-slave subjects but not free men, for they were still servants of the king. Towards the end of the nineteenth century *tai* became increasingly synonymous with 'free' in the modern sense.

In 1882 Prince Phichitpreechakorn, the elder brother of both Chulalongkorn and Damrong, in his play *I-Nao*, also used a concept of freedom characteristic of *farang* (Europeans).[51] The current Thai word for freedom – *seriphap* – appears for the first time as late as 1918, in the *Samutsan* magazine created by King Vajiravudh (r.1910–25) for the Royal Navy Club. King Rama VI had coined the word. He was one among the first generation of Siamese royal élites to study in Europe as a preparation for returning to rule the new and modernising Siam in its most 'civilised' form of government, the modern absolute monarchy. The word *seriphap* appeared in an article '*Seriphap hang tale*' (Freedom of the Seas).[52] King Vajiravudh concluded in his article that he did not agree with Germany's concept of freedom of the seas. Consequently he led Siam to side with the Allied Powers in the First World War.[53]

While Vajiravudh translated 'freedom' as *seriphap*, Prince Chantaburi, another of the linguistically aware élite, disagreed with his usage, arguing that in the original Pali, *seri* meant 'self-will, or independence'.[54] It had in addition a derogatory connotation similar to that of the English word 'licence'. However, Prince Devawong and the Supreme Patriarch were in favour of *seriphap*. Devawong, a senior minister of foreign affairs, supported Vajiravudh's *seriphap* by citing the use of the word *seri* by King Mongkut in the royal name given to Prince Narathipprapanpong. A word given by the linguistically alert King Mongkut could hardly have unsavoury implications. Actually it meant to let the prince be free (*itsara*) by himself, or self-reliance.[55]

At stake here were old and new concepts of power and freedom. *Itsaraphap* emphasises one's power over another, while *seri* implies one's power or authority over oneself. The former signifies unlimited scope of authority, the latter the limitation (in a sense, the subversion) of such authority.

But the significant transformation of the idea of modern freedom was the construction of freedom as Thai-ness. King Vajiravudh formulated his idea of Thai nationalism in a series of bitter debates with the urban intelligentsia about the meanings of of the concept.[56] Basing his official nationalism on a trinity of 'Nation, Religion and King', Vajiravudh argued that the existence and durability of the nation depended on the monarchy and the Buddhist religion. Buddhism was the guiding moral principle which every Thai must follow both in thought and practice. At the same time the monarchy was the defender of the Buddhist religion. These two crucial institutions would imbue and preserve the quality of Thai-ness in Thai citizens, which ultimately created and strengthened the Thai nation. The king also emphasised that the word *Thai* had a dual meaning. One was 'free'; another referred to the ethnicity of a people whose military capability and social cohesion had kept them a 'free' (sovereign, independent) people throughout their long history. This people later formed a political unit called the Thai nation. Gradually but strongly, the idea of free(dom) merged into, and was subsumed under, the concept of ethnic nationalism. Thus Thai means free and Thailand is the land of the free or independent nation.

The modern idea of freedom in Siam is essentially a construction of the royal élite in the era of modernisation or westernisation of Siam from the middle of the nineteenth century to the early twentieth century. In order to avert colonisation by Western powers, Siamese élites consciously constructed new systems of knowledge using Western models, but still based on their own past and tradition. The prospect of colonisation in Asia drove home to the royal élite a core sense of independence and freedom from domination by foreign powers. For colonisation appeared to them precisely as slavery – spelling not only loss of freedom of the Thai nation *per se* but, in a deeper sense, loss of their *itsaraphap* or sovereign power over their subjects.

For the Thai élite, freedom did not also mean the recognition of individual rights and rightful space for personhood in a society. On the contrary, freedom was conceptualised and formulated to be the essence of the Thai nation and race as an independent and sovereign state. Ultimately, Thai freedom was conceived to mean Thai-ness. The reinvention of 'slavery' and 'freedom' therefore provided solid ground for the coming of state nationalism and subsequently the strong nationalist policies of the later Thai governments. Of all these inventions and constructions of the idea of freedom, one thing is missing or obliterated: a notion of freedom as a positive social value for the common people.

Notes

The official name of the country in English was Siam until it was changed to Thailand in 1939. 'Siam' is therefore used in this chapter, while 'Thai' is used as the adjective for language, culture and people, though not for the state.

1 Orlando Patterson, *Freedom in the Making of Western Culture* (New York: Basic Books, 1991); see Chapter 1 of this volume.

2 *Itsaraphap* has been used at least since the Ayudhya Kingdòm (1351–1767). In *Kotmai tra sam duang* [The Three Seals Law], Article 1 of the law on slavery stipulates that fathers and masters, because they possess *itsaraphap*, are entitled to sell their children, wives or slaves. The present *Thai Dictionary* authorised by the Royal Institute defines *itsaraphab* as 'greatness in oneself; independence, not being subject to any one; being *thai*'. See *Potchanajukrom thai chaabab rajabandhityasathan* [Thai Dictionary Edition Royal Institute] (Bangkok, 1950; reprinted 1976), p. 1031.

3 Ironies of the British 'discovery' of slavery in India have been noted by Gyan Prakash. Finding slavery contrary to their post-Enlightenment legacy, they abolished it in 1843. 'In fact, what the British actually did',

he writes, 'although they were unaware of it, was to abolish their own creations.' See 'Terms of Servitude: The Colonial Discourse on Slavery and Bondage in India', in Martin A. Klein (ed.), *Breaking the Chains: Slavery, Bondage, and Emancipation in Modern Africa and Asia* (Wisconsin: University of Wisconsin Press, 1993), p. 131

4 See Yoneo Ishii, *A Glossarial Index of the Sukhothai Inscriptions* (Kyoto: Centre for Southeast Asian Studies, Kyoto University, 1972).

5 *Pramuan kotmai ratchakarn tee nung* [Collected Laws of Rama I] (hereafter referred to as *Kotmai tra sam duang* [The Three Seals Law]) (Bangkok: Ruenkaew Press, 1986), vol. 3, pp. 321–2.

6 See Akin Rabibhadana, *The Organization of Thai Society in the Early Bangkok Period, 1782–1873*, Southeast Asia Program Data Paper No. 74 (Ithaca, NY: Cornell University, 1969).

7 See *Potjananukrom Chabab Rajabanthitsathan* [Thai Dictionary Edition Royal Institute] (Bangkok, 1940, reprinted 1976), p. 912.

8 *Potjananukrom Chabab Rajabanthitsathan* [Thai Dictionary Edition Royal Institute] (Bangkok, 1982), p. 838.

9 *Sakdina*, literally 'power of the rice-fields', is defined as 'ruling power over the land' in the official *Thai Dictionary*. Since the Second World War, this word has been a source of heated political debates between the Left and Right in Thai society. See the meticulous and incisive discussion of the discourse of *sakdina* in Craig J. Reynolds, *Thai Radical Discourse: The Real Face of Thai Feudalism Today* (Ithaca, NY: Cornell University Press, 1987), Ch. 3.

10 Sombat Chantornwong, *Lokatasna sunthornphu* [Sunthornphu's World-View] (Bangkok: Matichon Press, 1994), p. 59.

11 See Chapter 2 in this volume. Other useful interpretations of Buddhist ideas of freedom include Bhikkhu P. A. Payutto, *A Buddhist Solution for the Twenty-First Century* (Bangkok: Sahadhamic Co. Ltd, 1993); Saneh Chamarik, 'Human Rights and Buddhism', in *Democracy and Development: A Cultural Perspective* (Bangkok: Local Development Institute, 1993).

12 For a detailed discussion and insight into Thai hierarchy and the application of the concept of patron–client see Barend J. Terwiel, 'Formal structure and informal rules: an historical perspective on hierarchy, bondage and the patron-client relationship' in Han Brummelhuis and Jeremy Kemp (eds), *Strategies and Structures in Thai Society* (Amsterdam: Anthropological-Sociological Centre, University of Amsterdam, 1984), pp. 19–38.

13 John Charvet, *A Critique of Freedom and Equality* (Cambridge: Cambridge University Press, 1981), p. 2.

14 Cf. Hegel's famous dictum that 'the Orientals knew only that one is free, the Greeks and Romans that some are free, while we know that all men absolutely, that is, as men, are free . . .' In thus apportioning degrees of freedom, Hegel of course conceived of it as *consciousness of the self*: G. W. F. Hegel, *Reason in History*, transl. Robert S. Hartman (New York: The Library of Liberal Arts, 1953), p. 24.

15 For more details see Akin Rabibhadana, *The Organization of Thai Society*.

16 See Chapter 3 in this volume, as well as Scott's *Weapons of the Weak: Everyday Forms of Peasant Resistance* (New Haven and London: Yale University Press, 1985).

17 For history of the Thai *thammasat*, see Yoneo Ishii, 'The Thai Thammasat', in M. B. Hooker (ed.), *Laws of South-East Asia* (Oxford: Oxford University Press, 1986); R. Lingat, 'Evolution of the Conception of Law in Burma and Siam', *Journal of Siam Society*, 38, 1 (1950). For the recent studies of the

thammasat, see Nai Pan Hla, transl., with Ryuji Okudaira, *Eleven Mon Dhammasat Texts* (Tokyo: Centre for East Asian Cultural Studies for Unesco, 1992).

18 Barry Hindess and Paul Hirst, *Pre-Capitalist Modes of Production* (London: Routledge & Kegan Paul, 1975), p. 113.

19 See also Thanet Aphornsuvan, 'Rabob that kab amnaj karnmuang nai prawatsat sangkom thai' [Slavery and Political Power in Thai Social History], in *Thai Khadi Suksa: Ruam botkwam pua sadang mutitachit kae pan-ek ying khun nion snidwong na ayudhya* [Essays in Gratitude to Col. Khun Neon Snidwong na Ayudhya] (Bangkok, 1990).

20 Akin Rabibhadana, 'Clientship and Class Structure in the Early Bangkok Period', in G. William Skinner and A. Thomas Kirsch (eds), *Change and Persistence in Thai Society* (Ithaca, NY: Cornell University Press, 1975), p. 106. See also Orlando Patterson, *Slavery and Social Death: A Comparative Study* (Cambridge, Mass.: Harvard University Press, 1982), where he shows that slaves in the Middle East could have great wealth and status.

21 Craig Reynolds, 'Buddhist Cosmography in Thai History with Special Reference to Nineteenth Century Culture Change', *Journal of Asian Studies*, 35, 2 (February 1976), p. 205.

22 *Kotmai tra sam duang* [The Three Seals Law], vol. 2, p. 312.

23 *Phra rajabanyat pikad kasian ayu luk that luk thai* [Laws Concerning the Limits of the Age of the Children of Slaves and of Free People, 1874] in *Kotmai laksana thaat* [Siamese Domestic Institutions, Old and New Laws on Slavery], transl. Samuel J. Smith (Bangkok: S. J. Smith's Office, 1880), p. 91. In northern Thailand women tended to be valued higher than men; this, however, applied more to free men than to slaves.

24 Andrew Turton, 'The Thai Institution of Slavery', in J. L. Watson (ed.), *Asian and African Systems of Slavery* (Oxford: Basil Blackwell, 1980), p. 271.

25 Phra aijakaan thaat, *kotmai tra sam duang* [The Three Seals Law], vol. 2, p. 312, quoted in Terwiel, 'Formal structures and informal rules', p. 29.

26 Ibid., p. 29; Turton, 'The Thai Institution of Slavery', p. 268.

27 See Craig J. Reynolds, 'Predicaments of modern Thai history', *South East Asia Research*, 2, 1 (March 1994), pp. 64–90.

28 Phra aijaakaan rubfong, *Kotmai tra sam duang* [The Three Seals Law], Art. 12; the same stipulation is also in Phra aijakaan thaat, Art. 90.

29 R. Lingat, *Prawatisat kodmai thai* [History of Thai Laws], vol. 2, (Bangkok: Foundation for Promotion of Social Sciences and Humanities Textbooks Project, 1983), p. 169.

30 Laksana thaat, Article 16, *kotmai tra sam duang* [The Three Seals Law], p. 81.

31 Another category of *phrai* in the *sakdina* system which belongs to the local masters instead of the king.

32 Akin Rabibhadana has contributed greatly to this understanding. See his *The Organization of Thai Society*.

33 See Akin Rabibhadana, *The Organization of Thai Society*; and Sombat Chantornvong, *Lokatasna sunthornphu*, p. 60.

34 See Seksan Prasertkul, The Transformation of the Thai State and Economic Change (1855–1945), PhD, Cornell University, 1989, pp. 50–1.

35 See the discussion of intellectual changes in the early Bangkok period in Nidhi Aeusrivongse, *Pakkai lae bairua* [Pen and Sail] (Bangkok: Amarin Printing, 1983); and Saichol Wannarat, Buddhism and Political Thought in the Reign of Rama I (1782–1809), Masters thesis, Chulalongkorn University, 1982.

36 David Engel, *Law and Kingship in Thailand During the Reign of King Chulalongkorn*, Papers on South and Southeast Asia, No. 9 (Michigan: University of Michigan, Center for South and Southeast Asian Studies, 1975), p. 4.

37 For an economic point of view on the abolition, see David Feeny, 'The Demise of Corvee and Slavery in Thailand', in Klein, *Breaking the Chains*, pp. 83–111.

38 It is interesting to note that Dr Samuel J. Smith, an American missionary who translated the Thai slave laws and royal proclamations concerning the abolition of slavery into English, had made Chulalongkorn's languages sound like Western abolitionists whose aim was clearly freedom for individuals from slavery as an institution. Smith translated the word *tai* as 'freedom'. Thus 'the law concerning the limits of the age of servitude and *freedom*'. In Thai it was the Law concerning the Limits of the Age of slave and free children [*kasian aayu 'luk that luk tai*']. It had nothing to do with 'freedom' of the slaves in a Western liberal sense at all. Ironically, the word *kasian* has later acquired the meaning of retirement for government officials. Therefore the first group of Thais who 'retired' from government control was slave children.

39 'The Laws Concerning the Limits of the Ages of Servitude and Freedom' in Samuel J. Smith, transl., *Kotmai laksana thaat*, p. 56.

40 Prince Damrongrajanuphap, Letter to Phya Anumanrajathon, 21 June B.E. 2482 (1939), *Ruang lerk that nai samai rajakarn ti ha* [Abolition of slavery in the Fifth Reign] (Bangkok, 1942), p. 27.

41 *Chotmaihet Sayamsmai*, No. 2, CS 1245 (B.E. 2426), p. 72. There was an interesting letter from one Ai Chin-Sud to the editor of *Sayam Samai* to complain about his imminent suffering resulting from the new anti-slavery law. Without selling his daughter, the father could not get the financial support and help from other well to do people because they did not trust him without the personal mortgage.

42 See Charnvit Kasetsiri, 'Pratya prawatisat thai' [Thai Philosophy of History], in Charnvit Kasetsiri and Suchart Sawadsri (eds), *Pratya prawatisat* [Philosophy of History] (Bangkok: Social Science and Humanities Textbooks Project Foundation, 1984), pp. 210–11.

43 Prince Damrongrajanuphap, 'Thatkhatha', part I, *Wachirayanvises*, no. 5, R.S. 109 (B.E. 2433), reprinted in Anumanrajathon (ed.), *Ruang lerk that nai ratchakarntiha* [On the Abolition of Slavery in the Reign of Rama V] (Bangkok: Bamrungnukulkit Press, 1956), pp. 4–6. Both in Thai words (italicised) and English usage (capitalised) I am using the word *tai* for ethnicity broader than Siamese borders, while Thai refers to the country. The pronunciations are identical.

44 Prince Damrong, *Laksana kan pokkrong prathed sayam tae boran* [Nature of Rule in Siam from Ancient Times] (Bangkok: Thammasat University Press, 1975, original lecture was in 1927), p. 11.

45 Ibid., p. 6.

46 See more details in Reynolds, *Thai Radical Discourse*. The counterattack on Jitr's *The Real Face of Thai Feudalism Today* can be seen in M. R. Kukrit Pramoj's *Farang Sakdina* [Western Feudalism] (Bangkok, 1961).

47 These three kings were greatly concerned with the written Thai language as the essence of their authority. In a penetrating article, Anthony Diller shows that before substantial Western cultural contact beginning in the middle of the nineteenth century, the Thai language had developed

differentiated registers. See Anthony Diller, '"Thai Syntax" and "National Grammar"', *Language Sciences*, 10, 2 (1988), p. 293.

48 As Engel has shown, the legal transformation in the Chulalongkorn reformation was no less important than the political, economic and educational ones. It was indeed crucial to the success of the other reforms. See David Engel, *Code and Custom in a Thai Provincial Court* (Tucson, Ariz.: University of Arizona Press, 1978).

49 Correspondence with Nidhi Aeusrivongse, 20 June 1993.

50 Matthew Phillip Copeland, Contested Nationalism and the 1932 Overthrow of the Absolute Monarchy in Siam, PhD, Australian National University, 1993, p. 210.

51 In his version of I-Nao, which was adapted from a Javanese story, Prince Phichit created four comic characters, all Siamese citizens, interestingly consisting of a Thai, a Chinese, a Laotian, and the last one, a *farang* or westerner. They were commenting on social questions, while waiting to see Prince I-Nao come into the city. The last comment was on happiness. The Thai asked who knew what happiness was. The Siamese-Chinese answered it was when one had a lot of money and lived longer because of the wealth. The Thai disagreed, saying having more money invited more sufferings (*thuk*) and living longer meant one would have to be *kheekha* (*slave*) in this life longer too. Therefore it was not real happiness. 'Mr Kok', the Siamese-*farang*, replied that happiness was when one is free and doesn't have to oppress others because 'free[dom] is in yourself'. It was clear that Phichit used ethnic characters of each to highlight their answers, which underlay their differing world-views. Here freedom was seen as a foreign concept. See *Prachum praniphon kromluang phichitpreechakorn* [Collected Writings of Prince Phichitpreechakorn] (Bangkok: Teeronasarn Press, 1950), p. 130.

52 *Samutsan*, June B.E. 2461 (1918), pp. 1–33.

53 At that time, at least five schools among the élite had undertaken the translation and adaptation of Western texts and ideas into Thai. These schools were headed by King Vajiravudh, by the Supreme Patriarch Prince Vajirayan, by Prince Nakornsawan, by Prince Chantaburi and lastly by Prince Bidhyalongkorn. This royal élite, mostly made up of kings, princes and senior ministers, invented Thai words not only for the legal codes but also for literary, political, religious, scientific, and philosophical texts. The new words and ideas would then circulate in books, newspapers and magazines. 'Kor kuan kid nai pasathai' [Thoughts on Thai Language], Prince Wanwaithayakorn, in *Chumnum praniphon khong prachaoworawongther krommun narathippongprapan* [Collected Works of Prince Narathip] (Bangkok, 1989), p. 441.

54 The Prince used these two words, 'self-will' and 'independence', in English.

55 Ibid., p. 441.

56 See a more detailed discussion of Thai nationalism in Scot Barmé, *Luang Wichit Wathakan and the Creation of a Thai Identity* (Singapore: Institute of Southeast Asian Studies, 1993), pp. 14-39. For a critique of the idea that the Thai nation was solely created by the royal élite, see Copeland, Contested Nationalism and the 1932 Overthrow of the Absolute Monarchy in Siam.

CHAPTER 9

The Idea of Freedom in Burma and the Political Thought of Daw Aung San Suu Kyi

Josef Silverstein

There is a serious political struggle in Burma today that turns on the idea of freedom. Since the military violently suppressed a peaceful democratic revolution on 18 September 1988, its leaders have ruled by martial law, allowing a free and fair election on 27 May 1990, in which the National League for Democracy was overwhelmingly chosen to form a new parliament and establish democratic rule. But the rejected military leadership refused to accept the decision of the people and did not allow the parliament to form; instead *it* proceeded to perpetuate its rule by pressuring delegates *it* selected, to a National Convention *it* formed, to write a constitution *it* dictated, to insure *its* goal would be achieved.[1]

Do the Burmese people have the freedom to decide how to be governed and by whom, or do those who seized power by force have the right to construct the political forms, make the rules and govern as they see fit? Is freedom, in the broadest sense, a part of Burmese thought and traditions or is it a relatively recent addition which is claimed only by the westernised intelligentsia and not by the majority of the people? Is freedom individual or collective?

These and other questions are not new; they were raised during the Burmese quest for independence from colonial rule and later in the struggle against authoritarianism from both the Left and the Right. When given the opportunity through free and open elections, an overwhelming majority of the Burmese people upheld the standard of freedom and popular rule against those who would deny it.

Two Sources of Freedom

Today there is a single dominant voice in defence of freedom and a return to democratic self-rule. When Daw Aung San Suu Kyi stepped forward in August 1988, in the midst of a popular peaceful revolution, instantly she became the leader who united the people in their quest for freedom and democracy. From the moment she moved into the political arena she spoke unflinchingly to those in power and challenged their right to rule and deny the freedom the people had won from the British four decades earlier. As the daughter of Burma's leader who brought the nation to the edge of independence from foreign rule in 1947, only to be assassinated before achieving that goal, she appeared to have picked up her father's mantle and was ready to lead Burma's second struggle for freedom – this time against the army her father created.

Daw Aung San Suu Kyi is nearing the end of five years of house arrest, during which she has been denied freedom to communicate with her party and followers; but in that time she has found ways of addressing them indirectly through her writings, publications and speeches of acceptance for awards given *in absentia* which were summarised or broadcast in full over international short-wave radio. Through her resolute determination to remain in Burma and share her people's struggle she demonstrates the personal cost she is ready to pay to help restore freedom and democracy to Burma. Despite her present isolation – which was partially lifted in 1992 for visits by her immediate family and again, in 1994, for a visit from a US Congressman – and the military's efforts to demean her in the eyes of the people, her stature has grown. Although she has been offered freedom if she would be willing to leave Burma and end her involvement in politics, she has refused.

It is the thesis of this chapter that the idea of freedom in Burma has two sources, one deeply embedded in Burma's religion and culture, the other imported from the West as part of the intellectual baggage of the British. By the beginning of the twentieth century the two streams had merged, and today the idea of freedom in Burma is a mixture of the two traditions.

A further argument is that Daw Aung San Suu Kyi's idea of freedom is in the mainstream of Burmese thought and therefore easily understood and widely accepted by the people. From the outset of her involvement in the nation's peaceful struggle, she offered a fresh vision of a free Burma where the people might enjoy self-rule and basic human and civil rights. The Burma military leaders and their supporters abroad often say that political freedom is an alien idea with no roots in Burma. But, as Daw Aung San Suu Kyi has argued, the idea of freedom in Burma has its root in the religion and the traditions of the people, even though it was not claimed in its own right before the advent of colonial rule.

Theravada Buddhism, the faith of an overwhelming majority of Burmese, centres on a basic contradiction: all living things are lashed to the wheel of rebirth but only man has the power and freedom to escape if he accepts the four noble truths, as taught by the Buddha, regarding suffering, attachment, impermanence and escape via the eightfold path. The Buddha taught that each individual is free to work out his own salvation.[2]

> Buddhism, the foundation of traditional Burmese culture, places the greatest value on man, who alone of all beings can achieve the supreme state of Buddhahood. Each man has in him the potential to realize the truth through his own will and endeavor and to help others to realize it.[3]

Through education and interaction with the *sangha*, the religious order, the young were taught to read and to learn how to live as the Buddha taught. The *sangha* was made up of monks whose social role was to live in an exemplary manner; through their morning begging rounds and acceptance of food offerings from the people, the monks made it possible for the givers to earn merit. The monks also conducted monastic schools where the young learned to memorise the teachings of the Buddha and were imbued with the fundamental principle that man is solely responsible for his own destiny. An important lesson the Buddha taught about freedom was that men must think for themselves and test the truth of the things they hear and are told as truth.

> Be ye not misled by reports or tradition or hearsay. Be not misled by proficiency in the collection of traditional sayings, nor by mere logic or inference, nor after considering reasons, nor after reflection on the approval of some theory, nor because it fits becoming, nor out of respect for a recluse who holds it to be true. But, Kalamas, when you know for yourselves: These things are unprofitable, these things are blameworthy, these things are censured by the intelligence; these things, when performed and undertaken conduce to loss and sorrow – then indeed do you reject them.[4]

Unlike Western religious organisations, the *sangha* was not a hierarchy of priests with powers and authority to intercede and grant forgiveness for sin or for not living as the Buddha taught.

Burmese Buddhists never made the intellectual leap from freedom in the religious realm to freedom in the political world. Although they believed that everyone and everything was subject to the law of impermanence and change, they did not speculate about alternative political forms in the secular world. Since escape from the wheel of rebirth was the guiding principle of the individual, his thoughts and actions were concentrated on actions in this existence which would improve those of the next. He found no reason to reflect on or concern himself with the political and social system in which he existed.

Burmese tradition incorporated the idea of a strong state under an absolute monarch. Buddhist political thought argues that men lived originally in a state of nature and needed no ruler to regulate their lives because they lived virtuously, respecting the rights of others and fulfilling their own obligations consciously. Over time their behaviour degenerated to anarchy and terror, and to overcome this they came together, elected one among them to be king and entrusted him with power to enforce the laws and maintain order. Kingship was seen as a reward for meritorious actions performed in past births. A good king was 'expected to be charitable, moral, sacrificing, penitent, nonwrathful, nonviolent, patient and harmless'.[5]

The Burmese tradition of an all-powerful king also had its roots in Buddhist thought; once monarchy was established, kings assumed unbridled authority and their power rested not on contract and election but on control of the military, wealth, territory and charisma – mystical powers that were embodied both in the office and the person.[6] Obedience to the ruler became a quasi-religious duty. The institution of kingship was imbued with absolute and overwhelming authority over all areas of human activity.

In theory, the state as a reflection of the king was strong and controlled from the centre; in practice, it left a great deal of room for individual freedom. Unlike China, where the bureaucracy formed a 'steelframe' which held the state together regardless of war and dynastic changes, in Burma, office-holding under the reigning king depended on his whim, and a commission to hold office could come to an end at any time, and certainly with the king's death. Each monarch could void all acts and orders of his predecessors, and each change of king saw an administrative breakdown as the king's appointees had to receive new commissions or be replaced before the office could be filled again.[7] Each new ruler adopted the system of his predecessor as his own, and never thought about how to improve and make it more lasting. The Burma state proved only to be as strong as the king who controlled it.

Freedom in this system was to be seen at village level. Even when the system was under a strong king, his representative had limited powers. He collected taxes, commanded performance of services and adjudicated legal disputes; in most other matters concerning the people's lives, he did not interfere. With only short periods of strong kings, the direct authority of the monarch was only sporadically felt by the local leaders and their followers, especially in areas lying at great distances from the palace; as a result the villagers controlled most of their own affairs.

Burmese village society was composed of two broad social classes: *ahmudan*, those who were obligated for military or other service; and *athi*, those who paid rent for land and were obligated for various services which might be demanded by their patrons or protectors. Apart from this there was mobility between classes and easy intermarriage.[8] The people were not tied to the land, and since the countryside was underpopulated, individuals could escape from too demanding patrons by moving to other villages and swearing allegiance to a new protector. Land could be owned and passed on to heirs.

Women in Burma were freer than most women in Asia. They did not take their husband's name in marriage, they could divorce and remarry with little or no stigma, and they could inherit and own property. If, in a religious sense, they were inferior to males – escape from the wheel of rebirth required that they be reborn a male before they could free themselves from *samsara* (the wheel of rebirth) – in ordinary day-to-day life they enjoyed high status and a great deal of control of their lives.

The minorities, living in the hills surrounding the Burman heartland, who accepted the nominal suzerainty of the Burman monarch, contributed to the myth of the powerful centralised state, but in fact they enjoyed great freedom through continuing to be governed in their traditional ways, practising and preserving their cultures and social institutions and using their own languages.

In traditional Burma, freedom was implicit in Buddhism and explicitly practised by Burmans and non-Burmans alike without ever being extracted and claimed as an independent good.

Freedom under Tutelage

British colonial rule spawned a revolution in thought and action. It introduced a whole new way of looking at politics and society. Because the colonial system was concerned only with the here and now and not with the hereafter, it challenged the fatalism of those who believed that nothing could be done about this existence and concerned themselves only with the next.

The British quickly proved that they were more efficient than their indigenous predecessors in establishing and maintaining authoritarian rule. Their system rested on important principles: that the state and its rulers were of this world; that authority was based on power and not divine inspiration; that the state and its officers could be challenged when either transcended the legal limits. The English did not come to Burma to introduce Western ideas of liberty and freedom; these and other ideas entered Burma as a byproduct of their authority and concern for the rule of law, property rights and order.

The priorities of the new system were to provide strong administration and domestic tranquillity in order to encourage investment,
trade, and the development of economic resources and profit. To run
the state as cheaply as possible, the British rulers encouraged private
investment, mainly from Europe, to develop and expand the economy,
and allowed Indians, with whom they had worked for more than two
centuries, to come to Burma and fill the lower administrative, police
and military ranks and serve as moneylenders to the peasants and
shopkeepers in the cities.

Church and state were separated; the English rulers, not wishing to
interfere or assume responsibility for an alien faith, cast the Buddhist
clergy adrift.[9] Monastic education continued in the rural areas under
the *sangha*, but the knowledge and skills it taught were largely unusable
for employment in government and business. To impart new ideas,
skills and language, the colonial rulers encouraged Christian churches
to establish schools and provide an English education. In addition to
maths, science and the English language, the missionary schools
included the study of British history, thought and institutions which
exalted the political success of the English in building a strong state at
home and an empire abroad. This was meant to inculcate respect for
and appreciation of what colonial rule meant.

The British had no intention of making Burmans into Englishmen
and assimilating them. The colonial rulers recognised that they were
displacing a value-system and social system with which the majority of
the people still identified, and that new Western ideas and practices
were dividing the local population between those who adopted the
new and those who held tightly to the old. Faced with the need for
peace, tranquillity and support in their colonies as they fought the First
World War, the colonial rulers sought to unite the contradictory ideas
of loyalty to empire and patriotism to Burma. Called the Imperial
Idea, the colonial officials theorised that,

> if . . . Burma . . . is still under tutelage and has not yet reached the full enjoy-
> ment of liberty and citizenship in the Imperial Commonwealth, [the student]
> should be taught not to regard his people as a conquered nation but to
> understand that England has assumed the task of education and govern-
> ment of his country not as a tyrant but as a trustee for civilization in order
> to . . . build up those conditions of liberty and opportunity for the individual
> in which the people can learn to govern themselves.
>
> It is from his own patriotism, his own attachment to the ideals and tradi-
> tions of his own people that [he] will come to appreciate the national feelings
> and ideas of other races in the Empire and will learn to regard them not as
> foreign barbarians . . . but as brothers . . .[10]

It was in this new and changing context that the idea of freedom
took on meaning for the Burman constitutional framework, which

theoretically applied to all: individual and group, ruler and ruled, indigenous and alien. To use and enjoy it required knowledge of the law, the political system, and experience.

The emerging westernised élite among the Burmans faced a dilemma as they sought to hold fast to their religious beliefs and culture while absorbing new ideas and values. Before the beginning of the present century, the new Burman élite began to use the political freedoms implicit in the new institutions in defence of tradition. In 1895 they sponsored non-clerical Buddhist schools with a Western curriculum modelled on the Christian missionary schools.[11] Early in the new century they formed the Young Men's Buddhist Association, on the Western model of the YMCA, and launched a campaign to revive Buddhism among Burmans and, later, to campaign against the desecration of and disrespect for religious buildings and areas by non-Buddhist visitors.

While the British found it convenient administratively to join Burma to India as a province, it quickly worked to their disadvantage politically as the emerging élite emulated the Indians in their own demands for political reform, greater participation in governance, and more freedom. By 1923 Burma, like India, had a partially elected Legislative Council and ministers in the Governor's Council; under the 1935 constitution Burma was separated from India and given responsible government, in which four Burmans served as prime minister before the British were defeated and expelled by the Japanese in the early stages of the Second World War.

Between the First and Second World Wars, freedom and political development went hand in hand but followed two different courses: while the urban population moved in the mainstream of constitutionalism, liberal democracy and independence, the rural population moved back to the values and institutions of the precolonial period.

The westernised Burmans in the mainstream exercised their freedom through party formation, voting, participation in parliament, and various direct actions. The younger Western-educated expanded the idea of freedom through the use of strikes to achieve political and social ends, the use of the Burmese language in writing and publication to revive interest and pride, the study and adaptation of Western literature to acquire world knowledge, and the mobilisation of workers and peasants for economic and social ends. Within this mainstream the competing ideologies of Europe – communism, fascism, nationalism, democracy and others – found adherents and inspired the formation of local political movements. The British tried to channel some of these developments within the institutional changes which gave Burmans greater participation in politics and also to curb those they saw as a threat to their rule and their political and economic interests.

Freedom also applied to speech, writing and publication. Burman newspapers written in Burmese were the first manifestation; Western novels adapted to Burman locales and given a local veneer followed and gradually gave way to Burman stories, characters and issues. By the end of the 1930s novels critical of foreign rule, modern Buddhist monks who cloaked the violations of vows under their yellow robes, and other local subjects indicated how widely freedom of speech had spread.

The young intellectuals used political freedom to form the Dobama ('We Burman') movement in the early 1930s. Its adherents challenged the Europeans, who demanded to be addressed with the salutation *Thakin* ('master'), by adopting it as a term of address for themselves. The Thakins began by advocating revival and updating of the Burmese language and quickly transformed its cultural message to a political nationalist one by advocating 'Burma for the Burmese'. They popularised their ideas through a patriotic song which eventually became the national anthem of independent Burma.[12]

Freedom in the mainstream meant many things personal, social, intellectual and political, which led to greater participation by the people through political organisations, elections, and direct action outside the legal limits. Together they reflected a fundamental change in the popular outlook towards politics. Man, they came to believe, could affect his political condition in this existence and it did not depend on his karma.

On the eve of the Second World War a few of the younger Burmans, led by Aung San, Daw Aung San Suu Kyi's father, secretly went abroad for military training under the Japanese with the intent of returning and liberating Burma.

A second stream of politically aroused Burmans looked in a different direction. Using their new-found political freedoms, they organised Wunthanu Athins, offshoots of the national General Council of Burmese Associations in the rural areas, against corruption, drinking, taxation and other government and private activities which were seen as contrary to traditional Burmese or Buddhist values. They rejected the emphasis placed on westernised political development by their urban counterparts and sought remedies to their own problems – the cultivation and sale of agricultural products in an economic system of landlords, tenancy, moneylending and the British system of taxation with its penalties of being displaced from the land under laws they did not fully understand and which always seemed to work against their interests.

Many of the Western-educated Wunthanu leaders found themselves and their followers more in tune with the politically active monks than with their urban counterparts. Contrary to the traditional restrictions on the *sangha* not to become involved in politics, the General Council Sangha Sametggi, a political organisation of monks, played a strong role in the rural areas mobilising and agitating against British rule and preaching that colonialism threatened Buddhism. While their sermons and political activity were rejected by conservative monks and Buddhist orders, they found a wide audience among the peasants, especially among women. Two monks in particular, U Ottama and U Wisara, gained national attention with their political sermons. Arrest and imprisonment only strengthened their hold on their followers, and death in gaol made them martyrs in the national struggle for independence.[13]

Out of this movement came the most direct challenge to British rule, the Saya San revolt in 1930. Led by an ex-monk, it sought to force the British out and restore the monarchy. By using magic and amulets and imitating some of the royal ritual to claim the former throne, the revolt, mainly in central and lower Burma, drew only modest rural support and hardly any from the urban areas. Its failure marked the end of inward and backward-looking movements.[14]

By the beginning of the Second World War, freedom was accepted as part of the human condition which found a legal and moral basis in the ideas, institutions and political processes introduced by the British. More important, the Western-educated Burman Buddhists came to realise that there was a connection between the political system and the right and ability to exercise freedom. Finally, they recognised that their political and economic fate in this existence depended on their involvement in and eventual control of the political process.

In the minority areas surrounding Burma proper, the people continued to live apart from the Burmans in the heartland under the colonial policy of divide and rule – especially in the Shan States, where the British created a gulf between the two by leading each in a different direction. While the Burmans moved along the constitutional line towards eventual dominion status, the Shan States were grouped together in a separate federation which reinforced the perpetuation of traditional rule. The changes in education and the opportunities to learn about and exercise political freedom were not available in the hill areas, where there were traditional patterns of behaviour and where only the sons of chiefs, who were educated in Western schools, acquired a different outlook.

The short interlude of Japanese control of Burma left a legacy which seemed to reverse the growing trend towards freedom. Just before the outbreak of the Pacific War, when Aung San secretly left Burma to seek foreign help in freeing his country from foreign rule he wrote, shortly after arriving in Japan, 'Blue Print for Burma', which convinced his hosts that he shared their ideas of a strong totalitarian state.

> What we want is a strong state administration as exemplified in Germany and Italy. There shall be only one nation, one state, one party, one leader. There shall be no parli[a]mentary opposition, no nonsense of individualism. Everyone must submit to the s[t]ate which is supreme over the individual.[15]

During the early war period he was not alone in employing the language of fascism. Dr Ba Maw, the wartime head of state, included it in his speeches and in the wartime Declaration of Independence. With the approval of his Japanese advisers, it said:

> The New State of Burma, is . . . established upon the principle of Burmese unity in one blood, one voice and one leader. It was national disintegration which destroyed the Burmese people in the past and they are determined that this shall never happen again.[16]

When Aung San's essay is read together with the total body of his writings and speeches of both the war and postwar period, it is clear that the ideas in 'Blue Print for Burma' were not central to his thought. The wartime statements and writings of Dr Maw, too, were a reflection of the times and a direct response to Japanese demands.[17] There is no evidence that dictatorship in place of freedom was the desire of other leaders and the people. The civilian leaders, assembled by the Japanese and directed to write a constitution, rejected restoring the monarchy and accepted a basic Japanese-dictated authoritarian law for the duration of the war. With the Kempetai threatening the people who showed any signs of resisting the 'New Order' and the Japanese army occupying the cities and countryside, there was little room for the people to express themselves, other than as directed.

Where Burmans were free, they expressed a different set of ideas and goals. In 1944 Burmese military and civilian leaders met secretly and formed a revolutionary organisation and issued a manifesto. It had two objectives: the expulsion of the Japanese and the writing of a constitution for a free Burma. They gave greatest emphasis to the building of a free society wherein the people would enjoy the freedom and rights common to people living in free societies as well as those drawn from their ancient traditions. The manifesto called for the freedoms of person, speech and thought; it also called for 'freedom to follow and develop one's own language and culture' and the right of everyone to 'obtain free supply of timber and bamboo for the construction of one's own dwelling house' and to fish freely for one's own consumption. It anticipated some kind of union with the hill peoples by calling for 'the state to provide adequate safeguards in respect of economic, social and political interests of the minorities . . .'[18]

The wartime goals of freedoms and rights were realised four years later in 1948 when a freely chosen constituent assembly wrote Burma's first constitution for their forthcoming independent state. In the light of this achievement the political writings of the war years must be seen in more than one way: they reflect Japan's ability to influence the public statements and writings of those who served under its rule, and they also reflect the wartime thought and writing of those Burmans who risked their lives to communicate their ideas about a truly free Burma in the modern world, once the war ended. If the wartime writings of Burma's leaders are included with all the other writings and speeches given over a lifetime, they will be seen and understood in the perspective of their times.

The political activity of the Burman heartland immediately after the war was not matched in the hill areas. But the war had its impact on the hill minorities and they were of different minds about their future. Some feared the prospect of an independent Burma under Burman rule and sought either independence or continued British rule. Others were willing to consider such a future and were prepared to discuss it with the new Burman leaders. In 1946, and again a year later, several leaders of different minority groups met in the Shan States to discuss their political future; at the second meeting several freely agreed to join the Burmans in forming an independent federal union.

The Karens, on the other hand, who traditionally feared domination by the Burmans and looked to the British for protection, remembered the assaults against their people by units of the young new Burma army shortly after the British were expelled in 1942. During the war years Aung San worked to convince the Karens that in a future independent Burma the two could live together peacefully and that the Karens could share power and enjoy equal status with the Burmans. At war's end, despite the efforts of Aung San, the Karens sought to opt out of the proposed union. The question of the political future of the Karens was not resolved at the constitutional convention; denied their right to self-determination, in 1949 a majority of Karens went into revolt.

As Burma entered the new era of independence in 1948, the idea of freedom was well established. The two traditions of freedom had come together: from the precolonial past people inherited the idea that they were free to determine their future destiny by the way they lived; from the colonial past they learned that government was not divinely ordained and unchangeable; instead, it was man-made and people were free to change it. Freedom to achieve things in this world became as real as freedom to achieve things in the next.

'In Quest of Democracy'

> I think it is important for every people to work for the preservation of their culture and religion. At the same time it must be remembered that a progressive nation should move with the times and avoid bigoted and narrow-minded attitudes.[19]

In these words Daw Aung San Suu Kyi expressed the unity in Burmese culture of the two traditions of freedom she had come to know through her education, her own reflection, and travel and living abroad. As a child growing up in Burma, she gained a deep understanding of Buddhism, Burmese traditions, and the Western liberal ideas which were part of modern Burmese culture and the Burmese language; from her education in India and England, her experiences of living and working in several areas of the world and her postgraduate studies in Japan, she acquired an extensive intellectual experience which broadened and deepened her perspective on the thought and culture of modern Burma.

The synthesis of the two traditions is clearly expressed in her essay 'In Quest of Democracy'.[20] Writing in 1988, at the time of the peaceful revolution in Burma and its suppression by the military, she found nothing new in the rhetoric of the opponents of freedom and democracy, who questioned the ability of the people to judge what is best for the nation and condemned the liberal ideas drawn from the West as un-Burmese. She argued that even without the sophisticated techniques and methods of political and economic analysis common in the West, the Burmese could find answers to the terrible political and socio-economic conditions in Burma by turning to the words of the Buddha on the causes of decline and decay – 'failure to recover that which has been lost, omission to repair that which has been damaged, disregard for the need of a reasonable economy and the elevation to leadership of men without morality or learning' – and applying them to their situation. Put in modern terms, she said: 'when democratic rights had been lost to military dictatorship sufficient efforts had not been made to regain them, moral and political values had been allowed to deteriorate without concerted attempts to save the situation, the economy had been badly managed, and the country had been ruled by men without integrity and wisdom.'[21] For her, the 1988 peaceful revolution was an attempt by the people to act as the Buddha taught and take back their right to rule and reverse the process of decline.

For Aung San Suu Kyi, the contradiction between Buddhism and dictatorship begins with the question about the nature of man. Buddhism, she argued, places the highest value on man, who alone has the ability to attain the supreme state of Buddhahood. 'Each man has in him the potential to realize the truth through his own will and endeavor and to help others to realize it.' But under despotic rule man is valued least, as a 'faceless, mindless – and helpless – mass to be manipulated at will'. Reflecting on this contradiction, she observed: 'It is a puzzlement to the Burmese how concepts which recognize the inherent dignity and the equal and inalienable rights of human beings, which accept that all men are endowed with reason and conscience and which recommend a universal spirit of brotherhood, can be inimical to indigenous values.'[22] If man is endowed with reason and has the innate ability to realise his potential, then the political system and social environment must allow him freedom to pursue that end. For Aung San Suu Kyi, only in a democratic society can man truly exercise his freedom. Democracy, she argues, acknowledges the right to differ as well as the duty to settle differences peacefully. Under democracy, 'protest and dissent can exist in healthy counterpart with orthodoxy and conservatism, contained by a general recognition of the need to balance respect for individual rights with respect for law and order'.[23]

The idea of law and order, she wrote, is frequently misused as an excuse for oppression. In Burmese, the idea is officially expressed as *nyein-wut-pi-pyar* (quiet-crouched-crushed-flattened). A prominent Burmese writer drew the conclusion that 'the whole made for an undesirable state of affairs, one which militated against the emergence of an alert, energetic, progressive citizenry'.[24] For Aung San Suu Kyi, law must be equated with justice, and order with the discipline of a people satisfied that justice has been done. For her this could only exist where the people's elected representatives make the laws and the administrators have no power to set them aside and replace them with new arbitrary decrees. Drawing on Buddhist precepts, she wrote that the concept of law was based on *dhamma* ('righteousness or virtue'), not on the power to impose harsh and inflexible rules on a defenceless people. Noting that the teachings of the Buddha centre on universal values of truth, righteousness and loving kindness and that Burmese associated peace and security with coolness and shade, she found the modern liberal democratic idea of rule under law in a Burmese poem:[25]

> The shade of the tree is cool indeed
> The shade of parents is cooler
> The shade of teachers is cooler still
> The shade of the ruler is yet more cool
> But coolest of all is the shade of Buddha's teachings.

Towards the end of her essay on democracy, Daw Aung San Suu Kyi wrote that 'in their quest of democracy the people in of Burma explore not only the political theories and practices of the world outside their country but also the spiritual and intellectual values that have given shape to their own environment'.[26]

Implicit in her writing and speeches is the idea that freedom is a universal idea – an idea which was given modern approval in the Universal Declaration of Human Rights which the United Nations adopted in 1948. As she noted, the Burma delegation to the world body voted for it with no reservations when it was adopted by the General Assembly. The vote was consistent with the thought and goals of the nation's founding fathers at the Anti-Fascist People's Freedom League pre-convention meeting, the constituent assembly, and the language included in the constitution for an independent Burma.[27] She referred frequently to the Declaration as a universal standard for all people, and maintained that until its content was inscribed in the basic law of the land and upheld by the government and respected by those with power, the nation and its people were not free.

But freedom is more than constitutional guarantees and institutional arrangements. It also is psychological. In an address which, because of her imprisonment, she could not deliver to the European Parliament in response to being awarded the Sakharov Prize for Freedom of Thought, she spoke to the peoples of Burma, who have lived under corrupt military rule since 1962, when she wrote that, as important as the traditional ideas of freedom are, man is not truly free if he lives in fear. 'It is not power that corrupts but fear. Fear of losing power corrupts those who wield it and fear of the scourge of power corrupts those who are subject to it.'[28] Fear, Aung San Suu Kyi wrote, stifles and slowly destroys all sense of right and wrong. Fear contributes to corruption; 'where fear is rife corruption in all forms becomes entrenched.'[29]

> The quintessential revolution is that of the spirit, born of an intellectual conviction of the need for change in those mental attitudes and values which shape the course of a nation's development . . . It is not enough merely to call for freedom, democracy and human rights. There has to be a united determination to persevere in the struggle, to make sacrifices in the name of enduring truths, to resist the corrupting influences of desire, ill will, ignorance and fear.[30]

Daw Aung San Suu Kyi has demonstrated her courage in the face of threat and has shown that she will not be intimidated or made fearful. It is her model of courage which has sustained the people who have looked to her for leadership since 26 August 1988, when, for the first time, she stepped forward and became their instant leader. She recalled something her father said in an earlier time of troubles:

> Democracy is the only ideology which is consistent with freedom. It is also an ideology that promotes and strengthens peace. It is therefore the only ideology that promotes and strengthens peace. It is therefore the only ideology we should aim for.[31]

She said that was the reason why she was taking part in the struggle for freedom and democracy.

The ideas and thoughts of Daw Aung San Suu Kyi are not offered as an example of those of a scholar or reflective thinker working in the abstract. Rather, she is an example of a special person who, because of her name and family, gained an immediate audience; but it was her words and ideas, which the people understood and related to, that vaulted her into the leadership of Burma's revolution against authoritarian rule. Despite the military's effort to isolate and erase her presence from the mind of the public, she continues to hold its loyalty because of her courage and because the message she continues to deliver is in the mainstream of Burmese culture and tradition.

Freedom in modern Burma is not contrary to tradition; it has been part of it from the very start. Burma was not frozen in time in the face of the British military victories and the imposition of colonial rule. The Burmese learned new meanings for freedom from the British and other Western sources and incorporated those new meanings into their own beliefs and values. By the end of the Second World War, the emergent élite spoke of freedom and democracy to an audience who understood and freely followed in the direction it led.

But Burma was not destined to have an easy transition from authoritarian rule to political freedom; even after independence in 1948, several rebellions erupted, challenging the democracy and authority of the constitution.

The military's seizure of power in 1962 met virtually no organised opposition in the Burman heartland until 1988; but during that period the rulers' efforts to root out the nascent and imperfectly formed democracy of their predecessors and create a totalitarian dictatorship with a population of 'rice-eating robots' failed because the memory of and desire for freedom remained alive in the minds of the people. The student-led peaceful revolution provided the means to release those pent-up memories, and the speeches of Daw Aung San Suu Kyi reacquainted them with the meaning of freedom and rekindled their desire to recover it. The peaceful revolutionaries and their new leader were effective because freedom was part of the Burmese tradition which the military dictators tried to erase and failed.

Notes

Note: 'Burman' refers to the ethnic people of Burma and 'Burmese' to Burma generally or to those people who are not ethnically Burman.

1 *Statement of U. Daniel Auna, Member of SLORC's National Convention Panel of Chairmen and Political Party Group on the Reasons why he left the Convention and came to the Liberated Area in Manerplaw*, Manerplaw, 1 May 1994 (Mimeo).

2 *Illustrated History of Buddhism* (Rangoon: Young Men's Buddhist Association, Kuthalawaddy Press, 1954), p. 52.

3 Aung San Suu Kyi, *Freedom From Fear and Other Writings* (London: Penguin, 1991), p. 174.

4 Winston L. King, *A Thousand Lives Away: Buddhism in Contemporary Burma* (Cambridge, Mass.: Harvard University Press, 1964), pp. 117–18.

5 Balkristna G. Gokale, 'Early Buddhist Kingship', *Journal of Asian Studies*, 26, 1 (November 1966), pp. 16–22.

6 Ibid., p. 18.

7 William J. Koenig, *The Burmese Polity: 1752–1819*, Michigan Papers on South and Southeast Asia, No. 34, Ann Arbor, Michigan University, 1990, pp. 92–3, 103–7.

8 J. S. Furnivall, *The Political Economy of Burma*, 2nd rev. edn by J. R. Andrus (Rangoon: Burma Book Club, 1938), pp. 38–9.

9 Donald Eugene Smith, *A History of Modern Burma* (Princeton: Princeton University Press, 1965), pp. 43–57.

10 John Cady, *A History of Modern Burma* (Ithaca: Cornell University Press, 1958), pp. 198–9.

11 Ibid., p. 178.

12 Khin Yi, *The Dobama Movement in Burma (1930–1938)*, Cornell Southeast Asia Program, Monograph 2, Ithaca, Cornell University, 1988.

13 Cady, *A History of Modern Burma*, p. 231; Smith, *A History of Modern Burma*, pp. 92–107.

14 Cady, *A History of Modern Burma*, pp. 309–18; Patricia Herbert, *The Hsaya San Rebellion (1930–1932) Reappraised*, Centre of Southeast Asian Studies, Working Paper No. 27, Melbourne, Monash University, 1982.

15 'Blue Print for Burma', Josef Silverstein (ed.), *The Political Legacy of Aung San*, Southeast Asia Program, No. 86, Ithaca, Cornell University, 1972, pp. 13–14. There is no original copy of this document in Aung San's hand. It was said to be a copy of a copy of an original by a Japanese confederate and was given prominence in 1968 by Dr Maung Maung, who, in writing a biography of General Ne Win, cited it as the theoretical basis for the military dictatorship then in existence in Burma. Maung Maung, *Burma and General Ne Win* (New York: Asia Publishing House, 1969), pp. 298–9.

16 'Declaration of Independence of Burma', *Burma*, 1, 1 (Rangoon: Foreign Affairs Association, Burma, September 1944), p. 99. For the views of this and the wartime constitution see Ba Maw, *Breakthrough in Burma: Memoirs*

of a Revolution, 1939–1946 (New Haven: Yale University Press, 1968), pp. 318–30.

17 Thakin Nu, *Burma Under the Japanese: Pictures and Portraits* (London: Macmillan & Co. Ltd, 1954), pp. 54–69.

18 Anti-Fascist People's Freedom League, *From Fascist Bondage to New Democracy: The New Burma in the New World* (Rangoon: Nay Win Kyi Press, 1946).

19 'In the Eye of the Revolution', Aung San Suu Kyi, *Freedom From Fear and Other Writings*, p. 208.

20 'In Quest of Democracy', ibid., pp. 167–79.

21 Ibid., pp. 168–9.

22 Ibid., p. 175.

23 Ibid., p. 176.

24 Ibid., pp. 176–7.

25 Ibid., p. 177.

26 Ibid., p. 178.

27 Ministry of Information, *Burma's Fight for Freedom* (Rangoon, 1948). See the chapter on the AFPFL Convention for the initial Fourteen Points the party hoped to have adopted as the basis for a new constitution, esp. articles 6, 7, p. 58; for the actual Seven Points Directive Resolution, see article 4, p. 93.

28 Aung San Suu Kyi, *Freedom From Fear*, p. 180.

29 Ibid., p. 181.

30 Ibid., p. 183.

31 'Speech at Shwedagon Pagoda', ibid., p. 200.

CHAPTER 10

Freedom and Élite Political Theory in Vietnam Before the French

Alexander Woodside

Western thinkers on the whole have hardly wanted to attribute much capacity for freedom of any kind to premodern 'Oriental' societies. Perhaps the lowest point comes, oddly enough, not in the famous analyses of Asian despotism by Plato or Montesquieu, but in Montaigne's sixteenth-century essay on the education of children. There Montaigne attributed to Plutarch the bizarre argument that 'the peoples of Asia' were subject to one-man rule because 'they did not know how to pronounce the single syllable, No'.[1]

The period of the Western penetration or conquest of Asian mandarinates like China or Vietnam in the 1800s was, supposedly, the worst moment of all in the polemical and derogatory exoticisation of Asian societies by Western 'Orientalist' thinkers. Yet this period also featured an interesting counterpoint to the previous centuries of disdain for Asian politics. Some French writers took note of the fact that Vietnam was governed not by a formally hereditary aristocracy but by a scholar class recruited through civil service examinations.[2] Breaking with the Montesquieu tradition which held that the lack of a hereditary nobility guaranteed 'a condition of denuded egalitarian servitude throughout Asia',[3] these nineteenth-century French writers proposed that the Vietnamese were indeed significantly free, in the sense that their political system was dominated by self-made men whose power came not from inherited estates and titles but from being able to write winning essays and poems in three-stage examinations. A book called *L'Annam et le Cambodge*, by C. E. Bouillevaux, published in Paris in 1874, was typical of what I would call this counterpoint literature. Bouillevaux wrote that Vietnam was 'an academic democracy', although it had a 'hereditary Caesar at its head' (the Vietnamese emperor or *vua*); traditional Vietnam was thus at worst 'a mixture of tyrannies and of precious liberties'.[4]

Any contemporary Western exploration of freedom in traditional Vietnam, therefore, follows in the footsteps of nineteenth-century Western writers who were more open-minded about this topic than we normally suppose. I do not wish to escape their influence. Rather I wish to ask – on the basis of Vietnamese writings of the eighteenth and early nineteenth centuries – to what extent the people who wrote and thought about human self-determination from within Vietnamese society at that time agreed even roughly with Frenchmen like Bouillevaux that mandarinates contributed to desirable forms of self-determination because of the restricted but genuine equality of opportunity they provided through examinations. There is a related question which is worth taking up first. To what extent did the Vietnamese who wrote and thought about human self-determination in this period do so in terms substantially different from those used by modern Vietnamese who live in the much more intellectually Western world of the twentieth century?

In the present primitive condition of Vietnam studies the most convenient guide to important Vietnamese thought in the eighteenth century (admittedly, male élite thought) is probably the writings of the single most formidable Vietnamese Neo-Confucian philosopher of that age, Le Quy Don (1726–84). Future research will need to match Le Quy Don's writings more broadly with the political themes implicit in the brilliant Vietnamese poetry written during his lifetime. The poetry may well have been a more widely influential channel of public meditation. So what follows are preliminary hypotheses based on a narrow textual focus.

Le Quy Don was a first-place palace examination degree winner when still in his twenties, a high official, the leader of a Vietnamese diplomatic delegation to China (1760), and a writer of books which are still in print (in romanised translation into colloquial Vietnamese) in Vietnam today. Indeed, in 1994 Hanoi you could buy second-hand copies of his works which have been annotated so heavily and emotionally by their recent owners that they have become the textual equivalents of graffiti-strewn rock stars' tombs in the West. Some Vietnamese, in short, maintain an anxious dialogue with this long-dead intellectual even as I write. Le Quy Don was an important spokesman for the eighteenth-century Vietnamese intelligentsia, but his influence is not confined to that century.

Sincerity and Self-determination

Let us begin with the extent of the congruence of Vietnamese notions of freedom in the precolonial and modern periods. One can find

superficial continuities in vocabulary. They mask dramatic discontinuities in attitude and in world-view. Writing in 1773, Le Quy Don
denounced the notion of human history through 'self-originating'
(*tu do*). This was the Sino-Vietnamese term which was eventually
adopted in Vietnam a century and a half later (under guidance from
Japanese and Chinese revolutionaries) to express the Western term
'freedom'. Le Quy Don thought it was a pernicious notion. He argued
that everything from the destinies of states (*quoc gia*) and scholars to
human names, facial appearances, behaviour, and even human
'motion and tranquillity', were determined in advance by an inex-
pressibly profound cosmos, and could not be 'self-originated' by living
people. For living people the most that was possible was the cultivation
of 'total sincerity' (*chi thanh*) and 'self-completion' (*tu thanh*). If one
cultivated them successfully the future could be morally foreknown
and foremanaged, though not actually created out of nothing.[5]

Le Quy Don had both political and cosmological reasons for fearing
the spread of the notion of something called *tu do*. The term clearly was
popular enough in Vietnam in the 1770s to frighten him. In politics,
the classical sense of the cosmic modesty of purely human affairs,
which Le Quy Don was upholding in his contrast between 'sincerity'
and the allegedly mistaken belief that the 'self' could 'originate' its
own destiny, was embattled in eighteenth-century Vietnam. Other
eighteenth-century texts, such as a famous hand-copied chronicle of
uncertain authorship about the Vietnamese politics of that era, depict a
Vietnamese society whose courtiers and generals had as much arro-
gance and as little piety as Renaissance Italy's soldiers of fortune or
marketplace ruffians. About fifteen years after Le Quy Don wrote,
for example, Vietnam's capital city of Hanoi (*Thang Long*) fell into
the hands of a Tayson peasant army general named Ngo Van So. The
general was memorably quoted in this text as bragging that he could
dispose of the great saints of heaven, or of the king of hell himself if he
came to earth, with just one sweep of his net.[6] There is reason to believe
that Le Quy Don feared such over-confident militarists' refusal to see
that the future could only be understood through a 'sincere' acceptance of their own connection to everything else about them. He
wanted to limit their mayhem. He feared the function of the idea of
tu do as a licence for military mayhem. Political stability and *tu do* could
not coexist in such a fractured kingdom.

Le Quy Don had other reasons for wanting to place limits on the
belief in the human capacity to create the future, as opposed to morally
foreknowing it. He thought the term *tu do* implied a rejection of the
cosmological unity of humankind with nature. He contrasted the
notion of 'self-origination' with the notion of 'total sincerity' because

the latter was a broad metaphysical-religious-psychological quality, derived from the classical text 'The Doctrine of the Mean' (*Trung dung*, a staple of the Vietnamese civil service examinations from AD 1434), which called for a rigorous individual ethical development based on full awareness of the essential interrelatedness of everything in the universe. Le Quy Don's Neo-Confucian universe was not a great machine, accessible to the expanding control of detached human observers. It was a place in which the properties of the human part of it were determined by the properties of all the other parts and vice versa. One wonders whether the positive redefinition of the term *tu do* in the mind of twentieth-century Vietnamese could have occurred without the concomitant introduction of the more humanly empowering mechanistic picture of the universe as understood in Newtonian physics. Political and cosmological thought went together.

But discontinuities concerning the imagination of freedom in precolonial and postcolonial Vietnam were not just a matter of different cosmologies. A second discontinuity lay in the fact that Neo-Confucian intellectuals of the Le Quy Don sort separated the cultivation of individual moral autonomy from the pursuit of material interests. They did not choose to see politics as an activity instrumental to the attainment of individual or group interests, as in so much early modern Western thought. In his 'Classified Discourse from the Library' (*Van dai loai ngu*) completed in 1773, and one of premodern Vietnam's most central works in political theory, Le Quy Don wrote that it was 'shallow' for the 'gentleman' (*quan tu*), the most important agent in Vietnamese politics, to struggle over one degree, or even half a grade, in the examinations-based civil service of that era. Rather, the 'gentleman' should seek to become so impermeably 'tranquil' or 'serene' (*tinh trong*) that he could suffer poverty without grieving about it, and retire temporarily from office without regretting it. Great deeds and long-term good fortune depended on acquiring this invisible armour of 'tranquillity', whose ideal intensity was such as to put Western terms like 'unflappable', as applied to politicians like Harold Macmillan, very much in the shade.

It is important to emphasise that Neo-Confucian 'tranquillity' at no time meant absolute detachment from politics. It was rather intended as preparation for the political. From of old, Le Quy Don wrote, the people who had carried out the greatest political enterprises had all had a background of lack of desire, or of self-willed 'calmness' (*dam bac*).[7] The separation of politics from desire was quite explicit in these passages. The key to successful state-building was proposed to be a desireless tranquillity which did not mind poverty or temporary political setbacks. Delayed gratification, not the promotion of rational individual interest, was the ideal key at least to political self-determination.

This stress on the principle of a politically engaged serenity for mandarins in eighteenth-century Vietnamese political theory does not come as close as one might think to the famous German interest in inner freedom or in freedom as interior self-development, unless one purges the German notion of such characteristic German or Western dualisms as the dualism between the world of the spirit and the world of the flesh. Neo-Confucian spirituality required its practitioners to be socially interactive in the present. The Vietnamese principle of serenity called for a curious (in Western eyes) mixture of simultaneous political withdrawal and political engagement. Practical political agency, and an inner consciousness that was not fully accessible to outsiders (including emperors), were supposed to be coessential.

What this meant in practice was that at any one time Vietnamese rulers' governments might harbour unknown numbers of transcendentally serene gentlemen who had the potential to withdraw from politics. To avoid defections, rulers had to treat officials as ends in themselves, not just as means to rulers' ends. Vietnamese mandarins hardly enjoyed legally guaranteed protection against abusive monarchs. But the monarchical abuses which did occur could be construed not necessarily as expressions of an eternally unchecked 'Oriental' despotic caprice but as expressions of royal frustration with the monarch's limited authority over endlessly engaging or disengaging self-possessed literati.

Of course every moral philosophy presupposes its own sociology and has its own social embodiment. In premodern Vietnam the ideal of the temporarily withdrawn, serene gentleman was very plainly a dignifying of the village schoolteacher with national political aspirations through the examinations or by other ways. Village schoolteachers with a strong sense of their own moral self-possession were every bit as much the embodiment of Neo-Confucian tranquillity in Vietnam in the eighteenth and nineteenth centuries as Manchester manufacturers were the embodiment of Samuel Smiles' self-help preachings in nineteenth-century England. I would suggest that this was not true, at least to the same degree, elsewhere in Confucian Asia. Far more research will be needed to illustrate more thoroughly the imaginative Vietnameseness of such classical archetypes in Vietnam as the Confucian gentleman. But we may assume that its content was every bit as Vietnamese to the Nghe An village elder in the eighteenth century as the content of the notion of the knight, or *ksatria*, was entirely Javanese in the understanding of eighteenth-century Javanese *prijaji*. One telltale sign is that while Vietnamese literature shared the Chinese literary tradition of mocking and satirising Buddhist monks, it quite consciously did not accommodate the sort of mockery of village schoolteachers that could be found in Chinese fiction of the Ming–Qing period. The tendency of classically educated Vietnamese literati to withdraw to the villages (as contrasted with the more politically controllable walled cities and towns of the Chinese gentry), and to teach in the villages while awaiting political change, gave Le Quy Don's ideal of the 'gentleman' who transcends immediate desire in order to outlast incompetent emperors a very lively grassroots immediacy.

A third discontinuity in the imagination of freedom in precolonial and postcolonial Vietnam has to do with the definition of the likeliest sources of interference with individual or family self-determination. In this period political theory was written from the point of view of the intellectuals who claimed the right to withdraw to the villages. They saw the prescriptive tranquillity of their withdrawal as being most threatened not by foreign invaders or national emperors but by local lawlessness and corruption. Besides Le Quy Don, the other great élite theorist of politics in Vietnam between 1750 and 1850 was Phan Huy Chu (1782–1840). His master work, 'The Classified Survey of the Institutions of Successive Courts' (*Lich trieu hien chu'o'ng loai chí*), was completed in 1819, and comprised forty-nine volumes of analysis of Vietnamese government offices, laws, political rituals, and foreign relations.[8] Phan Huy Chu's family was victimised by the Vietnamese civil wars at the end of the eighteenth century. For backing the wrong ruler, his father was publicly and savagely flogged in front of Hanoi's Temple of Literature in 1803 by agents of the first Nguyen emperor. Yet Phan Huy Chu, with every personal reason to detest abusive and brutal emperors, still thought weak emperors, not strong ones, were the biggest threat to the Vietnamese people's capacity to 'sustain themselves and nourish themselves' (*tu sinh tu nuoi*).

In 1819 Phan Huy Chu argued that the first priority in governing the world was for the master of a country to 'investigate' his entire domain, certify the actual numbers of households in it, discover clearly and recurrently which adult male taxpayers were 'strong' and which ones were old and feeble, and then use this information to ensure that taxes were 'balanced' and that poor people had occupations. The national ruler was not to transfer these responsibilities to the less impartial village chief.[9] Obviously Phan Huy Chu was not inclined to romanticise the power of village chiefs, or to see them as potential tribunes of their fellow villagers against the ravages of a national despotism. It was the abuses of local power and its authorities, who were closer to the governed and thus potentially more meddlesome, which he thought were most to be feared, not the abuses of emperors. But the Europeans who arrived in Vietnam in the 1800s were conscious of the way in which their own feudal magnates had restricted the power of irresponsible kings. These Europeans were the ones who idealised

Vietnamese village chiefs as the epitome of a sort of limited rustic democracy which might operate as an idiosyncratic Oriental counter-weight to the supposed 'despot' in the capital city.

The twentieth century has revolutionised the Vietnamese view of the likely sources of interference with both individual and now ethnic self-determination. The rise of anti-colonial nationalism inevitably found these sources of interference in the international arena, not within local village tyrannies. The key was provided by the great Chinese reformer and journalist Liang Qichao, under whose tutelage some of the most influential first generation of Vietnamese reformers studied in Japan in the early twentieth century. In the pioneering essay on freedom (*Lun ziyou*) which he published in his newspaper in May 1902, Liang praised freedom by writing that the saying 'Give me liberty or give me death' was the great source of the modern European and American people's capacity to build strong states.[10] Western historians of liberty, taking for granted the relative success and efficiency of their own modern nation-states, show little interest in analysing the relationship of various kinds of freedom to the survival of and competition between nation-states. Such Western analysts seem more interested in the freedom of class, race and gender communities within the nation-states they take for granted. So there remains even now a difference in agendas. Although the Vietnamese imagination of freedom in the twentieth century has come to be deeply influenced by both Western science's view of the cosmos and by the Western association of individual self-development with the pursuit of material interest, the moral and political agenda of the Vietnamese discussion of freedom, as in other Southeast Asian discussions of it, still has a separate starting-point.

Equality as Liberty

At this point it is worth returning to the extraordinary moment in the nineteenth century when Western observers of the premodern Vietnamese and Chinese mandarinates thought they saw in them indigenous Asian monuments to what westerners themselves celebrated as freedom.

The moment was extraordinary because the dominant Western approach to precolonial Asian governments had been to regard them as 'Oriental despotisms', meaning governments characterised both by an absence of political participation liberties and by an absence of legally guaranteed property rights. Such governments were thought to be barbaric; their leaders were often characterised with merciless mockery. Consider, for example, how a famous British journalist and

future British colonial administrator in Burma described the last independent king of Burma in 1882, four years before that king was
destroyed.

> His most glorious excellent majesty, the present ruler of the city of Mandalay
> . . . ruler of the sea and land, lord of the rising sun . . . and . . . king of all the
> umbrella-bearing chiefs, lord of the mines of gold, silver, rubies, amber, and
> the noble serpentine, chief of the . . . celestial elephant, and master of many
> white elephants . . . the sun-descended monarch . . . king of kings . . . the
> arbiter of existence, has a very bad character. He killed his brothers and
> sisters, and he drinks gin.'[11]

Freedom was usually conceded to precolonial Asian states only by
Western writers who despised liberalism and who preserved but
merely inverted Oriental despotism theory in order to do it. Tolstoy
was perhaps the best example. In 1906 Tolstoy said that he believed
that 'the peoples of the Orient were called to recover that liberty which
the peoples of the Occident had lost almost without chance of recov-
ery'. Tolstoy's reason for suggesting this was essentially that a 'member
of a despotic state may be entirely free, even in the midst of the most
brutal violence. But a member of a constitutional state is always a slave,
for he recognizes the legality of the violence done him'.[12]

But it was Western liberals, not illiberals like Tolstoy, who thought
they saw their own ideal of freedom reflected in the premodern
Vietnamese and Chinese civil service examination systems. At the
time they did so the word 'meritocracy' had just begun to be used in
Western languages. Michael Young dates its first restricted use in
English, in small-scale journals linked to socialism, to the 1860s.[13]
Aptitude tests and the other supposedly class-transcending ways by
which post-feudal industrial societies try to measure intelligence did
not even begin in the West until about 1905, with the work of Alfred
Binet. Thus British treaty port Sinologists like D. J. MacGowan under-
standably marvelled at the huge Chinese civil service examination sites
of the 1800s, which might accommodate up to 17,000 Chinese students
for their tests. MacGowan wrote in 1887:

> when, more than a score of centuries ago, feudalism and hereditary rule were
> abolished [in China], there was a Radical revolution (China's sole revolu-
> tion) which opened the way to rank and power of every qualified man . . . No
> institution or caste bars the way of the ambitious to take part in the govern-
> ment of the empire . . . The air of the examination hall is as free as the air of
> heaven, and there, in competition, labourers and rich men's sons are on an
> equality. Herein lies the secret of the success of Chinese administration.[14]

Invading French observers had the same reactions in Vietnam.
Reference has already been made to Bouillevaux's view in 1874 that

Confucian Vietnam was an 'academic democracy' in which whatever tyranny existed was mixed with precious liberties'. Other French Indochina hands who followed him extended this theme. Jean de Lanessan, in his *L'Indochine francaise* (published in Paris in 1889) wrote that the government of Vietnam could be considered as 'a monarchy without aristocracy, without clergy, without an official religion, with democratic institutions and a strong communal decentralization'; in a second book, *La colonisation française en Indochine* (1895), de Lanessan again commented on the 'profoundly democratic' nature of traditional Vietnamese social and political organisation, and suggested that it was impossible for Vietnamese rulers to exercise 'autocratic power' under those circumstances. J. Silvestre, in a book called *L'empire d'Annam et le people annamite* (1889), went even further. He proposed that precolonial Vietnam had a 'monarchical regime of liberty, equality, and property', and that to remove the 'Annamite' from this free and equal regime in order to subject him to the 'brutal' political order of French colonies would be wrong.[15]

In such comments, equality meant the presumed equality of opportunity of the Vietnamese mandarinate's civil service examinations. The association between liberty and this type of equality was the bedrock of the analysis. Nineteenth-century European liberals were confident about the dynamic interdependence of liberty and equality. They even assumed that the levelling of society into equality, which was what the Vietnamese examination system appeared to be doing, was actually a historical prerequisite for the growth of freedom. As Alexis de Tocqueville wrote in volume 2 of *Democracy in America*, 'among most modern nations, especially those of Europe, the taste for freedom and the conception of it only began to take shape and grow at the time when social conditions were tending toward equality, and it was a consequence of that very equality'.[16] One could dismiss this view as bucolically pre-industrial. It was published in 1840, preceding late nineteenth-century European industrial societies' discovery that industrial capitalism created new social disparities. Yet Max Weber's contemporary, the brilliant German sociologist Georg Simmel, could still write many years after Tocqueville that 'the basic metaphysical motif that finds expression during the eighteenth century in the practical demand for "freedom and equality" is this: the worth of each individual's configuration is based, to be sure, on him alone ... but along with that it is based on what the individual has in common with all others', and the recognition of this.[17]

There are many reasons why Western scholars today no longer share the nineteenth-century Western optimism that the traditional Vietnamese and Chinese civil service examination systems were the precocious Asian forcing-houses of modern freedoms. But one of them must surely be the decline of Western faith in the interdependency of freedom and equality itself. A neo-libertarian obsession has arisen which holds that liberty and equality are in a trade-off relationship.[18] One of the most egregious advocates of neo-libertarian thought, the anti-interventionist Nobel Prize–winning Austrian-British economist F. A. Hayek, even went so far as to argue (in *The Constitution of Liberty*, 1960) that almost all forms of equality destroy liberty, and that the hereditary transfer of property within the family from one generation to another actually serves the interests of a free society.[19]

I have two purposes in making this digression into Western thought in a chapter which is supposed to be about traditional Vietnamese values. One is to show that the Western scholars who analyse those values will find it hard to escape the disabling influence of the confusing fluctuations in more general Western views about the relationship between liberty and equality. Our contemporary tendency is to pay insufficient respect to an extraordinary Vietnamese historical institution: the civil service examinations which began in the eleventh century. This tendency is probably every bit as misguided as the nineteenth-century French tendency to celebrate the examinations was overstated.

My second purpose is to lament that modern Chinese and Vietnamese reactions to their historic civil service examinations have largely imitated the unstable and contradictory Western reactions I have just outlined. Unfortunately, my examples must be Chinese, for I know of no Vietnamese data which undermine their applicability. In his essay on freedom in 1902, Liang Qichao wrote that there were six great problems in the struggle for freedom, the first of which was the class struggle to wrest freedom from an entrenched aristocracy; he went on to say that this problem fortunately did not exist in China, because of China's edifying abolition of hereditary ministers and the 'base customs' of hereditary classes, at the end of the Warring States period.

On the other hand, when F. A. Hayek's most important Taiwanese disciple, Zhou Dewei, translated *The Constitution of Liberty* into Chinese in 1973, and tried to show that traditional Chinese culture was compatible with Hayek's theories, he ignored the post-aristocratic civil service examinations, and glorified instead the aristocratic China before 221 BC, which Liang Qichao had deplored. It was commendable that the ancestors of Confucius himself were aristocrats, Zhou wrote in 1973; the high ancestry of the great historian Sima Qian also explained his achievement. Although the West undoubtedly had more salutary examples of the strict link between heredity and achievement which a libertarian society must cherish, Zhou continued, pre-imperial aristocratic China nonetheless also demonstrated Hayek's point that hereditary family power was good and that levelling educational systems were questionable.[20]

Now the actual amount of equality of upward mobility which the Vietnamese examination system permitted was limited, although there was not the fear of downward mobility in nineteenth-century Vietnam that haunted examination-taking gentry families in Qing China. Charts of 'feudal land systems' adorn the walls of Vietnamese historical museums in the 1990s in the same way that charts of royal regalia, prahus and kerises adorn the walls of museums in the Malay world. What the Vietnamese wall charts show is that economic defeudalisation occurred far more slowly than the political defeudalisation implied by the examinations. Individual economic liberty of the sort found in early modern Europe was only rudimentary. Although Vietnam experienced an irreversible transition from a society of big hereditary estates owned by aristocratic families before the fifteenth century to a society of small peasant landowners after that century, the concept of 'private lands' (*tu dien, tu tho*) which we find in Vietnamese land registers was more communalistic and less individualistic than it sounds. In the nineteenth century 'private lands' might include the lands of Buddhist temples, lineage lands to maintain ancestral cults, village lands for 'feasting elders' or for 'sustaining orphans and people without families', village 'orthodox culture' group lands to finance Confucian ceremonies, village 'studies fields' to pay for the support of academically gifted village children, and collectively owned disciples' association lands for the support of teachers.

But if there was no complete breakthrough to any sort of absolute individual economic liberty, it is still true that the civil service examinations provided more political equality of opportunity than would have been found in most European societies before the French Revolution. Hence the admiration of them by even post-revolutionary French observers in the nineteenth century. Even the communist historian Tran Van Giau, with no love for what he must regard as the 'feudal' Vietnam before French colonialism, concedes that 30 to 40 per cent of the men who passed examinations in early nineteenth-century Vietnam were probably the sons of poor households.[21] The Vietnamese popular belief in the examinations' equality of opportunity is historically incontestable. It was so enormous that when the cash-starved Trinh lords who ruled northern Vietnam in the eighteenth century sold access to the examinations in 1750, allowing people to pay money to bypass the screening tests which selected candidates, the crowds of peasants, merchants, peddlers, and meat shop owners who allegedly fought to compete were so large that some people were killed at the gate of the examination site.[22] This was political corruption of the opposite kind from the English 'rotten boroughs' of the same century.

This sort of corruption broadened the popular sense of enfranchisement rather than diminishing it. It could occur easily, by rulers' fiat, in a country without any rigorously preserved sense of social 'estates'.

Transcendence, Mandarins and Serfs

The really difficult questions lie in intellectual history. Did late traditional Vietnamese thinkers themselves believe that any value remotely comparable to important Western definitions of 'freedom' was guaranteed or promoted in their lives by the existence of an examination-taking mandarinate?

The answer is a limited yes. For from the point of view of the Vietnamese officials who won bureaucratic jobs through the examinations, government service could be part of their search for a sort of transcendental self-actualisation as individuals.[23] This point cannot be understood if we adopt a crudely Weberian approach to bureaucracy which discounts distinctions between manipulative and non-manipulative social relations. As Richard Pipes showed many years ago, Max Weber, though a critic of Bismarck, got most of the premises of his political theory from the peculiar lessons of Bismarckian politics in Germany. Power forms the essence of politics; political bodies including bureaucracies are mainly concerned with the rational exercise of power. Regarding the state as a rational, factory-like 'enterprise', Weber overestimated the technical aspects of government – the administrative apparatus, financial arrangements, bureaucratic training and experience – and underestimated those features of the state which were only weakly paralleled, if at all, in the rationally organised enterprise. These included ideology and mass psychology.[24]

Vietnam was undoubtedly a bureaucratic kingdom in the early nineteenth century. Government offices were functionally differentiated, under six separate ministries which specialised in personnel appointments, tax collections, education and the management of foreign relations, war-making, the disposition and punishment of civil and criminal legal offences, and the superintendence of public works. Officials served statutory six-year terms in their positions. Higher officials investigated lower officials annually, preparing 'lists for awaiting promotion' (*hau thuong sach*) and 'lists for awaiting transfer' (*hau dieu sach*) for ministry heads to review. The whole operation was a more highly educated, more objectively selected meritocracy than the government of the present-day Socialist Republic of Vietnam, more than half of whose state functionaries are – by insiders' calculations – military men who depend on personal connections.[25] Yet nineteenth-century Vietnam had no equivalent of the Western term 'bureaucracy'.

In part, this was because traditional Vietnamese 'bureaucracy' was about the search for ultimate values, not just about rationally effective power. Being a means to an end, it could not be linguistically reified, as it was in Europe from the end of the eighteenth century. The bureaucracy was merely an institutional version of the millennial quest for 'worthies' (or Confucian élite, to use the deflationary Western term). The élite's brilliance had little ultimately to do with the systems of offices to which they might be temporarily linked. Putting it in inappropriate and anachronistic Western terms in order to clarify it, the Vietnamese political order was, in its own idealised view of itself, Arnoldian (the purpose of government was to discover and promote what Matthew Arnold would have called the 'best selves' among the educated male population) rather than Weberian (government as the planned rational distribution of powers of command among various agencies and office-holders, so as to achieve binding authority over the state's citizens).

That some bureaucrats might at least try to be moderate religious pilgrims would strike westerners weaned on Weber (or Balzac) as odd. But one of the great differences between the West and the Confucian civilisation of which Vietnamese élites were such a distinctive, nationally assertive part was that Confucian thought did not clearly separate, as did Western thought, the 'transcendental' world from the 'real' world. (What follows is inspired largely by Yu.)[26] There was no important religious division here fully comparable to the Western one between a kingdom of heaven (or Augustine's heavenly city) and earth-bound human society (Augustine's earthly city).

Since it has become fashionable recently to compare Confucianism to Protestant Christianity and its famous work ethic, it is worth recalling that Calvin wrote in 1536 that the spiritual kingdom of Christ and civil government were far removed from each other, and that it was 'a Judaic folly' to look for the kingdom of Christ among the things that make up this world. Such an argument would be unimaginable to Confucian thinkers who held that the ideal transcendental world, the 'Way' (*dao* or *Tao*), was immanent in daily human relations, which could not be conceptually divorced from it. Buddhism, which coexisted with Confucianism in Vietnam, is more problematic.[27] But Buddhism was more the religion of the village than the religion of mandarins as mandarins. Moreover, the Zen Buddhism which was so extraordinarily popular in medieval Vietnam also refused to dichotomise 'true' meaning from ordinary worldly meaning.

We could summarise the differences by suggesting that traditional Vietnamese Confucian thought, by not absolutely dichotomising the transcendental and real worlds, could not produce two absolute and antithetical notions of freedom, as in the Western Augustinian tradition. But it is not clear that the absence of absolutely dichotomised ideas of freedom in premodern Vietnam meant less real freedom for Vietnamese men (at least) to develop their mind-heart (the path of inner transcendentalism) by being politically active. One may concede that Western thought had a greater accumulation of conceptualisations of ideal or pure types of freedom, distinguished from – or in Confucian eyes, dangerously disaggregated from – daily grinding reality. On the other hand, the greatest Vietnamese thinkers (such as Le Quy Don) may well have been better than most of their Western counterparts at defining this-worldly forms of self-development with an internally transcendental flavour. To the degree that the civil service examinations provided access to such forms of self-development, within government service, to people without great wealth, they did maximise freedom.

It would be possible to argue that the mandarinate's maximisation of freedom did not stop at the élite level but extended to premodern Vietnamese society's underdogs: its serfs (*no ty*). No scholar has done a better job of expounding the provocative contrasts between European and Southeast Asian notions of slavery in the early modern period than Vicente Rafael. He shows us that when Spanish Franciscan missionaries in the Philippines explained the Ten Commandments in Tagalog in the late sixteenth century, they told their Filipino converts that Christians were all 'slaves of God'. But while enslavement arose from a perceived condition of indebtedness in both Tagalog and Spanish Christian culture, in Tagalog culture indebtedness was merely a determinant of differential status within a network of social relations. It was not a determinant of the general sinfulness of individual persons with respect to an absolutely outside transcendental realm and its life after death. The innovation of European Christianity lay therefore in giving slavery an existential absoluteness which it had not previously had and in 'introducing a different kind of temporal determinateness into the relationship between master and slaves'.[28]

Confucian Vietnam, like the pre-Catholic Philippines, lacked a belief in an absolutely outside transcendental realm as has been shown. Equally important, Vietnam's state orthodoxy, which required knowledge of the writings of the philosopher Mencius to be tested in the civil service examinations from the early fifteenth century on, held that all human beings were potentially good and were perfectible through education. Aristotle's claim that there are *by nature* both free people and slaves, and that slavery therefore naturally agreed with its exemplars, would have been as unimaginable to the Vietnamese as Calvin's sharp distinction between the kingdom of Christ and civil government.

The combination of the open-mindedness of Vietnamese Neo-Confucian orthodoxy with respect to the goodness of all human beings, and a civil service examination system which prevented at least the theoretical rigidification of the social structure, worked jointly to reduce the importance of serfdom in Vietnam after the fifteenth century. I need hardly add that it was in the interests of Vietnam's mandarinate-based monarchy to discourage serfdom, in order to protect the numbers of its unenslaved subjects who were taxpayers. But Vietnamese rulers could not have done this in a more politically feudal context, such as characterised Vietnamese history before 1400.

The Freedom of Political Gentlemen

In studying the evolution of serfdom in premodern Vietnam, our most important textual guides are the dynastic law codes. The most influential of these was the Le dynasty penal code (*Le trieu hinh luat*), whose roughly 720 surviving laws emerged gradually between the beginning of the dynasty (1427) and its end (1786).[29] One of modern Vietnam's most perceptive students of this code has suggested that forty-three of its laws, or about 6 per cent of the law code which we have now, dealt with household serfs and maidservants.[30] This percentage may be contrasted to what one finds in Malay codes of law, which typically devoted about a quarter of their total attention to questions of slavery.[31] An even more significant difference is that whereas the Malay codes had a clear body of law on slaves as property, the Le code treated serfs more as a legal element which constituted part of the public realm, but not as private property outside the state's normal sphere. There is not a single item in the entire law code which refers to the state paying damages to the owners of serfs whom the state reclaimed for its own purposes.

The ethnic Vietnamese serfs who did exist might be criminals who were being punished; poor people who had sold themselves into bondage, a practice occurring throughout Southeast Asia; or people like military deserters who had been illicitly converted into household menials by powerful mandarins, who lost their government positions if they were caught. The law code emphasised the protection of free commoners ('good people', *luong dan*; see Chapter 4 for the equivalent Chinese expression *liang ren* [respectable people]). It specified that whoever abducted another person and transformed him into his serf, or sold him as a serf to someone else, would be exiled to a distant region; if he had also robbed his victim of money, he would suffer execution by strangulation. Destitute orphans aged 15 and over were allowed voluntarily to sell themselves, but the transaction required not just a purchaser but a guarantor, witnesses, a scribe to draw up the contract and government officials to review the contract. Here serfdom was treated not as a state punishment but as a last-ditch remedy to bridge the gap between inadequate state welfare and the breakdown of family power. It was a sort of auxiliary device for community reintegration, reflecting harsh external circumstances, rather than a theorisation of the congenital moral debasement of certain groups of Vietnamese people. Politically, it was intended as a remedy against extreme marginalisation (that is, the destitution of orphans), not as a device for consolidating marginalisation.

This situation nevertheless had a more ugly underside. Vietnamese relations with the hill country minorities – the Tai, the Hmong, the Jarai, and many others – were the real test of the country's Neo-Confucian ethical universalism, the court's chosen ideology (not to mention Buddhist egalitarianism, also part of the religious landscape) and the real test as well of the authenticity of the social universalism of its civil service examinations. In practice, neither of these two universalisms covered the hill peoples. The result was sometimes the conversion of non-Vietnamese minorities into not merely serfs but full-fledged slaves for whom there was a free market.

Le Quy Don tells us that in the eighteenth century, when the Nguyen lords moved settlers from Quang Nam south to the 'thick forests' of the Mekong Delta to live and cultivate rice and areca palms, such settlers rounded up 'boys and girls' of the Malayo-Polynesian minorities and sold them as slaves, the price depending on whether they were 'real Moi' (black-skinned, with curled hair) or less real 'Moi' with whitish complexions. The 'real Moi' sold for twenty strings of cash each.[32] In this respect the labour supply crisis in Vietnam's southern frontier-lands clearly eroded whatever limited protection the ideology of the premodern mandarinate offered society's underdogs.

It has been suggested that the mandarin élite itself thought the civil service examinations offered them not merely upward mobility but the opportunity to pursue moral self-actualisation as individuals. Therefore the French association of freedom with the examinations in the nineteenth century really did correspond, if only superficially and accidentally, to traditional Vietnamese values which amounted in Confucian terms to the same thing. This suggestion must also be qualified. For late traditional Vietnamese intellectuals did not believe that latter-day mandarins had the creative autonomy of the wandering scholars who had taught thousands of students in private schools in the pre-Chinese 'China' of the age of Confucius. This was of course the classical golden age, revered for centuries by Asian literati from Korea to the Mekong River, which provided the imaginative seedbed of late traditional Vietnamese politics in the same way that ancient Greece and Rome provided it for westerners. Indeed Max Weber rightly identified these wandering scholars as a 'free and mobile stratum of literati' comparable to the philosophers of 'Hellenic antiquity'.[33]

Philosopher bureaucrats like Le Quy Don therefore posited an explicit tension between the morally autonomous gentleman (*quan tu*) and the average bureaucrat. Le Quy Don derived his notion of the gentleman from classical books which predated all mandarinates, such as 'The Book of Songs' (*Thi kinh*), composed perhaps about 600 BC, a collection of folk-songs from the aforementioned golden age whose function in Vietnam was as a kind of secondary religious text, rather like *hadith* for Islamic scholars in Java. In this respect Le Quy Don's ideal of freedom corresponded less to the equality-of-opportunity freedom the French thought they saw in Vietnam in the nineteenth century and more with the longings of idealistic medieval European monks for the poorer and purer and more authentic early days of the Christian Church, of Christ and his apostles, when there were no popes or bishops, and there was no dense scholastic vocabulary such as required Ockham's razor. The difference between nineteenth-century Vietnam and medieval Europe was that the 'gentleman' with such longings was far more likely also to serve as a bureaucrat in late traditional Vietnam. (Le Quy Don himself was the best example.) Radical monks were far less likely to become the bishops they mistrusted in medieval Europe.

Le Quy Don wrote in 1773 that the gentleman must have 'nine capabilities' (*cuu nang*). These included reading auguries well enough to found a successful state; serving as an envoy to foreign countries without being killed by their rulers; commanding an army successfully; choosing appropriate posthumous honorary names for deceased people; and making appropriate prayers on sacrificial occasions. What is striking about this litany of capabilities is that some were those of a ruler's servant. Others were those of an actual ruler. The boundaries were blurred. Le Quy Don drove the point home when he asserted that a government which chose its officials according to the nine capabilities of the gentleman would obtain officials who could replace the king in speaking on his behalf.[34]

The blurred boundaries between ruler and gentleman help to suggest the answer to the question why did the provincial literati not actually seize power from the emperor, like the 'third estate' in parts of Europe. Apart from the fact that they had little desire to demolish the power of the chief examiner who selected and promoted them, the literati's predisposition to search for this-worldly forms of transcendence blocked the explicit theoretical association of politics with individual or group interests, and thus made it difficult to separate the sphere of the ruler from the sphere of the gentleman. Mandarins of the Le Quy Don or Phan Huy Chu type saw themselves not in separate class terms but as imperial surrogates or second-hand imperial selves. There was a broad vicarious shared sense of rulership, as in Le Quy Don's image of the official who spoke for the ruler. It was this shared sense of rulership which allowed someone like Phan Huy Chu – a lowly northern scholar without even a high academic degree – to write an encyclopedic manual of government and politics, obliquely critical of the existing southern-based dynasty, and present it to the sitting Vietnamese emperor in 1821. One can imagine what might happen to a low-level Vietnamese Communist Party cadre who tried to present an unsolicited and critical theorisation of politics to the contemporary Vietnamese politburo; he might very well be gaoled for a long time. In 1821, however, a very different political script required the emperor Minh-mang to receive Phan Huy Chu's great work with simulated ecstasy, thank him for it, and reward him.

The reason for this was that the tension between the politically critical gentleman and the more obedient bureaucrat, who might be one and the same person, was a necessary one even from the point of view of emperors, who had to indulge it. The late traditional Vietnamese bureaucracy was not thought to have an immanent institutional capacity to preserve its own norms. Nobody in premodern Vietnam anticipated the assumption made by modern Western theorists of administration (Chester Barnard, Herbert Simon, Lyndall Urwick) that a bureaucratic organisation has a collective rationality superior to that of any of its individual bureaucrats.[35] Therefore even emperors accepted that the traditional Vietnamese government, however bureaucratic it was, required individual mandarins with relatively autonomous moral lives to renew it. Otherwise it would collapse. It could fairly be said that this was a limit on despotism, however fragile, and that, unfortunately for modern Vietnam, it vanished in the shipwreck of the traditional Vietnamese political order a century ago.

Notes

1   M. de Montaigne, *Essays*, transl. J. M. Cohen (London: Penguin, 1958), p. 62.
2   The Vietnamese civil service examinations were first held in AD 1075. The French finally ended them in 1919.
3   P. Anderson, *Lineages of the Absolute State* (London: Verso, 1979), p. 464.
4   N. van Phong, *La société vietnamienne de 1882 à 1902* (Paris: Presses universitaires de France, 1971), p. 189.

5 Le Quy Don, *Van dai loai ngu* [Classified discourse from the library], cf. 1773 work (Hanoi: Nha xuat ban van hoa, 1961), vol. 1, p. 72.

6 Nguyen Du'c Van and Kieu Thu Hoach (transl.), *Hoang Le nhat thong chi* [A chronicle of the polity of the imperial Le dynasty] (Hanoi, 1970), p. 338.

7 Le Quy Don, *Van dai loai ngu*, vol. 2, pp. 110–11.

8 Every postcolonial Vietnamese government, communist or non-communist, has seen to it that modern romanised editions of this work have appeared; the most recent modern edition, published in Hanoi in 1992, amounts to over 1200 pages.

9 Phan Huy Chu, *Lich trieu hien chu'o'ng loai chí* [A classified survey of the institutions of successive courts], 1819 work, transl. into modern Vietnamese by the Vien Su' hoc Viet-Nam [Vietnamese Historical Studies Institute] (Hanoi: Nhe xuat ban Su' hoc, 1962), vol. 3, 29, p. 53.

10 Li Huaxing and Wu Jiaxun (comp.), *Liang Qichao xuanji* [Selections from Liang Qichao] (Shanghai: Renmin chubanshe, 1984), pp. 223–33.

11 Shway Yoe (Sir James George Scott), *The Burman: His Life and Notions*, 1882 (New York: W. W. Norton & Co., 1963), p. 466.

12 Romain Rolland, *Tolstoy*, transl. Bernard Miall (New York and London: Garland Publishing Inc., 1972), pp. 280–1, 259.

13 Michael Young, *The Rise of the Meritocracy: An essay on education and equality* (London: Thames & Hudson, 1958), p. 153.

14 D. J. MacGowan, 'Chinese guilds or chambers of commerce and trades unions', *Journals of the China Branch of the Royal Asiatic Society*, 21, 3–4, 1886 (March 1887), p. 192.

15 Nguyen Van Phong, *La société vietnamienne de 1882 à 1902* (Paris: Presses universitaires de France, 1971), pp. 109, 65–6.

16 Alexis de Tocqueville, *Democracy in America*, 2 vols, publ. 1835 and 1840, ed. J. P. Mayer, transl. George Lawrence (New York: Doubleday & Co., Anchor Books, 1969), p. 505.

17 Donald N. Levine, *Georg Simmel on Individuality and Social Forms: Selected Writing* (Chicago and London: University of Chicago Press, 1971), p. 220.

18 David Held, *Political Theory Today* (Stanford: Stanford University Press, 1991), pp. 48–66.

19 F. A. Hayek, *The Constitution of Liberty* (Chicago: University of Chicago Press, 1960), pp. 85, 89–91.

20 Xiong Xijian, *Dangdai Zhonguo sichao shuping* [A review of the trends of thought in contemporary China] (Taibai: Wenjin chubanshe, 1992), pp. 36–7, 41–4.

21 Tran Van Giau, *Su' phat trien cua tu' tu'o'ng o' Viet-Nam tu' the ky' XIX den cach mang thang Tam* [The development of Vietnamese thought from the nineteenth century to the August Revolution] (Hanoi: Nha xuat ban khoa hoc xa hoi, 1975), pp. 23–4.

22 Phan Huy Chu, *Lich trieu hien chu'o'ng loai chí*, vol. 3, 26, p. 19.

23 It was also, of course, part of the creation or consolidation of their family fortunes.

24 Richard Pipes, 'Max Weber and Russia', *World Politics*, 8 (3 April) (Princeton: NJ, 1955), pp. 371–401.

25 Hoang Chi Bao et al., *Co' cau xa hoi-giai cap o' nu'o'c ta: ly luan va thu'c thien* [The social-class structure in our country: theory and practice] (Hanoi: Nha xuat ban Thong tin Ly luan. comp., 1992), pp. 186–7.

26 Yu Yingshi, *Zhongguo sixiang chuantong de xiandai quanshi* [A contemporary

exegesis of Chinese intellectual tradition] (Taibei: Lianjing chuban shiye gongsi, 1987).

27 When Vietnamese students read Thomas More's *Utopia* for the first time, it was almost certainly in its pioneering Chinese translation in Sun Yat-sen's revolutionary journal *Minbao* in Tokyo in September 1906. Since there was no commonly accepted term for 'Utopia' in Chinese at that time, the Chinese translator, Liao Zhongkai, rendered the very Catholic Thomas More's title as 'The Flower Garland World', *Huayan jie*, borrowing the name of a Buddhist sutra which concerned itself with escape from earthly hindrances through the calming of the mind.

28 Vicente L. Rafael, *Contracting Colonialism: translation and Christian conversion in Tagalog society under early Spanish rule* (Durham and London: Duke University Press, 1993), pp. 167–8.

29 See the magnificent English-language translation by Nguyen Ngoc Huy and Ta Van Tai, *The Le code: law in traditional Vietnam* (Athens, Ohio: Ohio University Press, 1987).

30 For this and for what follows I owe much to Tru'o'ng Hu'u Quynh, 'Tìm hieu che do no ty tho'i Le so' qua luat phap' [Toward an understanding through law of the serfdom system of the early Le period], 155, *Nghien cu'u lich su'* [Historical researches], Hanoi (March–April 1974), pp. 56–7.

31 Anthony Reid, *Southeast Asia in the Age of Commerce*, vol. 1 (New Haven: Yale University Press, 1988), p. 134.

32 Le Quy Don, *Phu bien tap luc* [Miscellaneous chronicles of the pacified frontiers], 1776 work (Hanoi: Nha xuat ban khoa hoc xa hoi, 1977), p. 345.

33 Max Weber, *The Religion of China*, transl. Hans H. Gerth (New York: The Free Press, 1951), p. 111.

34 Le Quy Don, *Van dai loai ngu*, vol. 1, pp. 235–7.

35 Sheldon S. Wolin, *Politics and Vision: Continuity and Innovation in Western Political Thought* (Boston: Little Brown & Co., 1960), pp. 376–83.

Index